GLENCOE
WORLD HISTORY
MODERN TIMES

Reading Essentials and Note-Taking Guide

Student Workbook

McGraw Hill **Glencoe**

To the Student

Glencoe World History: Modern Times **Reading Essentials and Note-Taking Guide** is designed to help you use recognized reading strategies to improve your reading-for-information skills. For each section of the student textbook, you are alerted to key content. Then, you are asked to draw from prior knowledge, organize your thoughts with a graphic organizer, and follow a process to read and understand the text. The **Reading Essentials and Note-Taking Guide** was prepared to help you get more from your textbook by reading with a purpose.

The McGraw-Hill Companies

 **Glencoe**

Send all inquiries to:
Glencoe/McGraw-Hill
8787 Orion Place
Columbus, OH 43240-4027

ISBN: 978-0-07-891012-8
MHID: 0-07-891012-9

Printed in the United States of America.
2 3 4 5 6 7 8 9 10   009   13 12 11 10 09

Table of Contents

Chapter 1 The First Civilizations and Empires, Prehistory–A.D. 500
Section 1: The First Humans 1
Section 2: Western Asia and Egypt 4
Section 3: India and China 7

Chapter 2 Ancient Greece and Rome, 1900 B.C–A.D. 500
Section 1: Ancient Greece 10
Section 2: Rome and the Rise of Christianity 13

Chapter 3 Regional Civilizations, 400–1500
Section 1: The World of Islam 16
Section 2: Early African Civilizations 19
Section 3: The Asian World 22
Section 4: Emerging Europe and the Byzantine Empire 25

Chapter 4 Toward a New World, 800–1500
Section 1: Europe in the Middle Ages 28
Section 2: The Americas 31

Chapter 5 Renaissance and Reformation, 1350–1600
Section 1: The Renaissance 34
Section 2: Ideas and Art of the Renaissance 37
Section 3: The Protestant Reformation 40
Section 4: The Spread of Protestantism 43

Chapter 6 The Age of Exploration, 1500–1800
Section 1: Exploration and Expansion 46
Section 2: The Atlantic Slave Trade 49
Section 3: Colonial Latin America 52

Chapter 7 Crisis and Absolutism in Europe, 1550–1715
Section 1: Europe in Crisis: The Wars of Religion 55
Section 2: Social Crises, War, and Revolution 58
Section 3: Response to Crisis: Absolutism 61
Section 4: The World of European Culture 64

Chapter 8 The Muslim Empires, 1450–1800
Section 1: The Ottoman Empire 67
Section 2: The Rule of the Safavids 70
Section 3: The Grandeur of the Moguls 73

Chapter 9 The East Asian World, 1400–1800
Section 1: China at Its Height 76
Section 2: Chinese Society and Culture 79
Section 3: Tokugawa Japan and Korea 82
Section 4: Spice Trade in Southeast Asia 85

Chapter 10 Revolution and Enlightenment, 1550–1800
Section 1: The Scientific Revolution 88
Section 2: The Enlightenment 91
Section 3: The Impact of the Enlightenment 94
Section 4: The American Revolution 97

Chapter 11 The French Revolution and Napoleon, 1789–1815
Section 1: The French Revolution Begins 100
Section 2: Radical Revolution and Reaction 103
Section 3: The Age of Napoleon 106

Chapter 12 Industrialization and Nationalism, 1800–1870
Section 1: The Industrial Revolution 109
Section 2: Reaction and Revolution 112
Section 3: National Unification and Nationalism 115
Section 4: Romanticism and Realism 118

Chapter 13 Mass Society and Democracy, 1870–1914
Section 1: The Growth of Industrial Prosperity 121
Section 2: The Emergence of Mass Society 124
Section 3: The National State and Democracy 127
Section 4: Toward the Modern Consciousness 130

Chapter 14 The Height of Imperialism, 1800–1914
Section 1: Colonial Rule in Southeast Asia 133
Section 2: Empire Building in Africa 136
Section 3: British Rule in India 139
Section 4: Nation Building in Latin America 142

Chapter 15 East Asia Under Challenge, 1800–1914
Section 1: The Decline of the Qing Dynasty 145
Section 2: Revolution in China 148
Section 3: Rise of Modern Japan 151

Chapter 16 War and Revolution, 1914–1919
Section 1: The Road to World War I 154
Section 2: World War I 157
Section 3: The Russian Revolution 160
Section 4: End of World War I 163

Chapter 17 The West Between the Wars, 1919–1939
Section 1: The Futile Search for Stability 166
Section 2: The Rise of Dictatorial Regimes 169
Section 3: Hitler and Nazi Germany 172
Section 4: Cultural and Intellectual Trends 175

Chapter 18 Nationalism Around the World, 1914–1939
Section 1: Nationalism in the Middle East 178
Section 2: Nationalism in Africa and Asia 181
Section 3: Revolutionary Chaos in China 184
Section 4: Nationalism in Latin America 187

Chapter 19 World War II, 1939–1945
Section 1: Paths to War.. 190
Section 2: The Course of World War II 193
Section 3: The New Order and the Holocaust 196
Section 4: Home Front and Aftermath of War... 199

Chapter 20 Cold War and Postwar Changes, 1945–1970
Section 1: Development of the Cold War 202
Section 2: The Soviet Union and Eastern Europe 205
Section 3: Western Europe and North America.. 208

Chapter 21 The Contemporary Western World, 1970–Present
Section 1: Decline of the Soviet Union.. 211
Section 2: Eastern Europe 214
Section 3: Europe and North America... 217
Section 4: Western Society and Culture 220

Chapter 22 Latin America, 1945–Present
Section 1: General Trends in Latin America 223
Section 2: Mexico, Cuba, and Central America 226
Section 3: The Nations of South America 229

Chapter 23 Africa and the Middle East, 1945–Present
Section 1: Independence in Africa 232
Section 2: Conflict in the Middle East 235

Chapter 24 Asia and the Pacific, 1945–Present
Section 1: Communist China 238
Section 2: South and Southeast Asia 241
Section 3: Japan and the Pacific 244

Chapter 25 Changing Global Patterns
Section 1: Challenges of a New Century... 247
Section 2: New Global Communities 250

The First Humans

Big Idea

After *Homo sapiens sapiens* spread throughout the world, the development of systematic agriculture led to the rise of early civilizations. As you read, create a chart like the one below listing six characteristics of a civilization.

Civilization	
1.	4.
2.	5.
3.	6.

Notes

Read to Learn

Before History (page 4)

Identifying Cause and Effect

Why do archaeologists and anthropologists have to study artifacts to get information about early peoples?

_____

_____

_____

_____

Prehistory is the period in history before writing was developed. To learn about prehistory, anthropologists study artifacts and human fossils (bones and other human remains). Archaeologists examine tools, art, weapons and other things that early humans left behind.

The earliest human-like creatures were called **hominids.** They walked upright and lived in Africa about 4 million years ago. *Homo erectus* existed beginning about 1.8 million years ago. It was probably the first hominid to migrate out of Africa. Around 200,000 years ago, *Homo sapiens* emerged. Two kinds of early humans descended from *Homo sapiens:* Neanderthals and *Homo sapiens sapiens.* Neanderthals lived between 100,000 B.C. and 30,000 B.C. They used many different stone tools, and buried their dead. *Homo sapiens sapiens* had an anatomy similar to that of people today. They probably spread out of Africa 100,000 years ago.

The Paleolithic Age lasted from about 2,500,000 B.C. to 10,000 B.C. During this period, humans hunted animals and gathered wild plants for their food. They were nomads, moving from place to place to find food. They lived in caves or shelters made of wood poles covered with animal hides. They knew how to use fire for warmth and to protect themselves from wild animals. The art of Paleolithic people, drawings on cave walls, can still be seen in parts of France and Spain.

The Neolithic Revolution *(page 7)*

Making Inferences

Why did civilizations arise first in river valleys?

_____

_____

_____

_____

The end of the last ice age was followed by the **Neolithic Revolution** between 8000 and 4000 B.C. The major change in human history during this period was the shift from hunting and gathering to planting and growing food on a regular basis. This is called **systematic agriculture.** People also began to tame and keep animals for meat, milk, and wool. This is called domestication. Some historians think these changes are the most important in all human history.

Systematic agriculture meant that people could settle down and live in farming villages. Here they built houses and other structures for storing food. In Neolithic villages, people had a simple culture, or way of life. In time, some villages became cities and developed civilizations. A **civilization** is a complex culture in which large numbers of people share common elements. Six of the basic characteristics of civilizations are: cities, government, religion, social structure, writing, and art. The first civilizations came about in river valleys, where a lot of farm land was available. Farmers could produce much food in these fertile lands to feed a large population, allowing others to become merchants or craftsmen. Governments developed that were responsible for protecting the people of their cities. Rulers and the upper class dominated society. Developments occurred in religion, writing, and architecture.

Section Wrap-up

Answer these questions to check your understanding of the entire section.

1. What two subgroups developed from *Homo sapiens?*

_____

_____

_____

2. About when did the Neolithic Revolution occur?

_____

_____

_____

Descriptive Writing

Using information from the text and your imagination, describe a day in the life of a Paleolithic boy or girl.

_____

_____

_____

_____

_____

_____

_____

_____

_____

_____

Western Asia and Egypt

Big Idea

Ancient civilizations rose along rivers in Western Asia and Egypt and gave humankind new technologies and belief systems. As you read, complete a chart like the one below listing the geographic locations of the civilizations of western Asia and Europe.

Western Asia	Egypt

 **Notes**

Read to Learn

Ancient Mesopotamia *(page 10)*

Evaluating Information

Why did the Mesopotamians learn irrigation?

_____

_____

_____

_____

Mesopotamia lay between the Tigris and Euphrates Rivers. Each spring, the rivers overflowed their banks, leaving layers of rich silt. People used irrigation and drainage ditches because they did not know when the rivers would overflow.

By 3000 B.C. a people called Sumerians had established several city-states in southern Mesopotamia. **City-states,** the basic units of Sumerian civilization, are cities that have control over the countryside around them. About 2340 B.C., these city-states were overrun by northerners, the Akkadians, led by Sargon, who created the first empire. An **empire** is a large political unit usually under a single leader that controls many peoples or territories. Hammurabi, a leader of Babylon, founded another empire in the region. His most famous achievement was the Code of Hammurabi, a collection of laws. Penalties for all offenses were severe, and varied according to the social class of the victim.

Among Mesopotamians, the Sumerians were important for inventing a writing system called cuneiform. Writing allowed them to keep records, pass on knowledge, and create literature. The Sumerians also invented the wagon wheel, made bronze, and used geometry to chart the movement of the stars.

 **Notes** | **Read to Learn**

Ancient Egypt (page 14)

Identifying the Main Idea

What were the different levels in Egyptian society?

_____

_____

_____

_____

Because natural barriers gave them a secure geographic position, Egyptians had a relatively stable society. King Menes united Egypt and created the first dynasty. A **dynasty** is a family whose right to rule is passed on within the family. Egyptian history is divided into three periods: the Old Kingdom, the Middle Kingdom, and the New Kingdom. After the New Kingdom, foreign powers ruled Egypt, which finally became a Roman province. In Egyptian society, the pharaoh was at the top with an upper class of nobles and priests below. Next were the merchants, artisans, and scribes. At the bottom were peasants who farmed and worked on building projects. Early Egyptian writing was called hieroglyphics. This system of pictures and abstract shapes was used in temples and tombs.

The Israelites (page 18)

Drawing Conclusions

How were the Israelites influential historically, despite their lack of political power?

_____

_____

_____

The Israelites were never a great political power, but their religion, known today as **Judaism,** was an important influence on Christianity and Islam. Historians believe that between 1200 B.C. and 1000 B.C., the Israelites emerged as a distinct group. Eventually, the tribes split into two kingdoms—the kingdom of Israel and the kingdom of Judah. Both were conquered, but the people of Judah survived and became known as Jews.

The Jews were **monotheistic,** believing in one God. They believed that all people had access to God. They also believed that when Moses led the Jews out of Egypt, God had made a covenant, or contract, with them based on their obedience to the Ten Commandments.

New Empires (page 20)

Identifying Cause and Effect

What caused the Persian Empire to fall?

_____

_____

_____

After Egypt declined, new empires arose. The first was the empire of Assyria on the upper Tigris River. In 612 B.C., the Assyrians were conquered by Chaldeans and Medes, peoples who lived in the East. Under the Chaldean King Nebuchadnezzar, Babylonia was for a time the most important state in this region, but in 539 B.C., it was conquered by the Persians, who built a new empire. The Persians lived in today's southwestern Iran. They were united by Cyrus. The Persian Empire became the largest empire in history to that time. In the 400s, fights over who should be king made the empire weak. It was conquered by Alexander the Great, the Greek ruler, in the 330s B.C.

Section Wrap-up

Answer these questions to check your understanding of the entire section.

1. Why was writing important to the Sumerians?

_____

_____

_____

2. How did geography affect Egyptian society?

_____

_____

_____

_____

_____

Expository Writing

Using information from this section, explain the religion of the Jews and their idea of the covenant.

_____

_____

_____

_____

_____

_____

_____

_____

_____

_____

_____

India and China

Big Idea

Civilizations in India and China developed unique philosophies, religions, and societal ideas. As you read this section, prepare a Venn diagram like the one below to show the similarities and differences between Hinduism and Buddhism.

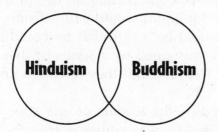

Hinduism   Buddhism

 **Notes** | **Read to Learn**

Early Civilization in India *(page 22)*

Identifying Cause and Effect

How did India's geography contribute to its many different societies?

_____

_____

_____

_____

India's diverse geography includes mountains, river valleys, a dry interior plateau, and fertile coastal plains. These different regions helped create diversity in its people, too. The Aryans, nomads from central Asia, moved into the area around 2000 B.C. Aryans were a group of peoples speaking Indo-European languages. Eventually they dominated most of India. Aryans believed society was divided into four *varnas* or social groups. In this rigid social system, or **caste system,** every Indian was believed to be born into a narrow social group defined by occupation and family network.

Hinduism is India's main religion. Early Hindus believed that Brahman, or God, was the ultimate reality that every person had to seek. By the sixth century B.C., Hindus believed in reincarnation, that their souls would be reborn after death in a different form. After many reincarnations, a person's soul finally unites with Brahman. In the sixth century B.C., a second religion, **Buddhism,** was founded by Siddhārtha Gautama. He believed that giving up worldly cares leads to wisdom and wisdom leads to nirvana, or reunion with the Great World Soul.

Two major empires, the Mauryan and Gupta, controlled early India. Trade prospered over the Silk Road from China to the Mediterranean Sea. In the late 400s, invasions weakened the empire.

 **Notes** | # Read to Learn

Early Chinese Civilizations (page 27)

Formulating Questions

What is a question that might be asked about the Han dynasty?

_____

_____

_____

_____

China's civilization began about 4,000 years ago. The Shang dynasty (1750 B.C. to about 1045 B.C.) had an organized government, a system of writing, and skill at making bronze vessels. In 1045 B.C., the ruler of one state, Zhou, revolted against the Shang. Zhou leaders established their own dynasty, the longest-lasting in Chinese history. Its rulers claimed that they had the **Mandate of Heaven.** This meant that the Zhou ruler had the authority of Heaven so long as he ruled according to the proper "Way," or **Dao.** If he did not, the kingdom would suffer from famine or other disasters. This would be a sign that he could be overthrown. For centuries, China was ruled by a series of dynasties. All claimed the Mandate of Heaven until they declined and were overthrown.

The Qin dynasty was founded by the leaders of one state, Qin, when Qin Shihuangdi declared he was emperor. He created a single monetary system and had a system of roads built. He expanded China's borders and built what was later called the Great Wall to keep out a nomadic people in the north. This wall was rebuilt in slightly different places many times. In 202 B.C., the Han dynasty emerged (202 B.C. to A.D. 220). Under the Han, population increased from 20 million to 60 million and a larger bureaucracy was needed. The Han emperors also expanded the Chinese Empire.

In China, the family was the basic social unit. One of the most important values was filial piety, or the duty of family members to follow the needs and desires of the male family head. Male supremacy was a key element and men were responsible for providing for families and serving as warriors and in public offices.

Chinese civilization reflects the ideas of Confucius, a philosopher who lived in the sixth century B.C. According to his system of ideas, **Confucianism,** people's lives would prosper if they acted in harmony with the universe. Proper behavior requires living according to the **Dao** or "Way," especially following one's duty to others. The interests of the family and community came before those of the individual. Parents should be loving, children should respect their parents, husbands should fulfill their duties, and wives should be obedient. Rulers should be benevolent and subjects loyal, while everyone should work hard. He also believed that government service should be open to all men of talent, not just to nobles.

Section Wrap-up

Answer these questions to check your understanding of the entire section.

1. What is reincarnation?

_____

_____

_____

2. What right did the Mandate of Heaven give to the people being ruled?

_____

_____

_____

Persuasive Writing

Describe the Chinese philosophy of Confucianism. Then explain why you think it does or does not help society.

_____

_____

_____

_____

_____

_____

_____

_____

_____

_____

_____

_____

Ancient Greece

Big Idea

For a long time, Greek life was centered around the polis. Alexander the Great's conquests spread Greek culture. Use a concept map like the one below to show the elements that contributed to the classical age of Greece.

Classical Age of Greece

 **Notes** | **Read to Learn**

Early Greek Civilization *(page 38)*

Identifying the Main Idea

What was the center of Greek life by 750 B.C.?

_____

_____

_____

_____

The earliest Greek civilization was at Mycenae on the mainland from about 1600 B.C. to 1100 B.C. Between approximately 1100 B.C. and 750 B.C., Greece went through its "Dark Age"—called this because there are few records of this time. Near the end of this period, the poet Homer wrote the *Iliad* and the *Odyssey*. These were **epic poems,** or long poems about heroes.

By 750 B.C., the city-state, or **polis,** became the focus of Greek life. The main gathering place of the polis was usually on a hill where there was a fortified area, the **acropolis.**

Some city-states had a **democracy,** or rule by the many. Others had an **oligarchy,** meaning rule by the few. These differences were clear in Sparta and Athens. In Sparta, people's lives were tightly controlled. Sparta's oligarchy was headed by two kings. A small council of elders decided on the issues presented to the all-male assembly. The assembly could not debate issues, only vote on them. In Athens, economic problems led to reform. In 508 B.C., Cleisthenes created a council of 500 that supervised foreign affairs, oversaw the treasury, and proposed laws to the assembly. The assembly had final authority to pass laws after open debate. Cleisthenes' reforms laid the foundation for Athenian democracy.

 **Notes** | **Read to Learn**

Classical Greece (page 43)

Identifying Cause and Effect

What caused the temporary alliance of Athens, Sparta, and other Greek city-states?

_____

_____

_____

_____

Classical Greece lasted from around 500 B.C. until 338 B.C. Between 499 B.C. and 479 B.C., the Greeks worked together to defeat two invasions by the Persians. Athens then led the Greek world. Athens had a **direct democracy** in which all citizens helped make government decisions.

Athens and Sparta were rivals for power. Their disputes led to the Great Peloponnesian War from 431 B.C. to 405 B.C. When it was over, the Athenian Empire was destroyed, the major Greek states were weaker, and Macedonia grew stronger.

During the Classical era, the arts flourished, becoming a main source of Western culture. Its art and architecture expressed the Greek ideals of reason, balance, and harmony. The Greeks pioneered Western drama. Greek tragedies explored themes people still struggle to understand—good versus evil, human nature, and human fate. Greek comedies entertained while criticizing society. The Greeks also excelled in philosophy, the love of and search for wisdom. Socrates, Plato, and Aristotle were three of the greatest philosophers of the Western world. They developed rational thought and raised questions about existence that are still debated.

Alexander and the Hellenistic Era (page 45)

Drawing Conclusions

What qualities did Philip and Alexander probably have in common?

_____

_____

_____

_____

In 359 B.C., Philip II became Macedonia's king. He was strong, ambitious, and he wanted to unite all Greece under his leadership. His son, Alexander the Great, took over the throne at the age of 20. He followed his father's dream, invaded the Persian Empire, and established control of it by 331 B.C. By 326 B.C., he was in India, where his armies faced many difficult battles. Alexander returned home where, in 323 B.C., he died.

Alexander created a new age, the Hellenistic Era. During this era, the Greek language and culture spread through trade to Southwest Asia and beyond. Because of power struggles the kingdom fell apart. Eventually there were four Hellenistic kingdoms. The rulers of these kingdoms encouraged many Greeks to colonize the cities of these regions. These cities became the means for spreading Greek ideas and language.

During this era, there were many cultural achievements. The city of Alexandria in Egypt, for example, was home to poets, writers, philosophers, and scientists. Greek architects and sculptors kept busy designing works in the new cities. There were also great advancements in the sciences, including astronomy and math.

Section Wrap-up

Answer these questions to check your understanding of the entire section.

1. What was the result of the Great Peloponnesian War?

_____

_____

_____

2. What effect on culture did Alexander the Great have?

_____

_____

_____

Expository Writing

In an essay, summarize the legacy of the ancient Greeks and explain why the Greeks have had such a strong influence on Western civilization.

_____

_____

_____

_____

_____

_____

_____

_____

_____

_____

_____

_____

_____

Rome and the Rise of Christianity

Big Idea

The Romans created a large and successful empire that spread Greco-Roman culture and, later, Christianity. As you read this section, complete a chart like the one shown below listing the government officials and the legislative bodies of the Roman Republic.

Officials	Legislative Bodies

 **Notes**

Read to Learn

The Rise of Rome *(page 48)*

Identifying Cause and Effect

What positive changes occurred during the Pax Romana?

_____

_____

_____

_____

Roman government was a **republic**, established in 509 B.C. In a republic, the leader is not a king and some citizens can vote. There were two classes, the patricians and the plebeians. The **patricians** were wealthy landowners who could vote and serve in office. The **plebeians** were less wealthy people who could vote but not serve in office. The Roman Senate, a group of about 300 patricians who served for life, was very important. There were other legislative bodies called assemblies.

Civil wars broke out between 82 and 31 B.C. as generals competed for loyalties. The Senate awarded Octavian, or Augustus, the title **imperator,** or commander in chief, in 31 B.C. The popular Augustus maintained power through his army. The Early Empire lasted from A.D. 14 to 180. From around 27 B.C. to A.D. 180, five so-called good emperors ruled and brought peace and prosperity—the *Pax Romana,* meaning Roman Peace. These emperors carried out positive policies and built aqueducts, bridges, roads, and ports. The Roman Empire was one of the greatest states the world had even seen, with more than 50 million people in three and a half million square miles of territory. The empire represented a vast trading network. Grains from Egypt reached the people of Rome, as did luxury items from the east, like silk.

Notes | Read to Learn

The Roman Empire (page 52)

Predicting

What would most likely have happened to the Roman economy if the slaves were suddenly freed?

_____

_____

_____

The Romans excelled in architecture and built on a large scale. They also had a golden age of literature with works by Virgil and Livy. The use of slaves was very common in the Roman Empire. Greek slaves often became tutors, musicians, and doctors. Slaves of all nationalities worked on farms, built roads and public buildings, and worked in households.

One of Rome's major contributions to later generations was its system of law. The Twelve Tables, created for the simple agricultural society of early Rome, later developed into civil law for Roman citizens. When law cases arose between Romans and non-Romans, a new set of laws developed—the Law of Nations. The Law of Nations prepared the way for an idea of universal law based on reason.

The Rise of Christianity (page 55)

Comparing and Contrasting

How was Christianity different from the Roman state religion?

_____

_____

_____

Christianity began as a religious movement within Judaism. Christianity spread because of apostles, followers of a Jewish teacher named Jesus. It also spread through writings and the establishment of churches all over Asia Minor. By A.D. 100, Christian churches could be found in all the major cities of the eastern empire as well as in some parts of the western empire.

Romans disliked Christianity because it opposed worship of the state gods and emperors. Christians who refused to worship with other Romans faced the possibility of death. Under Theodosius the Great (A.D. 378 to 395), however, Christianity became the official religion of the Roman Empire.

End of the Empire (page 58)

Formulating Questions

What is one question that is not answered in the section?

_____

_____

_____

During the third century, the Roman Empire suffered from civil wars and economic decline. By the end of the century, however, the emperors Diocletian and Constantine took steps to reverse the empire's decline. Constantine built a new capital at Constantinople. Now the Roman Empire was divided into two parts: Rome, capital of the Western Roman Empire, and Constantinople, capital of the Eastern Roman Empire.

German tribes from the north began to invade the western empire beginning in the late 300s. The year 476 marks the accepted date for the fall of the Western Roman Empire. In this year, the Germanic head of the army deposed the emperor. Germanic kingdoms then replaced the Western Roman Empire, but the Eastern Roman Empire continued to thrive.

Chapter 2, Section 2

1. How was Athens a direct democracy?

_____

_____

_____

2. What kinds of work did slaves do in ancient Rome?

_____

_____

_____

Under which government do you think it was best for ordinary citizens to live: that of ancient Greece or ancient Rome? Support your position with specific details from the text.

_____

_____

_____

_____

_____

_____

_____

_____

_____

_____

_____

The World of Islam

Big Idea

In the 600s, the Arabian prophet Muhammad created the religion of Islam, which led to great changes in the social and political systems of Southwest Asia. Use a chart like the one below to identify the achievements of Islamic civilization.

Achievements of Islamic Civilization

Notes

Read to Learn

Rise of Islam (page 90)

Predicting

Predict what would happen to Islam after Muhammad died.

_____

_____

_____

_____

The Arabs were a Semitic-speaking nomadic people who lived in the desert lands of the Arabian Peninsula. Muslims believe Muhammad, a prophet, received revelations from Allah. These were written down to form the Quran, the holy book of the religion of **Islam.** The followers of Islam are known as Muslims. They believe that there is only one God, Allah, and that Muhammad is his prophet.

Because they had so little success in convincing the people of Makkah to accept Islam, Muhammad and his followers moved to Madinah (Medina). This journey became known as the *Hijrah,* and became year 1 in the Islamic calendar. Muhammad won over new believers in Madinah and returned to Makkah in 630 with a force of ten thousand men. The city surrendered and most townspeople converted to the new faith. During a visit to the Kaaba, Muhammad declared it a sacred shrine of Islam. All Muslims are encouraged to make a pilgrimage to Makkah, known as the hajj. Muhammad died in 632, just as Islam was spreading throughout the Arabian Peninsula.

Like Judaism and Christianity, Islam is monotheistic. To fulfill their obligation to obey the will of Allah, Muslims follow the Five Pillars of Islam. Those who follow the law are guaranteed a place in eternal paradise.

 **Notes** | **Read to Learn**

Islamic Empires (page 92)

Making Generalizations

What happened to the Arab Empire under the Umayyads?

_____

_____

_____

_____

Muhammad had been both a religious and a political leader, but he never named a successor. After Muhammad's death, Abū Bakr was named **caliph,** or successor to Muhammad. Under Abū Bakr, Syria, Egypt, and other parts of northern Africa were added to the new Arab Empire. By 650, the Arabs had conquered the entire Persian Empire.

In 661, Mu'āwiyah moved the capital from Madinah to Damascus in Syria. He also made the office of caliph, called the caliphate, hereditary in his family. This established the Umayyad dynasty.

In 750, Abū al-'Abbās overthrew the Umayyad dynasty and set up the Abbasid dynasty, which lasted until 1258. The capital city at Baghdad became the center of an enormous trade empire that extended into Asia, Africa, and Europe. Over time, the Abbasid rulers became corrupt and provinces broke away from their rule. In Egypt, the Fatimids established a new dynasty, dividing the Muslim Empire. In 1055, a Turkish leader captured Baghdad and commanded the entire empire. His title was **sultan,** "holder of power." It was the Mongols who finally ended the Abbasid caliphate when they destroyed Baghdad. Now Cairo, Egypt, was the new center of Islam.

Islamic Culture (page 96)

Determining Cause and Effect

How did Muslim scholars make it possible for Europeans to sail to the Americas?

_____

_____

In the Arab Empire there was a fairly well-defined upper class of ruling families, senior officials, nomadic elites, and wealthy merchants. In philosophy and science, the Arabs made an important contribution by translating and preserving the works of Greek philosophers. Arabic scholars also wrote down their own ideas about these works. In math, the Muslims refined the numerical system of India, which included the concept of zero. Muslim scholars also studied and named stars. They perfected the astrolabe, which made it possible for Europeans to sail to the Americas.

Muslims brought major changes to the culture of Southwest Asia through both literature and architecture. Their most famous works of literature are the _Rubaiyat_ of Omar Khayyam and _The 1001 Nights_. The best examples of Islamic architecture are the Muslim mosques, or houses of worship.

Answer these questions to check your understanding of the entire section.

1. What event marks the beginning of the Islamic calendar?

_____

_____

2. Who was the first caliph, or successor to Muhammad?

_____

_____

Using information in the summaries and your imagination, describe a city of the Arab Empire.

_____

_____

_____

_____

_____

_____

_____

_____

_____

_____

Early African Civilizations

Big Idea

The expansion of trade led to migration and the growth of new African kingdoms and societies. Using a chart like the one below, list the African kingdoms discussed in this chapter and whether they were in north, south, east, or west Africa.

Kingdom	Location

 **Notes** | **Read to Learn**

The Emergence of African Civilizations (page 98)

Drawing Conclusions

Africa is 40 percent desert, 10 percent rain forest, and 40 percent savanna, where the rainfall is unreliable. What effect would this have on food production?

_____

_____

_____

_____

The first African civilizations—Egypt, Kush, and Axum—arose when people mastered farming. Around 1000 B.C. Nubia became the independent state of Kush. Kush flourished as a major trading state from about 250 B.C. to A.D. 150. It declined when the new power of Axum emerged.

Axum's culture combined Arab and African traditions. In about A.D. 330, King Ezana converted to Christianity and made it the official religion of the state. In much of North Africa, the Arabs were in control, however. Arabs had taken control of Egypt in 641 and soon they controlled the entire North African coast. Muslim trading routes were established along the coast near Axum. For several centuries, the Christians in Axum and the Muslims were peaceful neighbors, but in the 1100s, the Muslim states wanted control of profitable trade in ivory and slaves. They tried to take control of the inland trade routes in Axum, but Axum fought back.

Kingdoms in West Africa (page 100)

Determining Cause and Effect

Why was salt prized by the Ghanians?

_____

_____

_____

As early as A.D. 500, the trading kingdom of Ghana emerged in the upper Niger River valley. With access to large gold deposits, Ghana was very wealthy. Muslim merchants from North Africa brought metal goods, textiles, horses, and salt to Ghana. These items were exchanged for gold. Salt was especially important to Ghanaians because people needed it to replenish their bodies and to preserve food. Ghana soon became an enormous trading empire.

The kingdom of Mali in West Africa arose after Ghana declined. Mali was founded by Sundiata Keita, who united his people in 1240. Like Ghana, Mali based its wealth and power on the gold and salt trade. Mansa Mūsā, who ruled from 1312 to 1337, doubled the kingdom's size and created a strong central government.

By the 1400s, another West African kingdom, Songhai, exceeded Mali in power. Its ruler, Sunni Ali, led many military campaigns to expand his kingdom. His conquests allowed the empire to gain control of the valuable gold and salt trade. In the late 1500s it began to decline.

Societies in East and South Africa (page 101)

Making Inferences

Why might east Africa flourish more quickly than in southern Africa?

_____

_____

As early as 1000 B.C. many people who lived near the Niger River migrated to East Africa and the Congo River basin. They spoke dialects of the **Bantu** language and eventually reached the East African coast and began to take part in the trade there. Around the seventh century A.D., Muslim traders from the Arabian Peninsula settled along the eastern coast and set up trading ports like Mogadishu, Mombasa, and Kilwa. The southern half of Africa developed more slowly than the north. Zimbabwe, which grew rich on the gold trade and flourished from 1300 to 1450, was one of the wealthiest states in the south.

African Society and Culture (page 103)

Drawing Conclusions

Why was the lineage group important?

_____

_____

Most early Africans lived in small villages. Their sense of identity came through family and **lineage groups.** The lineage groups, which were communities of extended family units, made up the basic building blocks of African society. Different African societies shared the belief in a number of gods, the power of diviners (people who were believed to have the power to predict events), and the importance of ancestors. African art usually reflected these religious beliefs.

Section Wrap-up

Answer these questions to check your understanding of the entire section.

1. What products did Axum trade?

_____

_____

_____

2. What were the basic building blocks of African society?

_____

_____

Summarize the influence of gold on the growth of African kingdoms.

_____

_____

_____

_____

_____

_____

_____

_____

_____

_____

_____

The Asian World

Big Idea

The diverse landforms of Asia influenced the development of distinct cultures. Using a diagram like the one below, identify all the civilizations that were affected by Mongol expansion.

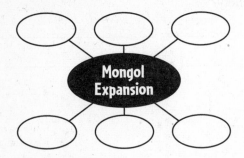

 **Read to Learn**

China Reunified (page 106)

Predicting

What do you think happened to the Mongol Empire once it was broken into khanates?

_____

_____

_____

_____

During the Tang dynasty (618 to 907), emperors made major reforms. They began to use exams again to recruit officials for the civil service. They also created a more stable economy by giving land to the peasants.

In 960, the Song dynasty came to power. Their rule lasted until 1279 and was a time of prosperity and cultural achievement. In the 1200s, the Mongols who lived in the Gobi desert in the north overthrew the Song and created a new Mongol dynasty. Until the end of the Song dynasty, Chinese government was based on a monarchy that relied on a large bureaucracy.

Under Genghis Khan, the Mongols brought almost the entire Eurasian landmass under one ruler, creating the largest land empire in history. When he died in 1227, his heirs divided the empire into khanates. Each khanate was ruled by a son of Genghis Khan. Genghis Khan's grandson, Kublai Khan, overthrew the Song dynasty in 1279. He established a new Chinese dynasty, the Yuan dynasty, and China prospered. The Mongols were eventually overthrown and the Ming dynasty began.

The centuries between the Tang and Ming dynasties—roughly 600 to 1600—are often seen as the great age for Chinese art and literature. During the Song and Mongol dynasties, many landscape artists used the Dao, or Way, to paint nature.

 **Notes** | **Read to Learn**

The Emergence of Japan *(page 110)*

Analyzing Information

How much power did the emperor have under the shogunate?

_____

_____

_____

By 794, instead of the central government having great power, powerful families dominated rural areas. They began to hire military men for protection. This new class of military servants were called **samurai.** The samurai fought on horseback and wore a helmet and armor. The samurai lived by a strict code, known as **Bushido,** or "the way of the warrior."

By the end of the 1100s, rivalries between aristocratic families led to almost constant civil war. Minamoto Yoritomo created a strong centralized government by having a **shogun** as ruler. Called a shogunate, this form of government allowed the emperor to rule in name, while the shogun held true authority.

Japanese spiritual beliefs included worship of *kami,* spirits that were believed to live in nature. The Japanese also revered their ancestors. Gradually these beliefs evolved into a religion called **Shinto,** which is still found in Japan today.

India After the Guptas *(page 112)*

Drawing Conclusions

Why were the Rajputs unsuccessful at resisting Maḥmūd of Ghazna?

_____

_____

Islam became a force in India at a time when the country was politically divided. The Rajputs, Hindu warriors, fought against the Ghazna leader Maḥmūd without success. That was because the Rajputs' elephants could not match the cavalry of the invaders. By 1200 the Muslims dominated northern India. They created a new Indian state known as the Sultanate of Delhi.

Civilization in Southeast Asia *(page 114)*

Analyzing Information

Which aspects of life in Southeast Asia did Chinese and Indian cultures influence?

_____

_____

Between 500 and 1500, a number of states emerged in Southeast Asia. Many of them modeled their governments on either China or India. In the tenth century the Vietnamese overthrew the Chinese, but they continued to use the Chinese model of government. Vietnam named itself Dai Viet (Great Viet) and adopted state Confucianism.

Angkor, or the Khmer Empire, was the most powerful state in the region for several hundred years. The Burmese peoples established the kingdom of Pagan to the west of the Thai in the eleventh century. Both the Thai and Burmese cultures drew on Indian models in politics and in cultural matters. Chinese and Indian cultures influenced not just political forms in Southeast Asia, but art and architecture, too.

Section Wrap-up

Answer these questions to check your understanding of the entire section.

1. What reforms were instituted by the Tang dynasty?

_____

_____

_____

_____

2. Which Southeast Asian state was influenced by Chinese culture?

_____

_____

_____

_____

Expository Writing

Briefly summarize the role of the samurai in early Japan.

_____

_____

_____

_____

_____

_____

_____

_____

_____

_____

Europe and the Byzantine Empire

Big Idea

The western European states were formed by the Germanic peoples, the legacy of the Romans, and the Christian Church. Byzantine rulers continued an empire in the East. Use a table like the one below to list the differences between the systems of feudalism and kingdoms.

Feudalism	Kingdoms

 **Notes**

Read to Learn

European Kingdoms and Feudalism (page 118)

Formulating Questions

What is a question that could be asked about the Carolingian Empire?

_____

_____

_____

By 500, the Western Roman Empire had been replaced by German states. As the official Roman state fell apart, the Christian church played an increasingly important role in the new European civilization. This was due to its organization and teachings. Charlemagne (768–814) ruled the Frankish Kingdom and expanded his territory into much of western and central Europe. This was the Carolingian Empire. After Charlemagne died in 814, his empire began to fall apart. People then turned to local landed aristocrats to provide them with protection in return for service. This led to a new political and social system called **feudalism.** In what came to be known as the feudal contract, a **vassal** swore an oath of allegiance to his lord and promised to provide him with military service. In return, the lord granted his vassal a fief, or piece of land that would support the vassal and his family.

In time, kings began to strengthen their position at the expense of the nobles. These kings laid the foundations for the European kingdoms that have dominated Europe ever since. In England, many nobles resented the growth of the king's power. During King John's reign, they rebelled and in 1215 forced the king to sign the **Magna Carta,** or Great Charter, limiting his power.

Notes | Read to Learn

Byzantine Empire and Crusades *(page 123)*

Determining Cause and Effect

How did Justinian influence the modern-day legal system in Europe?

_____

_____

_____

Analyzing Information

Why was the First Crusade considered a success?

_____

_____

_____

_____

Despite the collapse of the western part of the Roman Empire in the fifth century, the Eastern Roman Empire continued to exist. It was centered in Constantinople. When Justinian became ruler of the Eastern Roman Empire in 527, he was determined to reestablish the Roman Empire in the entire Mediterranean world. By 552, he had succeeded, but after his death in 565, the empire fell apart again. Justinian's most important contribution was his codification of Roman law, which resulted in *The Body of Civil Law.* This code of Roman laws was also used in the West and became the basis for much of the legal system of Europe.

By the 700s, after a defeat by Islamic forces and problems on its northern frontier, the Eastern Roman Empire had shrunk. Now it consisted only of the eastern Balkans and Asia Minor (modern-day Turkey). Historians call this small Eastern Roman Empire the Byzantine Empire, a civilization that lasted until 1453. The Byzantine Empire was both a Greek and a Christian state. Greek was the official language, not Latin, and the Eastern Orthodox Church was the official church. Under the Macedonians, who ruled from 867 to 1081, the empire expanded again to become the largest it had been since the beginning of the seventh century. In 1071, however, the Seljuk Turks defeated Byzantine forces at Manzikert, and Emperor Alexius I turned to Europe for military aid.

From the eleventh to the thirteenth centuries, European Christians carried out a series of military campaigns to regain the Holy Land (the ancient region of Palestine) from the Muslims. These expeditions, known as the **Crusades,** came about because the Byzantine emperor Alexius I had asked for help in defending his lands against the Seljuk Turks. Pope Urban II agreed to the request, seeing an opportunity to give papal leadership to the cause of liberating the Holy Land from non-Christians.

The First Crusade was the only successful one. The crusaders captured Jerusalem in 1099 and set up four crusader states. Although supplied with provisions from Italian port cities, these states could not hold out against the surrounding Muslims. In 1187, Jerusalem fell to Muslim forces led by Saladin. It is not certain what effect the Crusades had on Europe. They probably increased trade wealth in Italian port cities. They also helped break down the feudal system because kings took the role of levying taxes to raise Crusading armies. As feudalism broke down, strong states emerged.

Section Wrap-up

Answer these questions to check your understanding of the entire section.

1. What played an increasingly important role in European affairs once the Western Roman Empire fell?

_____

_____

_____

_____

2. What was Justinian's most important contribution?

_____

_____

_____

_____

_____

Informative Writing

Using information from the text and your imagination, explain why a man would choose to be a vassal.

_____

_____

_____

_____

_____

_____

_____

_____

_____

_____

_____

_____

_____

Chapter 4, Section 1 (Pages 132–141)
Europe in the Middle Ages

Big Idea

New farming practices led to population growth, and architectural innovation made Gothic cathedrals possible. Use a chart like the one below to show the effects of the growth of towns on medieval European society.

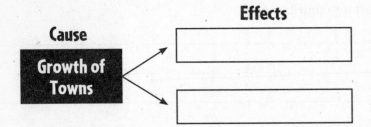

Cause

Growth of Towns

Effects

Notes

Read to Learn

Peasants, Trade, and Cities *(page 132)*

Determining Cause and Effect

Why did a money economy emerge during the High Middle Ages?

_____

_____

_____

_____

During the High Middle Ages (1000–1300), Europe's population expanded from 38 to 74 million because there was greater peace and stability after the Viking invasions and because food production increased. A **manor** was a lord's agricultural estate that the peasants farmed. More and more peasants became **serfs,** or peasants legally bound to the land. Serfs had to provide labor services, pay rents, and be under the lord's control. By 800, probably 60 percent of the people of Western Europe were serfs. The seasons determined peasant activities.

Trade became more important in the 1000s and 1100s. The demand for gold and silver coins grew until a **money economy**—an economic system based on money rather than barter—emerged. Trading companies and banking firms were set up to manage the exchange of goods. All of this was part of the rise of **commercial capitalism,** a system in which people invested in trade and goods to make profits.

New cities were founded and the urban population grew with trade. Cities and towns manufactured many items, from cloth and metalwork to shoes. In the 1100s, craftspeople began to organize themselves into guilds, or business associations. By the 1200s, there were guilds for almost every craft, and they played a leading role in the economy.

 **Notes** | **Read to Learn**

Medieval Christianity and Culture *(page 135)*

Drawing Conclusions

Why were convents appealing to women?

_____

_____

_____

_____

In the thirteenth century, during the papacy of Pope Innocent III, the Catholic Church reached the height of its political power. From about 1050 to 1150, a number of new monastic orders were formed: the Cistercians, Benedictines, Franciscans, and Dominicans. Many women, especially aristocrats, became nuns, took religious orders, and lived in convents. Most of the learned women of the Middle Ages were nuns.

The Church also created a court called the **Inquistion** to find and try heretics—people who deny Church doctrines. To ordinary Catholics in the High Middle Ages, sacraments, or Christian rites, were very important. Sacraments were seen as necessary for salvation, and only the clergy could administer them.

During the eleventh and twelfth centuries, there was an increase in church building. Innovations led to a new architectural style, Gothic, which allowed churches to have higher ceilings and more windows than the earlier Romanesque style. At university, students studied the liberal arts. After that, students could study law, medicine, or theology—the study of religion and God. Latin was the universal language in Europe at this time, used in the Church and universities. By the 1100s, new literature was being written in the vernacular. That is the everyday language of a particular region, such as Spanish, German, and French.

The Late Middle Ages *(page 139)*

Synthesizing Information

Which sates attempted to form strong monarchies?

_____

_____

_____

In the 1300s, the Black Death hit Europe. Bubonic plague was the most common form of the Black Death. It usually followed trade routes and so appeared first in port cities. As many as one-third to one-half of a total European population of 75 million had died by 1351. The death of so many people had severe effects on the economy. Trade declined, and a shortage of workers drove up the price of labor.

Another crisis concerned the Church. After 1377, a period began with two competing popes. The Italian cardinals elected an Italian pope, while some French cardinals elected a French pope. This was called the Great Schism. From 1378 until 1417, both lines of popes claimed to be the true Christian leaders.

The 1300s also had war and political instability. The Hundred Years' War between England and France (1337–1453) was the most violent struggle during this period. By the fifteenth century, many rulers tried to reestablish strong central control. Some historians call these reestablished states **new monarchies.** This didn't happen with the Holy Roman Empire, however, in part because of religious differences.

Section Wrap-up

Answer these questions to check your understanding of the entire section.

1. Why was the clergy so important to ordinary people in the Middle Ages?

_____

_____

_____

_____

2. What were some examples of vernacular language?

_____

_____

_____

Informative Writing

Using information from the text, trace the development and progress of the Great Schism. What effects did it have?

_____

_____

_____

_____

_____

_____

_____

_____

_____

_____

_____

Early American Civilizations

Big Idea

The Maya, Aztec, and Inca developed sophisticated civilizations in Mesoamerica and South America. As you read, create a separate chart, like the one shown here, for each of the cultures discussed in this section.

People	
Location	
Religion	
Architecture	
Year/Reason Declined	

Notes   Read to Learn

Early Civilizations in Mesoamerica (page 144)

Formulating Questions

What is a question that could be asked about the Toltec?

_____

_____

_____

_____

In North America, diverse cultures developed, including the Inuit, Mound Builders, Anasazi, Plains Indians, and Iroquois. One of the earliest civilizations in Mesoamerica was the Olmec civilization, which appeared around 1200 B.C. The Maya civilization flourished between A.D. 300 and 900. They built remarkable temples and pyramids and developed a complicated calendar, known as the Long Count. The Maya civilization eventually included much of Central America and southern Mexico and was made up of city-states. The Maya created a sophisticated writing system based on hieroglyphs.

Another civilization in central Mexico was the Toltec. The Toltec extended their control into Maya lands in Guatemala and the northern Yucatán. They built pyramids and palaces. They also introduced metalworking to Mesoamerica.

The Aztec founded their capital, Tenochtitlán, on the modern site of Mexico City by 1325. Along with the city-states of Tetzcoco and Tlacopan, the Aztec formed a Triple Alliance that helped them dominate much of Mesoamerica. The Aztec ruled over much of what is modern Mexico through local lords, who paid Aztec kings **tribute**—goods or money subjects pay to a conqueror. By 1500, almost four million Aztec people lived in the Valley of Mexico and surrounding valleys. Most were farmers, landless laborers who worked the nobles' estates, or slaves.

 **Notes** | **Read to Learn**

South American Civilizations (page 148)

(page 148)

Analyzing Information

Why did the Inca empire rely on forced labor?

_____

_____

_____

_____

In South America, the Inca civilization ultimately dominated the region, but before they gained power, there were earlier peoples who developed their own cultures. The people of the Chavin, Nazca, and Moche cultures built cities and left behind ruins and artifacts as evidence of their existence.

The Inca people, however, became the most powerful in early South America. In the 1440s, their ruler Pachacuti and his successors, Topa Inca and Huayna Inca—the word *Inca* means "ruler"—extended Inca rule as far as Ecuador, central Chile, and the edge of the Amazon basin. At its height, the Inca Empire ruled almost twelve million people. The empire was built on war, so all young men were required to serve in the army, which had as many as 200,000 soldiers. A noble was sent out to govern newly conquered areas. Subjects were instructed in the Inca language, Quechua.

The empire relied heavily on forced labor. As needed, workers were moved to work on road and building projects. Using these resources, the Inca built an extensive road system that went from modern-day Columbia to a point south of present-day Santiago, Chile. Social roles were rigidly defined. For example, men and women chose a marriage partner from their own social group. A few women might be priestesses, but most worked in the home. Most Inca were farmers, growing potatoes and corn and living in stone or adobe homes near their fields. In mountain farms they practiced high-altitude agriculture, in which the land was leveled into terraces and careful irrigation practices were followed.

The Inca constructed great buildings and temples in their capital, Cuzco. Stones were fitted together without mortar to withstand frequent earthquakes. The technique is seen in the ruins of Macchu Picchu, a city built 8,000 feet (2,400 m) above sea level. The Inca had no writing system, but they kept accurate records by using a system of knotted strings called the **quipu.** The lack of a complete writing system, however, didn't prevent Inca cultural achievements.

Answer these questions to check your understanding of the entire section.

1. What ancient city was built on the site of modern-day Mexico City?

_____

_____

_____

2. How did the Inca keep records?

_____

_____

_____

Explain what the cultural advancements of the early civilizations in Mesoamerica and South America were, and what they suggest.

_____

_____

_____

_____

_____

_____

_____

_____

_____

_____

_____

_____

The Renaissance

Big Idea

Between 1350 and 1550, Italian intellectuals believed they had entered a new age of human achievement. As you read, use a web diagram like the one below to identify the major principles of Machiavelli's work *The Prince*.

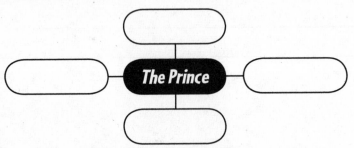

The Prince

**Notes**   **Read to Learn**

The Italian Renaissance *(page 162)*

**Analyzing Information**

What was reborn during the Renaissance?

_____

_____

_____

_____

The Italian Renaissance lasted from about 1350 to 1550. *Renaissance* means "rebirth." It had three main characteristics. First, Italy was largely an **urban society.** In this urban society, a **secular,** or worldly, viewpoint grew. Second, the Renaissance was an age of recovery from the disasters of the plague, political instability, and the decline of Church power. There was a rebirth of interest in ancient Roman culture that affected both politics and art. Third, people in the Renaissance emphasized individual ability. The Renaissance affected the wealthy more than ordinary people, but even they could see the art that decorated the churches and public buildings.

Italy had not developed a centralized monarchical state. Instead, independent city-states played important roles in politics. Milan, Florence, and Venice had all prospered from trade. The Visconti family and then Francesco Sforza ruled Milan. Sforza conquered the city with **mercenaries**—soldiers who sold their services. Venice was a republic, but in name only. The Medici family ruled Florence except for a time when a Dominican preacher named Girolamo Savonarola took power.

Both the French and the Spanish tried to conquer Italy, fighting each other in Italy for 30 years. The Spanish under Charles I sacked Rome and left the Spanish a dominant force in Italy.

Machiavelli on Power *(page 165)*

Comparing and Contrasting

How were Machiavelli's principles different from those stressed in the Middle Ages?

_____

_____

_____

_____

One of the most influential works on political power in the Western world was *The Prince,* written by Niccolò Machiavelli. Machiavelli's work concerned how to get and keep political power. During the Middle Ages, many writers had stressed how a ruler should behave based on Christian principles. Machiavelli, in contrast, believed that morality had little to do with politics. He believed that human nature was basically self-centered and that since a prince acted on behalf of the state, he should not be restricted to moral principles. Machiavelli believed that a leader must do good when possible, but evil when necessary, and that the end result justifies the means of achieving it.

Renaissance Society *(page 166)*

Comparing and Contrasting

What were the differences in the Renaissance classes?

_____

_____

_____

_____

Renaissance society was still divided into classes, or estates. Nobles dominated society even though they made up only 2 to 3 percent of the population. The ideal noble was described in *The Book of the Courtier,* written by Baldassare Castiglione. The book said that nobles had to be born, not made. They were to have a classical education and serve their prince effectively and honestly. Castiglione's principles guided European social and political life for hundreds of years. Peasants still made up 85 to 90 percent of the total European population. Most peasants were no longer serfs. Townspeople during the Renaissance included patricians, who had wealth. Beneath them were the burghers—the shopkeepers, artisans, and guild members. Below the burghers were the workers, who earned pitiful wages, and the unemployed. Both groups lived miserable lives.

Family bonds were a source of security. Parents arranged marriages for children, paying a **dowry** to the husbands of their daughters. The father-husband was the center of the family and had absolute authority over his children until he died or formally freed them. Children became adults when their fathers went before a judge to free them. This could happen when the children were in their early teens to their late twenties.

Section Wrap-up

Answer these questions to check your understanding of the entire section.

1. What does the word *renaissance* mean?

_____

_____

_____

2. Which two European countries tried to conquer and dominate Italy?

_____

_____

_____

Persuasive Writing

Which principles do you think would lead to the best government—Machiavelli's or those of the Middle Ages? Explain why.

_____

_____

_____

_____

_____

_____

_____

_____

_____

_____

_____

_____

Ideas and Art of the Renaissance

Big Idea

Humanism was an important intellectual movement of the Renaissance and was reflected in the works of Renaissance artists. As you read, use a chart like the one below to describe the three pieces of literature written by Dante, Chaucer, and de Pizan. What was the primary importance of each of their works?

Divine Comedy	The Canterbury Tales	The Book of the City of Ladies

Notes

Read to Learn

Italian Renaissance Humanism (page 170)

Making Inferences

Why might some writers use their local vernacular?

_____

_____

_____

_____

Humanism was based on the study of the ancient Greek and Roman classics. Humanists studied grammar, rhetoric, poetry, moral philosophy, and history. Petrarch looked for forgotten Latin manuscripts and started searches in monastic libraries throughout Europe. In Florence, humanists took an interest in civic life. They believed that intellectuals had a duty to live lives of service to their state. Humanists emphasized the use of classical Latin, though some writers wrote in the **vernacular**—the language spoken in their own regions. In the Italian vernacular, the poet Dante wrote the *Divine Comedy.* It was a long poem about an imaginary journey to Paradise, or Heaven. The English writer Geoffrey Chaucer wrote *The Canterbury Tales* about a group of pilgrims traveling to Canterbury. Each pilgrim represented part of English society. Chaucer's dialect became the ancestor of the modern English language. A Frenchwoman, Christine de Pizan, wrote to defend women. *The Book of the City of Ladies* denounced men who said that women were unable to learn.

Read to Learn

Renaissance Education (page 172)

Making Inferences

What subjects do you study that were not part of the liberal arts schools of the humanists?

_____

_____

_____

Renaissance humanists believed that education could change human beings. They wrote books on education and started schools. Education became more secular, or less focused on religion. Liberal studies (liberal arts) were at the core of the schools. To enable individuals to reach their full potential for virtue and wisdom, humanists had students study history, moral philosophy, poetry, mathematics, and other subjects. The humanists wanted to create individuals who follow a path of virtue and wisdom, and who could persuade others to follow the same path. They also wanted to prepare the sons of aristocrats for leadership roles. A few female students studied history, poetry, and how to ride and dance. They were told not to learn mathematics or rhetoric. Humanist schools were the model for education of Europe's ruling classes until the twentieth century.

Italian Renaissance Art (page 173)

Identifying the Main Idea

How did artists' paintings change during the Renaissance?

_____

_____

_____

Renaissance artists sought to imitate nature. A **fresco** is a painting done on fresh, wet plaster with water-based paints. Masaccio, in Florence, made great strides in using perspective in his frescoes. Painters explored perspective, the organization of outdoor space, movement, and human anatomy. Leonardo da Vinci, Raphael, and Michelangelo worked during the High Renaissance, a period between 1490 and 1520. Leonardo mastered realistic painting. Raphael created great beauty in his madonnas (paintings of the Virgin Mary). Michelangelo created such masterpieces as the ceiling of the Sistine Chapel in Rome.

The Northern Artistic Renaissance (page 175)

Drawing Conclusions

Why was the use of detail important to the artists of northern Europe?

_____

_____

Like the artists of Italy, the artists of northern Europe wanted to portray their world realistically. Because their churches were smaller, they emphasized the use of detail. The most important northern school of art was in Flanders, in the Low Countries. The Flemish painter Jan van Eyck was among the first to use and perfect the technique of realistic oil painting.

By 1500 northern artists had begun to study in Italy. A German artist, Albrecht Dürer, was greatly influenced by them. Dürer tried to achieve a standard of ideal beauty that was based on a careful examination of the human form.

Section Wrap-up

Answer these questions to check your understanding of the entire section.

1. What Renaissance work served as the ancestor of the modern English language?

_____

_____

_____

2. Who are the three artists most associated with the High Renaissance?

_____

_____

_____

Using information from the text, choose a scene in your mind, such as your classroom or your bedroom, and imagine how a northern European artist would have painted it. Describe this painting. Remember that northern European artists used oil paints.

_____

_____

_____

_____

_____

_____

_____

_____

_____

_____

_____

_____

_____

The Protestant Reformation

Big Idea

In northern Europe, Christian humanists sought to reform the Catholic Church, and Protestantism emerged. As you read, use a diagram like the one below to identify steps that led to the Reformation.

Steps Leading to the Reformation

 **Notes** | **Read to Learn**

Prelude to Reformation (page 176)

Analyzing Information

What did the Christian humanists think that people should do in order to become more pious?

_____

_____

_____

_____

During the second half of the fifteenth century, the new classical learning of the Italian Renaissance spread to northern Europe. From that came a movement called **Christian humanism.** Its major goal was reform of the Catholic Church. The Christian humanists believed in the ability of human beings to reason and improve themselves. They thought that by reading the basic works of Christianity and the classics, people could become more pious, or inwardly religious. The best-known Christian humanist, Desiderius Erasmus, thought that Christianity should show people how to live good lives. He thought that external forms of medieval religion, such as relics and fasts, were not all that important.

Erasmus and others were calling for reform of the Church for several reasons. One was corruption. Many popes acted as political and military leaders rather than as spiritual leaders. Many church officials used their church offices to gain wealth. Also, many parish priests were ignorant of their spiritual duties. Ordinary people wanted **salvation,** or acceptance into Heaven. The Church made this process mechanical. People could collect relics to gain salvation. Or, they could buy an **indulgence,** a certificate of release from all or part of their punishment for sin. A popular movement called Modern Devotion also contributed to an environment where people would be receptive to ideas that went against the Church.

 **Notes**

Read to Learn

Martin Luther *(page 179)*

(page 179)

Determining Cause and Effect

What led to Luther's writing of the Ninety-five Theses?

_____

_____

_____

Martin Luther was a monk and a professor at the University of Wittenberg, in Germany. Through his study of the Bible, he came to believe that human beings could never do enough good works to earn salvation. Instead, they could be saved if they had faith in God, because God was merciful. This idea, called justification (being made right before God) by faith alone, became the chief teaching of the Protestant Reformation. In 1517 Luther posted an attack on the selling of indulgences, called the Ninety-five Theses, on the door of the Castle Church in Wittenberg. Thousands of copies were printed and spread to all parts of Germany.

By 1520 Luther was calling on German princes to overthrow the papacy in Germany and establish a reformed German church. He also attacked the Church's system of sacraments and called for clergy to marry. The Church excommunicated Luther in 1521. He was also required to appear before the emperor, Charles V. Charles thought he could convince Luther to change his ideas, but Luther refused. Luther was made an outlaw within the empire. A revolution occurred, with German rulers taking power over the Catholic churches. Luther set up a new service to replace the mass. Luther's doctrine soon became known as **Lutheranism.**

Politics in the German Reformation *(page 181)*

(page 181)

Drawing Conclusions

After the Peace of Augsburg, were the German people able to choose whether to be Catholic or Lutheran?

_____

_____

_____

_____

The fate of Luther's movement was closely tied to political affairs. The Holy Roman emperor was Charles V, who was also Charles I of Spain. Charles wanted to keep his large empire under the control of his dynasty, the Hapsburgs. He also wanted to keep the empire united by keeping it Catholic. However, conflict with France over territory led to more than 20 years of wars.

The pope was on the side of the French king, which made things harder for Charles. Further, Germany was a land of several hundred territorial states. They all owed loyalty to the emperor, but many had freed themselves from his authority.

By the time Charles V was able to bring military forces to Germany, the German princes were well organized, and Charles was unable to defeat them.

In 1555 the Peace of Augsburg ended religious warfare in Germany. Under it, the German states were free to choose between Catholicism and Lutheranism. Subjects did not have the right to choose their own religion; instead, their ruler chose it for them.

Answer these questions to check your understanding of the entire section.

1. What was the major goal of Christian humanism?

_____

_____

_____

2. What was the political structure of Germany during the Protestant Reformation?

_____

_____

_____

Expository Writing

Using information from the text, explain how politics influenced the fate of Lutheranism.

_____

_____

_____

_____

_____

_____

_____

_____

_____

_____

_____

The Spread of Protestantism

Big Idea

Different forms of Protestantism emerged in Europe as the Reformation spread, and the Catholic Church underwent a religious rebirth. As you read, use a diagram like the one below to list some of the reforms proposed by the Council of Trent. Beside each, give the Protestant viewpoint to which it responded.

Council of Trent	Protestant Viewpoint
	←
	←
	←

Notes | Read to Learn

Divisions in Protestantism (page 182)

Determining Cause and Effect

What made John Calvin influential?

_____

_____

_____

_____

Divisions quickly appeared among Protestants. Relics and images were abolished. All paintings and decorations were removed from the churches. Ulrich Zwingli sought an alliance with Luther and the German reformers, but they were unable to agree on the meaning of the sacrament of Communion.

In 1531 there was a war between the Protestant and Catholic states in Switzerland. Zwingli was killed and leadership passed to John Calvin. Calvin's writings made him very influential. His doctrine was very close to Luther's, but he put more emphasis on the power of God, which led him to believe in **predestination.** Predestination meant that God had already decided who would be saved and who would be damned. This belief gave Calvinists great conviction and made them determined to spread their faith.

Among other reforms, Calvin created a special court for enforcing moral discipline. Citizens of Geneva were punished for "crimes" such as dancing, drunkenness, or playing cards. Calvinism became established in France, the Netherlands, Scotland, and central and eastern Europe. Calvinism was now the most important and dynamic form of Protestantism.

 **Notes** | # Read to Learn

Reformation in England *(page 184)*

Drawing Conclusions

How did the need for a male heir contribute to the English Reformation?

_____

_____

_____

The English Reformation was rooted in politics, not religion. King Henry VIII needed a male heir and wanted to marry a woman who might give him one. The pope was unwilling to **annul** (declare invalid) his first marriage. Henry got England's own church courts to do so. Henry married again, but the child was a girl, who later became Elizabeth I. In 1534, at Henry's request, Parliament finalized the break between the Catholic Church in England and the pope.

The Act of Supremacy made the king the head of the Church of England. Henry dissolved the monasteries and sold their land and possessions to wealthy landowners and merchants for money and support. He kept the doctrine of the church close to Catholic teachings.

During the reign of Edward VI, church officials moved the Church of England in a Protestant direction. When Edward died his older sister, Mary, a Catholic, tried to restore Roman Catholicism. She had some Protestants burned as heretics. England became even more Protestant, however.

Anabaptists *(page 185)*

Identifying the Main Idea

What did Anabaptists believe?

_____

_____

Radicals known as Anabaptists thought that the state should have no power over the church. They believed in complete separation of church and state. Anabaptists believed in adult baptism, not the baptism of children. They considered all believers to be equal, and any member of the community was eligible to be a minister. Anabaptists refused to hold political office or bear arms. Other Protestants and Catholics regarded them as dangerous radicals who should be persecuted.

Reformation and Society *(page 186)*

Drawing Conclusions

How did Protestantism affect women and Jews?

_____

_____

The Protestants developed a new view of the family. Both monasticism and the requirement for celibacy for the clergy had been abolished. The love between man and wife was praised. However, women were supposed to obey and bear children. Jews fared little better. Luther expected Jews to convert to Lutheranism. When they did not, he wrote that their synagogues and homes should be destroyed. In papal states, Jews who would not convert to Christianity were segregated into ghettos.

Catholic Reformation

Making Inferences

How did the Catholic Reformation affect Catholics?

_____

_____

_____

The Catholic Church also underwent a reformation. The Society of Jesus, known as the Jesuits, were very successful in restoring Catholicism to parts of Germany and eastern Europe.

Pope Paul III appointed a Reform Commission in 1537, which blamed the Church's problems on the corrupt policies of the popes. Paul III also started the Council of Trent. This group of church officials met on and off for 18 years. They reaffirmed traditional Catholic teachings that both faith and good works were needed for salvation. They upheld the seven sacraments and celibacy of the clergy. They forbade the selling of indulgences. The Roman Catholic Church was again unified and strong.

Section Wrap-up

Answer these questions to check your understanding of the entire section.

1. What religious doctrine is associated with John Calvin?

_____

_____

_____

2. How did the Protestant view of marriage and family affect the clergy?

_____

_____

_____

Expository Writing

Compare and contrast the beliefs of the Anabaptists with other Protestants of their time.

_____

_____

_____

_____

_____

_____

_____

Exploration and Expansion

Big Idea

Europeans began exploring the world in the fifteenth century, and several nations experienced economic heights through worldwide trade. As you read, use a chart like the one below to list the explorers and lands explored by each European nation.

	Explorers	Lands Explored
Portugal		
Spain		
England		
France		
Netherlands		

 **Notes**

Read to Learn

Motives and Means (page 194)

Making Inferences

Knowing what Christopher Columbus went on to do, how do you think he felt about the writings of Marco Polo?

_____

_____

_____

Between 1500 and 1800, Portugal, Spain, the Dutch Republic (the Netherlands), England, and France expanded into the rest of the world.

Europeans had long been attracted to Asia. Marco Polo had visited the Chinese court of Kublai Khan, and many, including Christopher Columbus, read his written accounts of the journey. In the fourteenth century, conquests by the Ottoman Turks made it difficult to travel by land to the East. People then began to think about going to Asia by sea. People wanted to expand trade, especially for spices, which were needed to preserve and flavor food. They were quite expensive when they came over land through Arab middlemen. Europeans also wanted to find precious metals. Further, many Europeans wanted to spread their religion to native peoples. They also wanted adventure. By the second half of the fifteenth century, European monarchs had the power and resources to expand, while technology had developed that would enable long sea voyages.

 **Notes** | # Read to Learn

A Race for Riches *(page 196)*

Drawing Conclusions

Why did more voyages follow da Gama's route?

_____

_____

_____

_____

Beginning in 1520, Portuguese fleets began probing southward along the western coast of Africa. They discovered a new source of gold. Vasco da Gama went around the Cape of Good Hope (the southern tip of Africa) and cut across the Indian Ocean to India. He took on a cargo of spices, took it home, and made a profit of several thousand percent. Of course, many more voyages followed this route.

Portuguese fleets took control of the spice trade from the Muslims. They defeated a combined fleet of Turkish and Indian ships off the coast of India. Admiral Alfonso d'Albuquerque set up a port at Goa. Then he sailed into Melaka, on the Malay Peninsula. From Melaka, the Portuguese launched expeditions to China and the Spice Islands. Although they got control of the spice trade, the Portuguese had neither the people nor the desire to colonize Asian regions.

Europeans knew the world was round, so Christopher Columbus persuaded Queen Isabella of Spain to finance an expedition west to find Asia. In 1492 Columbus reached the Americas, believing he had reached Asia. In 1519 Ferdinand Magellan sailed around South America into the Pacific Ocean and on to the Philippines. Magellan was killed, but is still remembered as the first person to circumnavigate the world.

Both Spain and Portugal feared that the other might claim territories. They signed the Treaty of Tordesillas in 1494. It gave Portugal the unexplored territories east of a line through the Atlantic Ocean and gave Spain the territories to the west of the line. This gave Spain rights to almost all of the Americas.

John Cabot explored the New England coastline for England. Portuguese sea captain Pedro Cabral landed in South America in 1500. Amerigo Vespucci described voyages to the Americas, whose name came from Vespucci's first name. The new territories already had flourishing civilizations of millions of people, but Europeans saw them as opportunities for conquest and exploitation.

Read to Learn

The Spanish Empire (page 198)

Determining Cause and Effect

How did the advanced technology of the Spanish affect their conquests of the Aztec and the Inca?

_____

_____

_____

_____

The Spanish conquerors of the Americas were called **conquistadors.** They had advanced firearms, skills, and determination. In central Mexico, the Aztec had ruled for a century. In 1519 a Spanish force under Hernán Cortés marched to the magnificent Aztec capital, Tenochtitlán. The Aztec were astounded to see men on horseback with firearms, cannons, and steel swords. Eventually, the Spanish took the Aztec king, Montezuma, hostage and began to pillage the city. Although at first the citizens drove the Spanish out, they suffered a smallpox epidemic because they had no immunity to European diseases. Other Aztec city-states helped the Spanish reconquer the city. The Spanish then destroyed it.

The Inca Empire was flourishing in 1530, when Francisco Pizarro landed on the Pacific coast. He had only a few men, but like the Aztec, the Inca were awed by his weapons and horses. The Inca also experienced a smallpox epidemic, and their emperor died. Pizarro captured the emperor's son, Atahuallpa, and executed him. He then captured the Inca capital at Cuzco. Pizarro established a new capital at Lima for a new colony of the Spanish empire.

By 1550 much territory in Mexico, Central America, and South America had been brought under Spanish control. Queen Isabella declared Native Americans to be her subjects. She granted to Spanish settlers in the Americas the ***encomienda,*** the right of landowners to use Native Americans as laborers.

Spanish settlers used Native Americans for forced labor. This, combined with European diseases, took a fearful toll on Native American lives. In Mexico, for example, the population dropped from 25 million in 1500 to 1 million in 1630.

Spaniards and Native Americans intermarried and created a new people. Traces of the original culture remain today. Colonists raised sugar, cotton, vanilla, and livestock to send to Europe. Europeans brought horses, cattle, and wheat to the Americas. Potatoes, cocoa, corn, tomatoes, and tobacco were shipped to Europe. The exchange of plants and animals between the Old and New Worlds, known as the **Columbian Exchange,** transformed economic activity in both worlds.

Comparing and Contrasting

How did the Spanish empire in Latin America differ from the English economy in North American colonies?

_____

_____

New European rivals began to challenge the Portuguese and the Spaniards by the beginning of the seventeenth century. The English established trade relations with India, as did the Dutch. The Dutch also traded in the Caribbean and settled on the North American continent in the Hudson River valley. After 1660, however, the English seized this colony of New Netherlands and renamed it New York. Canada became a French colony in 1663, but by the early eighteenth century, France had ceded some of its American possessions to the English. By this time, the English had control over most of the eastern seaboard of North America. Compared to the enormous empire of the Spanish in Latin America, the North American colonies still remained of little importance to the English economy.

Section Wrap-up

Answer these questions to check your understanding of the entire section.

1. Why were Europeans willing to make dangerous voyages of exploration?

_____

_____

_____

2. Describe the details of the Treaty of Tordesillas.

_____

_____

_____

Using information from the text, explain how Spanish colonization affected the Native American peoples.

_____

_____

_____

_____

_____

_____

_____

The Atlantic Slave Trade

Big Idea

European expansion affected Africa with the dramatic increase of the slave trade. As you read, use a table like the one below to identify economic and political factors that caused the slave trade to be profitable. List the economic and political effects of the trade.

Economic/Political Factors	Economic/Political Effects

Notes

Read to Learn

Trade, Colonies, and Mercantilism *(page 202)*

Drawing Conclusions

What were two reasons for the high demand for enslaved people?

_____

_____

_____

_____

European nations established many trading posts and colonies in the Americas and in the East. A **colony** is a settlement of people living in a new territory, linked by trade and government control with the parent country. **Mercantilism** was a set of economic principles. Mercantilists thought that the prosperity of a nation depended on having a large amount of gold or silver. To achieve this, countries tried to have a favorable **balance of trade.** This is the difference between what a nation imports and what it exports. Exports brought in gold or silver, so governments stimulated new industries with **subsidies,** or payments.

Sugarcane **plantations,** or large agricultural estates, were set up in Brazil and the Caribbean islands. Enslaved persons were taken from Africa, becoming part of the **triangular trade.** European merchant ships carried European manufactured goods to Africa, where they were traded for enslaved people, who were shipped to the Americas and sold. This part was called the **Middle Passage.** The Europeans then bought tobacco, molasses, sugar, and raw cotton in the Americas and shipped them back to Europe.

In the eighteenth century, 6 million enslaved Africans were exported. There was a very high death rate. Many died on the journey, and many more died of diseases to which they had no immunity when they arrived.

Effects of the Slave Trade *(page 205)*

Analyzing Information

What group of Europeans began the condemnation of slavery?

_____

_____

_____

_____

The slave trade was a tragedy for its victims. In addition, it led to the depopulation of some areas, and it deprived many African communities of their youngest and strongest men and women. It led to increased warfare in Africa. Coastal or near-coastal African chiefs, armed with guns acquired from the slave trade, increased their raids and wars on neighboring peoples. Very few Europeans cared.

The slave trade had a devastating effect on some African states. Benin in West Africa, for example, was a brilliant and creative society until it was pulled into the slave trade. As population declined and warfare increased, the people of Benin lost faith in their gods, their art deteriorated, and human sacrifice became more common. It became a corrupt and brutal place. It took years to discover the brilliance of the earlier culture.

The use of enslaved Africans remained largely acceptable to European society. Europeans continued to view Africans as inferior beings fit chiefly for slave labor. Not until the Society of Friends, or Quakers, began to condemn slavery in the 1770s did European feelings against it begin to build. The French did not abolish slavery until the French Revolution in the 1790s. The British ended the slave trade in 1807 and abolished slavery throughout the empire in 1833. But slavery continued in the United States until the Civil War of the 1860s.

Section Wrap-up

Answer these questions to check your understanding of the entire section.

1. How did the discovery of the Americas change the demand for enslaved persons?

_____

_____

_____

2. On what kind of power were the new social structures based?

_____

_____

_____

Expository Writing

Describe the effects of the slave trade on Benin.

_____

_____

_____

_____

_____

_____

_____

_____

_____

_____

_____

Colonial Latin America

Big Idea

Portugal and Spain reaped profits from the natural resources and products of their Latin American colonies. As you read, create a diagram like the one below to summarize the political, social, and economic characteristics of Colonial Latin America.

Colonial Latin America

Read to Learn

Colonial Empires in Latin America *(page 208)*

Making Inferences

How much respect did the Spanish and the Portuguese have for their conquered peoples?

_____

_____

_____

_____

In the sixteenth century, Portugal dominated Brazil, and Spain established a huge colonial empire that included parts of North America, Central America, and most of South America. A new civilization called Latin America arose. At the top of the social scale were **peninsulares,** officials who had been born in Europe and who held all important government positions. Below them were the **creoles,** who were descendants of Europeans born in Latin America. Below them were **mestizos,** the offspring of marriages between Europeans and Native Americans. The offspring of Europeans and Africans were called **mulattoes.** The multiracial groups were considered inferior to peninsulares and creoles. At the very bottom of the scale were Native Americans and enslaved Africans.

The colonies provided wealth to Spain and Portugal by sending them gold, silver, sugar, tobacco, diamonds, and animal hides. Farming was done on large estates owned by Spanish and Portuguese landowners and worked by Native Americans. Native Americans were forced to pay tribute and provide labor. In Peru, the Spanish used the **mita,** a system that allowed authorities to draft native labor for the silver mines.

The kings, being far away, appointed officials called viceroys to oversee the colonies. The Catholic Church played a powerful role, as Catholic missionaries established many missions and villages where they both converted and controlled Native Americans.

Section Wrap-up

Answer these questions to check your understanding of the entire section.

1. What goods did the colonies send to Europe?

_____

_____

_____

2. What effect did Catholic missionaries have on Native Americans?

_____

_____

_____

Expository Writing

Describe the social scale in Latin America.

_____

_____

_____

_____

_____

_____

_____

_____

_____

_____

_____

Europe in Crisis: The Wars of Religion

Big Idea

Religious and political conflicts erupted between Protestants and Catholics in many European nations. As you read, complete a chart like the one below comparing the characteristics of Spain, England, and France.

	Spain	England	France
Government			
Religion			
Conflicts			

 **Notes** | **Read to Learn**

Spain's Conflicts (page 218)

Drawing Conclusions

Why did Protestantism as practiced by Elizabeth Tudor satisfy most people?

_____

_____

_____

_____

By 1560 Calvinism and Catholicism were highly **militant,** or combative, religions. The greatest supporter of Catholicism was King Philip II of Spain. Philip inherited Spain, the Netherlands, and parts of Italy and the Americas. To control them, he insisted on strict conformity to Catholicism. Spain led an alliance against the Turks and defeated them at the Battle of Lepanto in 1571. But his attempts to control the Netherlands caused opposition from the nobles. Philip sent many troops, but the struggle continued until 1609.

Elizabeth Tudor took the English throne in 1558. She was a Protestant and was named as head of both church and state. Her religion was moderate enough to satisfy most people. Elizabeth tried to keep the powers of Spain and France balanced by always supporting the weaker one in any conflict. Finally, in 1588, Philip sent an **armada,** a fleet of ships, to invade England. The English ships were faster and better and defeated the armada. It limped home, battered by storms. Spain was weaker by the end of Philip's reign in 1598. War had bankrupted it, its armed forces were out of date, and the government was inefficient.

 **Notes** | **Read to Learn**

The French Wars of Religion (page 221)

Determining Cause and Effect

Why did Henry IV convert to Catholicism?

_____

_____

_____

French kings were Catholic, and they persecuted Protestants. Between 1562 and 1598, the French fought civil wars known as the Wars of Religion. Huguenots were French Protestants influenced by John Calvin. They made up only about 7 percent of the population, but of the nobility, 40 to 50 percent were Huguenots. They fought with an extreme Catholic party known as the ultra-Catholics. Battles raged for 30 years. Finally, in 1589, Henry of Navarre succeeded to the throne of France. He became King Henry IV. He was also the Huguenot political leader and believed he would never be accepted by Catholic France. So he converted to Catholicism. When he was crowned king in 1594, the fighting came to an end.

Henry IV issued the Edict of Nantes in 1598. The edict said that Catholicism was the official religion of France. However, it also gave Huguenots the right to worship and to enjoy all political privileges such as holding public offices.

Section Wrap-up

Answer these questions to check your understanding of the entire section.

1. Who were Huguenots?

_____

_____

_____

2. Who was the greatest supporter of Catholicism?

_____

_____

_____

Expository Writing

Explain what the Edict of Nantes said and accomplished.

_____

_____

_____

_____

_____

_____

_____

_____

_____

_____

_____

Social Crises, War, and Revolution

Big Idea

Social, economic, and religious conflicts challenged the established political order throughout Europe. As you read, use a chart like the one below to identify which conflicts were prompted by religious concerns.

Religious Conflicts

 **Notes**   **Read to Learn**

Crises in Europe (page 222)

Determining Cause and Effect

Why did witchcraft hysteria begin to decline by 1650?

_____

_____

_____

_____

From 1560 to 1650, Europe had severe economic and social crises. One major economic problem was **inflation,** or rising prices. By 1600 there was an economic slowdown. Less silver was coming from the silver mines, so Spain's economy, which depended on silver, declined. Also, ships were being attacked by pirates, and Spain had lost many artisans and merchants when it expelled the Jews and Muslims. Italy was also declining economically. Population in Europe grew in the sixteenth century, but it began to decline by 1650 due to wars, famine, and plague.

A belief in **witchcraft,** or magic, disturbed society. Traditional village culture had included a belief in witches for centuries. However, the religious zeal of the Inquisition and the hunt for heretics extended to witchcraft. Possibly more than a hundred thousand people were charged with witchcraft. More than 75 percent of these were women, and most were single or widowed and over 50 years old. Accused witches were tortured severely. Therefore, they usually confessed to allegiance to the devil and practices such as casting evil spells. The witchcraft hysteria began to lessen by 1650 because fewer people believed in evil spirits.

The Thirty Years' War (page 224)

Drawing Conclusions

Why did religious disputes continue even after the Peace of Augsburg?

_____

_____

_____

The Peace of Augsburg in 1555 allowed religious disputes to continue in Germany. This was because the peace settlement did not recognize Calvinism. The Thirty Years' War, which began in 1618, concerned religion, but it was also a struggle for territory. It began with Catholic forces led by the Hapsburg Holy Roman emperors fighting with Protestant nobles in Bohemia. The nobles were primarily Calvinist. Denmark, Sweden, France, and Spain entered the war, and it became more political. Finally, it was a struggle between France and Spain and the Holy Roman Empire for European leadership.

The war officially ended with the Peace of Westphalia in 1648. The Peace divided the more than 300 states of the Holy Roman Empire into independent states and gave them power to determine their own religion and foreign policy. This brought an end to the Holy Roman Empire as a political entity.

Revolutions in England (page 225)

Making Inferences

How did religious issues in England affect American history?

_____

_____

_____

_____

When Queen Elizabeth I of England died in 1603, the throne passed to her cousin, James I. James believed that he ruled by the **divine right of kings.** This meant that his power came from God. Parliament thought that it and the king should rule England together. The conflict came to a head after James's son, Charles I, was king. Charles also believed in the divine right of kings. He tried to curb the power of Parliament and also to add more ritual to the Church of England. In 1628 Parliament passed a Petition of Right limiting the king's powers, but Charles ignored it.

England slipped into civil war in 1642. Royalists, called Cavaliers, fought parliamentary forces, called Roundheads. Parliament won, led by Oliver Cromwell. Cromwell led Parliament to execute Charles I in 1649. Then Parliament abolished the monarchy and the House of Lords and established a **commonwealth,** or republic. However, after Cromwell died in 1658, Charles I's son, Charles II, was restored to the throne.

Charles was Protestant, but sympathetic to Catholics. When he died, his brother James became king. James II tried to make England more Catholic. Parliament waited for James's Protestant daughters to succeed him, but when James had a son English nobles invited William of Orange (husband to James's daughter Mary) to invade England. England had undergone the "Glorious Revolution." William and Mary accepted the throne, along with a Bill of Rights. The Bill, based on the Petition of Right, laid the foundation for a limited, or constitutional, monarchy.

Answer these questions to check your understanding of the entire section.

1. Which people were most likely to be accused of witchcraft?

_____

_____

_____

2. What happened to Germany as a result of the Thirty Years' War?

_____

_____

_____

Trace England's movement from kings who thought they ruled by divine right to constitutional monarchy.

_____

_____

_____

_____

_____

_____

_____

_____

_____

_____

_____

Response to Crisis: Absolutism

Big Idea

France became the greatest power of the seventeenth century. Prussia, Austria, and Russia also emerged as great European powers. As you read, complete a chart like the one below summarizing the accomplishments of Peter the Great.

Reforms	Government	Wars

 **Notes**

Read to Learn

France under Louis XIV (page 228)

Analyzing Information

On what did Louis XIV spend so much money?

_____

_____

_____

_____

Absolutism is a system in which a ruler holds total power. In seventeenth-century Europe, absolutism was tied to the divine right of kings. It was believed that a king's power came from God and that he was accountable only to God.

Louis XIV was only four when he came to the throne. Until he was 23, France was run by Cardinal Mazarin. When Mazarin died, Louis XIV took complete control. He called himself the Sun King. Louis undermined the power of nobles to make national policy. He bribed important people in the provinces to make sure his policies were carried out at the local level. He tried to convert the Huguenots to Catholicism by destroying their churches and closing their schools. Many Huguenots fled. Louis spent much money building palaces, maintaining the royal court at Versailles, and fighting wars. He created a huge army that fought four wars. France followed a policy of mercantilism to finance Louis's expenditures. But when he died in 1715, France had many debts and many enemies.

 **Notes** | # Read to Learn

Absolutism in Central and Eastern Europe (page 231)

Determining Cause and Effect

Why did Frederick William, the Great Elector, create such a large army?

_____

_____

_____

_____

After the Thirty Years' War, there were over 300 independent German states. The state of Prussia was ruled by Frederick William. He realized that Prussia was small and had no natural barriers to enemies. He created an army that was the fourth-largest in Europe. To pay for it, he set up the General War Commissariat to levy taxes. The Commissariat bureaucracy became the elector's instrument for governing the state. Many of its officials also served in the army. In 1701 Frederick William's son Frederick gained the title of King. Elector Frederick III became King Frederick I.

The Austrian Hapsburg's had long served as emperors in the Holy Roman Empire. The Thirty Years' War dashed their hopes of creating an empire in Germany. So they created a new empire in eastern and southeastern Europe. The core of the new Austrian Empire was present-day Austria, the Czech Republic, and Hungary. But the Austrian monarchy never became a highly centralized, absolutist state. It was made up of too many national groups. No common feeling tied all the groups together except for service to the Hapsburgs.

Peter the Great (page 232)

Drawing Conclusions

How did Ivan the Terrible get his name?

_____

_____

_____

_____

A new Russian state emerged in the fifteenth century, around the principality of Muscovy. In the sixteenth century, Ivan IV was the first to take the title of **czar,** the Russian word for *caesar.* Ivan expanded the territories of Russia eastward and crushed the power of the Russian nobility, known as **boyars.** He was known as Ivan the Terrible because of his ruthless deeds.

In 1598 Ivan's dynasty came to an end, and a period of anarchy began. It ended in 1613 when the national assembly chose Michael Romanov as the new czar. Peter the Great became czar in 1689. Peter visited the West and determined to Europeanize Russia. He was eager to borrow European technology to improve his army. Peter created the first Russian navy. He divided Russia into provinces so the central government could rule more effectively. When he died in 1725, Russia was a great military power and an important European state.

Culturally, Peter emphasized Western manners taught in Russia. He insisted that Russian men shave off their beards and shorten their coats. Upper-class women could remove their face-covering veils and enter society. The sexes could now mix for conversation and dancing. Peter also began the construction of St. Petersburg as a "window to the West."

Section Wrap-up

Answer these questions to check your understanding of the entire section.

1. What is absolutism?

_____

_____

_____

2. What state had the fourth-largest army in Europe during the 1600s?

_____

_____

_____

Descriptive Writing

Using information from the text and your imagination, describe how life for an upper-class man or woman would have changed under Peter the Great.

_____

_____

_____

_____

_____

_____

_____

_____

_____

_____

_____

The World of European Culture

Big Idea

Art and literature reflect people's spiritual perceptions and the human condition. As you read, complete a chart like the one below summarizing the political thoughts of Thomas Hobbes and John Locke.

Thomas Hobbes	John Locke

Read to Learn

Art after the Renaissance (page 236)

Making Inferences

How did baroque churches and palaces reflect a search for power?

_____

_____

_____

_____

The artistic Renaissance came to an end when a new movement, **Mannerism,** emerged in Italy. Mannerism rejected Renaissance principles of balance, harmony, and moderation. The rules of proportion were ignored, and elongated figures were used to show suffering, heightened emotion, and religious ecstasy.

The **baroque** movement replaced Mannerism. Baroque artists tried to combine classical ideals with spiritual feelings. Their work also reflected a search for power. Baroque churches and palaces were magnificent and richly detailed. Kings wanted people to feel awe when they looked at them. Baroque painting was known for its use of dramatic effects. Perhaps the greatest figure of the baroque period was the Italian architect and sculptor Bernini. Bernini completed St. Peter's Basilica in Rome. Caravaggio, from Italy, and Peter Paul Rubens, from the Spanish Netherlands, were noted Baroque painters. Artemisia Gentileschi was prominent, though less well-known than male artists. She was the first woman to be elected to the Florentine Academy of Design.

 **Notes** | # Read to Learn

Golden Age of Literature *(page 238)*

Determining Cause and Effect

Why did Elizabethan playwrights write to please everyone?

_____

_____

_____

_____

In England, a cultural flowering took place in the late 1500s and early 1600s. The period is often called the Elizabethan Era, as much of it took place during the reign of Elizabeth I.

Drama expressed the energy of the time. The most famous dramatist of all was William Shakespeare. Because Elizabethan audiences included all the classes, playwrights wrote to please everyone. In his comedies and tragedies, he showed keen insight into human psychology and a remarkable understanding of the human condition. Shakespeare also wrote sonnets, a style of poetry.

In Spain, Miguel de Cervantes wrote the novel *Don Quixote*. By using two main characters, a knight and his earthy squire, Cervantes showed the duality of human character. The knight is a lofty idealist. The squire is a realist. They come to appreciate each other's point of view.

Spanish plays were so popular that every large town had a public playhouse, including Mexico City in the New World. Playwright Lope de Vega wrote perhaps 1,500 plays that set the standard for others. Lope de Vega wrote to please people, but his writing was of very high quality.

Political Thought *(page 240)*

Comparing and Contrasting

What was the difference between how Hobbes and Locke viewed life before society was organized?

_____

_____

_____

_____

Thinkers in the seventeenth century were concerned with order and power. Thomas Hobbes wrote a work called *Leviathan*. Hobbes claimed that before society was organized, life was brutal, nasty, and short. He thought that humans were guided by a ruthless struggle for self-preservation, not moral ideals or reason. People formed states to keep themselves from destroying one another. The ruler should have absolute power, and rebellion should be suppressed.

John Locke wrote *Two Treatises of Government* in 1679 and 1680. Locke believed that before society was organized, humans lived in a state of equality and freedom. All humans had certain **natural rights,** rights with which they were born. These included rights to life, liberty, and property. People established a government to protect their rights and judge those that violated them. If the government failed to protect citizens' natural rights, the people had the right to remove or alter the government.

Locke was not an advocate of democracy, but his ideas were used by the Americans and the French to support demands for constitutional government, the rule of law, and the protection of rights.

Section Wrap-up

Answer these questions to check your understanding of the entire section.

1. What form of literature particularly flourished in England and Spain in the late sixteenth and early seventeenth centuries?

_____

_____

_____

2. What are natural rights?

_____

_____

_____

Expository Writing

Explain why the artistic Renaissance came to an end and was replaced by Mannerism.

_____

_____

_____

_____

_____

_____

_____

_____

_____

_____

The Ottoman Empire

Big Idea

The Ottoman Empire grew strong as it expanded its borders. As you read, create a chart to show the structure of the Ottoman society. List groups in order of importance.

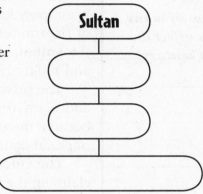

Sultan

Notes

Read to Learn

Rise of the Ottoman Turks (page 248)

Synthesizing Information

Selim I conquered Arabia. What cities did he then control that helped him in his claim to be caliph?

_____

_____

_____

_____

In the early fourteenth century, the Osman Turks began to expand and build the Ottoman dynasty. First, the Ottomans expanded westward to control two straits, the Bosporus and the Dardanelles. These straits connect the Black Sea and the Aegean Sea, which leads to the Mediterranean. Then the Ottomans expanded into the Balkans. The Ottoman rulers, called **sultans,** created a strong military led by **janissaries** recruited from the local Christian population and converted to Islam.

Under the leadership of Mehmed II, the Ottomans bombarded Constantinople with cannons. The Ottomans took the city and made Constantinople their new capital. They renamed it İstanbul.

By 1517, Sultan Selim I had taken control of Mesopotamia, Egypt, and Arabia. Selim now controlled several of Islam's holy cities, including Jerusalem, Makkah, and Madinah. He declared himself the new caliph—the successor to Muhammad. Where possible, the Ottomans administered their conquests through local rulers. They appointed officials called **pashas** to collect taxes and maintain law and order.

The Turks eventually moved into Austria and the western Mediterranean until the Spanish defeated a large Ottoman fleet in 1571. The Ottomans laid siege to Vienna, but were repulsed by a European army and were then pushed out of Hungary. They retained the core of their empire, but would never again threaten central Europe.

The Ottoman World (page 250)

The Ottoman Empire was one of the empires often called a **"gunpowder empire."** Gunpowder empires were formed by outside conquerors who unified the regions they conquered. A gunpowder empire's success was largely based on its mastery of firearm technology. At the head of the Ottoman system was the **sultan,** who was the supreme authority both politically and militarily.

The private domain of the sultan was the **harem,** where he and his wives resided. When a son became sultan, his mother became queen mother and often had power as an adviser. An imperial council helped govern. It was led by the **grand vizier.**

The Ottomans were Sunni Muslims. Ottoman sultans began claiming the title of caliph in the sixteenth century. They gave part of their religious duties to a group of religious advisers called the **ulema.** This group administered the legal system and the schools. The Ottomans were generally tolerant of non-Muslims, who made up a significant minority. Non-Muslims paid a tax, but were allowed to practice their religion or convert to Islam. In some areas, such as present-day Bosnia, many converted.

In addition to the ruling class, there were four main occupational groups: peasants, artisans, merchants, and pastoral peoples. Merchants were the most privileged class. All land was ultimately owned by the sultan.

Under the Ottomans, women had a somewhat better position than other Muslim women. Women were allowed to own and inherit property. They could not be forced into marriage and were sometimes allowed to divorce.

Problems in the Ottoman Empire (page 253)

The Ottoman Empire reached its height under Süleyman I, called Süleyman the Magnificent. After Süleyman's death, sultans became less involved in government, ministers exercised more power, and corruption grew.

Change in the empire was also brought about by the exchange of Western and Ottoman ideas and customs. Officials and merchants began to imitate Europeans in their clothes, furniture, and art. Some sultans attempted to outlaw certain Western goods, such as coffee and tobacco.

The economy was troubled by inflation and the imbalance of trade between the empire and Europe. The Ottomans did not invest in manufacturing and could not compete with European manufactured goods. The declining economy left little money for military expansion.

Answer these questions to check your understanding of the entire section.

1. What steps did the Ottomans take to build a strong military?

   _____

   _____

   _____

2. How did the Ottomans treat non-Muslims in their empire?

   _____

   _____

   _____

Expository Writing

What problems caused the weakening of the Ottoman Empire?

_____

_____

_____

_____

_____

_____

_____

_____

_____

_____

_____

_____

The Rule of the Safavids

Big Idea

The Safavids used their faith as a unifying force. As you read this section, use a Venn diagram like the one below to compare and contrast the Ottoman and Safavid Empires.

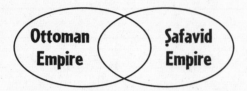

Ottoman Empire   Safavid Empire

 **Notes** | **Read to Learn**

The Safavid Empire (page 256)

Synthesizing Information

What was the religious reason that the Ottoman Turks fought the Safavids?

_____

_____

_____

After the empire of Timur Lenk (Tamerlane) collapsed, the area extending from Persia into central Asia fell into **anarchy** (lawlessness and disorder). At the beginning of the sixteenth century, a new dynasty—the Safavids—took control. This dynasty was founded by Shāh Esmā'īl. A **shah** was a king.

In 1501 Esmā'īl seized much of Iran and Iraq. He was a Shia Muslim, and sent Shia preachers to try to convert the Sunni Turkish tribes. The Ottomans and the Safavids fought several times. As the Safavids tried to consolidate their rule, they required conversion to the Shia faith from the largely Sunni population. Many Sunnis were either killed or exiled.

From 1588 to 1629, the Safavids reached their heights. Shāh 'Abbās strengthened the army, which he armed with the latest weapons. He fought with the Ottomans and regained Azerbaijan. However, after his death, the Safavid dynasty began to decline. Shia religious elements gained power at court and in society. Intellectual freedom declined as people were forced to conform to traditional religious beliefs, called religious **orthodoxy.**

During the early empire, Persian women had considerable freedom. Now they were forced to wear veils and live in seclusion.

Read to Learn

Life under the Ṣafavids *(page 259)*

Determining Cause and Effect

Why did the shahs need to keep the roads fairly clear of thieves and bandits?

_____

_____

_____

_____

Under the Ṣafavids, Persia was a mixed society with a combination of Persian and Turkish elements. The Shia eagerly supported the Ṣafavid rulers. The shahs declared Shia Islam to be the state religion. Shahs were more available to their people than rulers elsewhere. They firmly controlled the power of the landed aristocracy. Appointment to senior positions in the bureaucracy was based on merit rather than birth. The shahs supported trade and manufacturing. They kept the roads fairly clear of thieves and bandits. This was important because most goods moved by horse or camel caravans.

Ṣafavid Persia was probably not as prosperous as its neighbors, the Moguls and the Ottomans. Hemmed in by European sea power to the south and the land power of the Ottomans to the west, Ṣafavids found trade with Europe difficult.

Knowledge of science, medicine, and mathematics under the Ṣafavids was equal to that of other societies in the region. Silk weaving and carpet weaving flourished. There was a great demand for Persian carpets in the West. Persian painting showed soft colors and flowing movement. Persian painter Riza-i-Abbasi created exquisite works.

Section Wrap-up

Answer these questions to check your understanding of the entire section.

1. In what way was Persia under the Ṣafavids a mixed society?

_____

_____

_____

2. What art forms flourished under the Ṣafavids?

_____

_____

_____

Expository Writing

Explain the causes and effects of the decline of the Ṣafavid Empire.

_____

_____

_____

_____

_____

_____

_____

_____

_____

_____

_____

_____

_____

_____

The Grandeur of the Moguls

Big Idea

A country's society and its culture reflect the shared heritage of its people.
As you read, create a chart listing the accomplishments and weaknesses of
the Mogul rulers.

Ruler	Accomplishments	Weaknesses

Read to Learn

The Mogul Dynasty (page 262)

Analyzing Information

Was India a strongly centralized state under the Moguls?

_____

_____

_____

_____

Bābur, the founder of the Mogul dynasty, came to India from present-day Afghanistan. Bābur captured Delhi and established power in the plains of North India. By 1605 Bābur's grandson, Akbar, had brought Mogul rule to most of India. The empire was actually a collection of semi-independent states held together by the power of the emperor. Akbar was humane. He was a Muslim, but had a policy of religious tolerance.

Many lower-ranking officials were Hindus. These local officials, called **zamindars,** sometimes came to have considerable power in their local districts. Indian peasants had to pay about one-third of their harvest in taxes, but the taxes were reduced in hard times.

Akbar was succeeded by his son, Jahāngīr, who gradually lost interest in government. His successor, Shāh Jahān, expanded his territory. However, his treasury was nearly empty, and he had to raise taxes to pay for his military campaigns and extensive building projects. Most of his subjects lived in poverty.

Shāh Jahān's son, Aurangzeb, tried to eliminate evils such as the practice of **suttee,** where a widow was required to burn herself to death on her husband's funeral pyre. However, he ended the practice of religious tolerance, causing many protests from Hindus. There were revolts, and after he died India became increasingly divided and vulnerable to attack.

Life in Mogul India *(page 265)*

Distinguishing Fact from Opinion

What words tell you that the beauty of the Taj Mahal in comparison to other buildings is the author's opinion?

_____

_____

_____

_____

The Moguls were foreigners in India. They were also Muslims ruling a mostly Hindu population. The blend of influences on ordinary Indians was complicated. For example, women had played an active role in Mogul society. But the Moguls also placed restrictions on women according to their interpretation of Islamic law. Hindus adopted some of these practices, such as isolating women. Some Hindu practices, such as suttee and child marriage, remained unchanged. In the Mogul era, a wealthy nobility and a prosperous merchant class emerged.

Under the Moguls, Persian and Indian influences came together in a new and beautiful architectural style. This style is best symbolized by the Taj Mahal, which Shāh Jahān built in the mid-seventeenth century. It took more than 20 years to build and caused taxes to rise enough to drive many Indian peasants into complete poverty. The Taj Mahal may be the most beautiful building in India and possibly the entire world. It has monumental size and brilliance and also delicate lightness.

Painting in Mogul India blended Persian and Indian styles. Akbar strongly supported the arts and encouraged artists to imitate European art forms, including the use of perspective and lifelike portraits.

Europeans Come to India *(page 267)*

Making Inferences

What was the British attitude toward India?

_____

_____

_____

_____

The arrival of the British hastened the decline of the Mogul Empire. British ships carried Indian-made cotton goods to the East Indies, where they were traded for spices. The British success attracted the French, who established their own forts.

Sir Robert Clive, an aggressive British empire builder, served as the chief representative in India of the East India Company, a private company that acted on behalf of the crown. Clive fought any force that threatened the Company's power and ultimately restricted the French to the fort at Pondicherry and a few territories on the southeastern coast.

In 1757 Clive led a small British force to victory over a Mogul-led army in the Battle of Plassey in Bengal. Victory gave the East India Company the power to collect taxes from lands in the area around Calcutta.

Many East India Company officials offended both their Indian allies and the local population, who were taxed heavily to meet the Company's growing expenses.

Answer these questions to check your understanding of the entire section.

1. Who founded the Mogul dynasty?

_____

_____

_____

2. In what ways was Akbar a humane ruler?

_____

_____

_____

Using information from the text and your imagination, describe what you imagine the Taj Mahal to look like.

_____

_____

_____

_____

_____

_____

_____

_____

_____

_____

_____

_____

_____

_____

China at Its Height

Big Idea

China preferred to keep its culture free of European influences. As you read, complete a diagram like the one below to compare and contrast the achievements of the Ming and Qing dynasties.

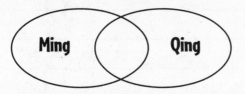

 **Notes** | # Read to Learn

---

The Ming Dynasty *(page 274)*

Determining Cause and Effect

What factors caused the decline of the Ming dynasty?

_____

_____

_____

_____

The Mongol dynasty in China was overthrown in 1368, and the Ming dynasty began. The Chinese strengthened the Great Wall and renovated the Grand Canal. Ming rulers ran an effective government using a centralized bureaucracy staffed with officials chosen by the civil service examination system. They set up a nationwide school system. Manufactured goods were produced in workshops, and new crops were introduced. It was an era of greatness for China.

In 1406 construction of the Imperial City in Beijing was begun, and soon the capital was moved there from Nanjing. Zheng He led naval voyages into the Indian Ocean and to the eastern coast of Africa. The voyages were profitable and informative but were halted as an unworthy activity.

In 1514 a Portuguese fleet arrived. The Chinese looked down on the Europeans as just a new kind of barbarian, who sometimes behaved outrageously. But some cultural exchange took place. Jesuit missionaries had brought instruments such as clocks that impressed the Chinese. The Europeans were impressed with Chinese civilization, including the teachings of Confucius, the printing and availability of books, and Chinese architecture.

Internal power struggles, government corruption, high taxes, and a major epidemic brought decline to the Ming dynasty. Then the Manchus, who lived northeast of the Great Wall, conquered Beijing and began the Qing dynasty.

 **Notes** |  **Read to Learn**

The Qing Dynasty *(page 277)*

Copyright © Glencoe/McGraw-Hill, a division of The McGraw-Hill Companies, Inc.

Analyzing Information

How did the Manchus change the appearance of the Chinese?

_____

_____

_____

_____

To identify rebels, the Manchu (Qing) government ordered all males to adopt Manchu dress and hairstyles. Men had to shave their foreheads and braid their hair into a pigtail called a **queue.** The Manchus were gradually accepted as legitimate rulers, even though they were ethnically and culturally different from the Chinese. The Manchus made up only 2 percent of the population, and they kept their distinction legally. The Manchu nobility had large landholdings and received revenues from the state treasury.

Other Qing were organized into separate military units, called **banners.** These were the chief fighting force of the empire. Chinese were allowed into the imperial administration, but mostly in the lower posts. However, the sharing of power won Chinese support for the Qing.

Perhaps the greatest emperor of the Ming and Qing dynasties was Kangxi, who ruled from 1661 to 1722. He was very hard-working and calmed unrest along the frontiers by force. He was devoted to justice and a patron of the arts and letters. Christian missionaries worked hard during his reign, converting several hundred officials and an estimated 300,000 ordinary Chinese. Kangxi's successor began to suppress Christian activities.

Another ruler, Qianlong (1746–1795), expanded China to its greatest physical size. Under his reign, China was prosperous, but decay was beginning. Corruption, high taxes, and the pressure of population growth led to unrest. The White Lotus Rebellion took place and was expensive to put down.

China was restricting trade with Europeans at this time. The British wanted more trade and access to more of China. Chinese exports to Britain were greater than Chinese imports from Britain, which Britain did not like. However, the Chinese refused to expand trade.

1. Who was perhaps the greatest ruler of the Ming and Qing dynasties?

_____

_____

_____

2. How did the Chinese regard the Europeans?

_____

_____

_____

Descriptive Writing

Describe the voyages of Zheng He in a journal entry as if you were a passenger on one of the ships. Use all five senses in your description.

_____

_____

_____

_____

_____

_____

_____

_____

_____

_____

_____

_____

Chinese Society and Culture

Big Idea

Chinese society was organized around the family. As you read, show the organization of the Chinese family by using a concentric circle diagram like the one below.

Husband, Wife, and Family

Notes

Read to Learn

Economy and Daily Life (page 280)

Determining Cause and Effect

Why didn't China develop commercial capitalism?

_____

_____

_____

_____

Between 1500 and 1800, nearly 85 percent of the Chinese people were small farmers. Population grew sharply between 1390 and the 1700s. This was because the Qing dynasty provided peace and stability, and the Chinese had acquired a faster-growing species of rice. More people meant less land available, which led to unrest and revolts. There was some growth in manufacturing, and trade in silk, porcelain, and cotton goods expanded. However, China did not develop **commercial capitalism,** where private business is based on profit, as did Europe. The government firmly controlled trade and manufacturing, and put higher taxes on them than on farming. This was because they were considered to be inferior occupations to farming.

Chinese society was organized around the family. Often, three or four generations lived under the same roof. Beyond the extended family was the **clan,** which consisted of dozens, or even hundreds, of related families. Clans were linked by a clan council of elders and common social and religious activities. Women were considered inferior to men. Only males could have a formal education or inherit property. Women could not get divorces, but men could if the wife did not produce sons. The mobility of women was restricted by footbinding. Bound feet were a status symbol. The process, begun in childhood, made the feet appear smaller and was very painful. Women with bound feet could not walk, yet were more marriageable. Perhaps one-half to two-thirds of the women in China had their feet bound.

Notes | Read to Learn

Chinese Art and Literature (page 283)

Analyzing Information

What literary form begin to develop during the Ming dynasty?

_____

_____

_____

_____

The economic expansion that took place under the Ming dynasty enabled more people to buy books. Also, advances in paper manufacturing encouraged the growth of printing. The beginnings of the modern Chinese novel lie in the Ming era. One novel, *The Golden Lotus,* is considered by many to be the first realistic social novel. It depicts the corrupt life of a wealthy landlord who cruelly manipulates those around him for sex, money, and power. *The Dream of the Red Chamber* by Cao Xueqin is still generally considered to be China's most distinguished popular novel. It tells of the tragic love between two young people caught in the financial and moral collapse of a powerful Chinese clan.

There was an outpouring of artistic brilliance during the Ming and Qing dynasties. In architecture, this is demonstrated in the Imperial City, home of the emperors in Beijing. The Imperial City is an immense compound surrounded by six and one-half miles (10.5 kilometers) of walls. It is a maze of apartments, offices, banquet halls, and spacious gardens. Commoners were not allowed there, so it came to be called the Forbidden City.

The decorative arts also flourished. Possibly the most famous of all the arts of the Ming Era was blue-and-white **porcelain.** Europeans admired and collected it. Different styles were produced under the reigns of different emperors.

Section Wrap-up

Answer these questions to check your understanding of the entire section.

1. What caused the shortage of land under the Qing dynasty?

_____

_____

_____

2. What Chinese item did Europeans admire and collect?

_____

_____

_____

Descriptive Writing

Using information from the text and your imagination, describe a morning in the life of a Chinese girl living in the Forbidden City.

_____

_____

_____

_____

_____

_____

_____

_____

_____

_____

_____

_____

Tokugawa Japan and Korea

Big Idea

Political unification often results in warfare and difficult economic and social changes. As you read, categorize the different elements of Japanese culture using a diagram like the one below.

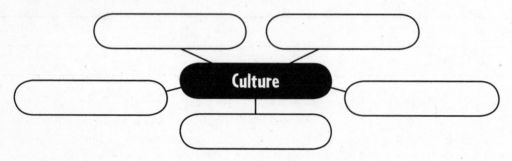

Notes | Read to Learn

Political Changes in Japan (page 284)

Making Inferences

How might the Tokugawa have used firearms?

_____

_____

_____

_____

By the end of the fifteenth century, Japan was in chaos. **Daimyo,** heads of noble families, controlled their own lands and warred with their neighbors. Oda Nobunaga seized the imperial capital of Kyōto and unified the central part of modern-day Japan. Nobunaga was succeeded by Toyotomi Hideyoshi, who, by 1590, had persuaded most of the daimyo to accept his authority. After Hideyoshi's death, Tokugawa Ieyasu, the daimyo of Edo (modern-day Tokyo) took control. Later, he took the title of shogun. Tokugawa shoguns remained in power at their capital of Edo until 1868. This long period was called the "Great Peace."

Portuguese traders arrived in Japan in 1543. The Japanese liked European goods such as tobacco, clocks, eyeglasses, and firearms. Jesuit missionaries converted thousands of Japanese to Christianity. However, when the Jesuits destroyed local shrines, Hideyoshi prohibited Christian activities. Under Ieyasu, missionaries were expelled and Christians were persecuted. Of the merchants, only a small Dutch community was allowed to remain in Japan.

During the Great Peace, the state was divided into about 250 territories called **hans,** each ruled by a daimyo. The shogun controlled the daimyo with the **hostage system.** When the daimyo was away at home, his family had to stay in Edo to insure the daimyo's loyalty to the shogun.

 **Notes** | # Read to Learn

The Tokugawa Era *(page 287)*

Synthesizing Information

How were the Chinese and the Japanese similar in regard to the rights of women?

_____

_____

_____

_____

By 1750 Edo was one of the largest cities in the world. Banking flourished, and paper money became the normal medium of exchange for business transactions. Most peasants, however, were experiencing rising costs and taxes and many peasant revolts against high taxes occurred.

Under the Tokugawa, Japan's class system became rigid. Rulers established strict legal distinctions between the four main classes: warriors, peasants, artisans, and merchants. Below these classes were Japan's outcasts, the *eta*. Intermarriage between classes was forbidden.

The rights of women were restricted. Male heads of households had broad authority over property, marriage, and divorce. Parents arranged marriages. However, women were generally valued for their roles as childbearers and homemakers among the common people.

New cultural values began to appear. The greatest Japanese poet, Matsuo Basho, wrote in the seventeenth century. In theater, Kabuki, which emphasized action, music, and dramatic gestures, emerged. Women were forbidden to appear on stage, so women's roles were acted by men.

Korea: The Hermit Kingdom *(page 289)*

Comparing and Contrasting

How are the Korean and English alphabets alike?

_____

_____

_____

_____

The Yi dynasty in Korea began in 1392 when Yi Song-gye, a great military strategist, overthrew the Koryo dynasty. The Yi patterned their society after the Chinese to the north but kept their own identity. One significant characteristic of Korean culture was their development of a unique alphabet, Hangul. Japanese and Chinese writing uses thousands of characters, or symbols. Hangul, however, is a phonetically based writing system, using one letter for each sound, as English does. Hangul is still largely the standard writing system in Korea.

A Japanese force invaded Korea as a first step to invading China, killing skilled workers and devastating farms. In response, Korean rulers sought to limit contact with foreign countries. Korea was largely untouched by European merchants or Christian missionaries. It earned the name "the Hermit Kingdom."

Korea was still recovering from the Japanese invasions when the Manchus attacked in the early seventeenth century. Korea surrendered, and the Yi dynasty became subject to China.

Answer these questions to check your understanding of the entire section.

1. Describe Japan's class system under the Tokugawa.

_____

_____

_____

2. What influence did Europeans have on Korea under the Yi dynasty?

_____

_____

_____

Explain the advantages and disadvantages that the Japanese felt they encountered with the Europeans.

_____

_____

_____

_____

_____

_____

_____

_____

_____

_____

_____

Spice Trade in Southeast Asia

Big Idea

Europeans struggled to control the profitable spice trade in Southeast Asia. As you read, use a chart like the one below to list reasons why the destructive effects of European contact in Southeast Asia were only gradually felt.

European Contact in Southeast Asia

 **Notes**

Read to Learn

Emerging Mainland States (page 290)

 **Analyzing Information**

Which style of king ruled by Confucian teachings?

_____

_____

_____

In 1500 mainland Southeast Asia was a relatively stable region. However, conflict between the Thai and the Burmese resulted in the Thai having to move their capital south to Bangkok in 1767. The Vietnamese spread to the coast and then took control of the Mekong delta. By 1800 the Khmer monarchy had virtually disappeared.

Four styles of monarchy emerged. In Burma, Thailand, Laos, and Cambodia, Buddhist kings were considered superior to other human beings and served as the link between human society and the universe. Javanese kings maintained the balance between the sacred and material worlds. Islamic sultans were found on the Malay Peninsula and the small coastal states of the Indonesian Archipelago. A sultan was head of state and defender of the faith. He staffed his **bureaucracy** (nonelected government officials) mainly with aristocrats. The Vietnamese emperor followed the Chinese model and ruled by Confucian teaching, which said the ruler was to treat subjects with love and respect.

The Arrival of Europeans (page 292)

Determining Cause and Effect

Why were mainland states in Southeast Asia better able to resist European influence?

_____

_____

_____

Since ancient times, spices had been highly valued. They were used as medicines and to preserve foods, as well as to flavor them. Sometimes only meat preserved with salt and pepper kept people from starving. Ginger, cloves, cinnamon, and nutmeg were also highly prized. European countries, therefore, competed to find a sea route to the Indies in order to get spices. Portugal first found the gateway when Vasco da Gama sailed to India. Then Portugal seized Melaka and occupied the Moluccas, known to Europeans as the Spice Islands. However, the Portuguese had only enough military and financial resources to establish small settlements as trading posts.

In the early 1600s, the Dutch began seizing Portuguese forts along the trade routes. They gradually pushed the Portuguese out of the spice trade. Then they drove out the English traders until England was left with a single port on the coast of Sumatra. The Dutch brought the entire island of Java under its control and closed access to the Spice Islands.

The arrival of the Europeans had less impact on the **mainland states** of Southeast Asia. These were part of the continent, not peninsulas or off-shore islands. Mainland states were better able to resist because they had strong monarchies and more political unity. Also, Europeans were more determined to control the non-mainland states, because these had the spices.

Section Wrap-up

Answer these questions to check your understanding of the entire section.

1. Which islands did Europeans call the Spice Islands?

_____

_____

_____

2. Which Europeans eventually gained control of the spice trade?

_____

_____

_____

Describe a meal of meat and bread without the use of spices. Then describe the same meal if the cook used the spices mentioned in the summary.

_____

_____

_____

_____

_____

_____

_____

_____

_____

_____

_____

_____

Chapter 10, Section 1 (Pages 302–309)
The Scientific Revolution

Big Idea

The Scientific Revolution gave Europeans a new way to view humankind's place in the universe. As you read, use a table like the one below to chart the contributions of scientists to a new concept of the universe.

Copernicus	
Kepler	

Notes | **Read to Learn**

Causes of the Scientific Revolution *(page 302)*

Determining Cause and Effect

How did the study of Greek influence the way Europeans viewed Aristotle?

_____

_____

_____

_____

In the Middle Ages, educated Europeans relied on a few ancient authorities, especially Aristotle, for their scientific knowledge. During the Renaissance, humanists studied Greek as well as Latin. This gave them access to other ancient authorities, such as Ptolemy, Archimedes, and Plato. This in turn let them know that some ancient thinkers had disagreed with Aristotle. This and other developments encouraged new ways of thinking. Technical problems that required careful observation and accurate measurements, such as calculating the weight that ships could hold, stimulated scientific activity. The invention of new instruments, such as the telescope and the microscope, made fresh discoveries possible. Above all, the printing press helped spread new ideas quickly and easily.

Explorers began to search for scientific discoveries instead of wealth and glory. James Cook used a chronometer, which calculated the precise location of a ship, to map Australia's coastline. He also discovered that eating fresh fruit prevented scurvy.

Mathematics played a key role in the scientific achievements of the sixteenth and seventeenth centuries. The foundation for trigonometry was laid. The decimal system was introduced and a table of logarithms was invented. This made calculation easier. Many great thinkers were also great mathematicians who believed that the secrets of nature were written in the language of mathematics.

Scientific Breakthroughs (page 304)

Drawing Conclusions

How did the Catholic Church try to block progress in scientific thought?

_____

_____

_____

_____

The ancient astronomer Ptolemy had constructed a **geocentric** model of the universe that placed Earth at the center. All the heavenly bodies but Earth were made of light.

In 1543 Nicolaus Copernicus published his theories, which said that the Sun was the center of the universe (it was **heliocentric**) and that the planets revolved around it. Johannes Kepler supported this model when he used detailed astronomical data to confirm it.

Galileo Galilei was the first European to make regular observations of the heavens by using a telescope. He discovered that the heavenly bodies were not made of light, but composed of material substance, as Earth was.

The Church ordered Galileo to abandon the Copernican idea his research supported. However, most astronomers had accepted the heliocentric conception of the universe by the 1640s. Then Isaac Newton defined three laws of motion. Part of his argument was the **universal law of gravitation.** This law stated that every object in the universe was attracted to every other object by a force called gravity.

Women's Contributions (page 307)

Making Inferences

How did keeping scholarship as the domain of men help to restrict the rights of women?

_____

_____

Many women contributed to the Scientific Revolution, even though scholarship was the domain of men. Margaret Cavendish, had no formal education in the sciences, but she wrote a number of works on scientific matters, some of which criticized the idea that humans were masters of nature.

Between 1650 and 1710, women made up 14 percent of all German astronomers. The most famous female astronomer, Maria Winkelmann, was rejected for the position of assistant astronomer at the Berlin Academy. Though she was well-qualified, she was a woman and did not have a university degree. Scientific work was considered to be mainly for males.

Philosophy and Reason (page 308)

Determining Cause and Effect

How did the Scientific Revolution influence the Western view of humankind?

_____

_____

_____

_____

The Scientific Revolution influenced the Western view of humankind. French philosopher René Descartes developed a system of thought called **rationalism.** He believed that the mind and the body, indeed all matter, were separate. Matter could therefore be viewed as dead, or inert, and could be investigated by the mind.

Francis Bacon created the **scientific method** for learning about nature. He taught that scientists should use **inductive reasoning**—starting with detailed facts and then proceeding toward general principles. Scientists were to observe natural events, propose explanations, and use systematic observations and organized experiments to test the explanations.

Section Wrap-up

Answer these questions to check your understanding of the entire section.

1. What is the main difference between the geocentric and heliocentric models of the universe?

_____

_____

_____

2. What force did Newton identify?

_____

_____

_____

Explain Francis Bacon's scientific method.

_____

_____

_____

_____

_____

The Enlightenment

Big Idea

Enlightenment thinkers, or philosophers, believed all institutions should follow natural laws to produce the ideal society. As you read, use a diagram like the one below to list some of the main ideas introduced during the Enlightenment.

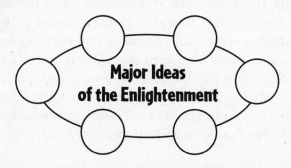

Major Ideas of the Enlightenment

Notes

Read to Learn

Path to the Enlightenment (page 310)

Analyzing Information

Why did Locke think that giving people the right influences could make a difference in society?

_____

_____

_____

_____

The Enlightenment was an eighteenth-century philosophical movement of intellectuals who were greatly impressed with the achievements of the Scientific Revolution. They thought they could apply reason and the scientific method to gain an understanding of all life. Two men from the seventeenth century—John Locke and Isaac Newton—influenced the Enlightenment. Locke thought that people were born with blank minds. Therefore, they were molded by their observations and experiences. If given the right influences, people could be changed to create a new society.

Newton thought of the world as a machine, created by a mechanic, God. God then allowed the world-machine to run according to natural laws that could be uncovered through systematic investigation. Enlightenment thinkers believed that by applying Newton's methods, they could discover the natural laws that governed society. If all institutions followed these natural laws, the result would be an ideal society.

 **Notes** | **Read to Learn**

Ideas of the Philosophes *(page 312)*

Making Inferences

How did the philosophes affect the Unites States Constitution?

_____

_____

The intellectuals of the Enlightenment were called **philosophes.** They came chiefly from the nobility and the middle class. They thought the role of philosophy was to change the world. A spirit of rational criticism was to be applied to everything, including religion and politics.

Montesquieu studied governments. He believed that England's government had three branches: the executive (the monarch), the legislative (Parliament), and the judicial (the courts). He believed that this **separation of powers** gave the government a system of checks and balances. American philosophes worked this idea into the United States Constitution.

Voltaire championed **deism,** a religious philosophy built on the idea that God had set the world in motion and allowed it to run without his interference. Diderot published a 28-volume *Encyclopedia* that spread Enlightenment ideas.

New Social Sciences *(page 313)*

Identifying the Main Idea

What did the Pysiocrats believe?

_____

_____

The founders of the modern social science of economics are believed to be the Physiocrats, a French group, and Scottish philosopher Adam Smith. The Physiocrats believed that if individuals were free to pursue their own economic self-interest, all society would ultimately benefit. The state, therefore, should not interfere in the economy. This doctrine became known as **laissez-faire.** The best statement of laissez-faire was made by Adam Smith when he published *The Wealth of Nations* in 1776.

The Spread of Ideas *(page 315)*

Comparing and Contrasting

How were Rousseau's thoughts different from other Enlightenment thinkers?

_____

_____

In his work *The Social Contract,* Rousseau presented the idea that through a **social contract,** an entire society agreed to be governed by its general will. Rousseau also argued that education should foster, not restrict, children's natural instincts. Unlike many Enlightenment thinkers, Rousseau believed that emotions, as well as reason, were important to human development. He sought a balance between heart and mind, emotions and reason.

Mary Wollstonecraft advanced the strongest statement for the rights of women. In *A Vindication of the Rights of Women,* Wollstonecraft argued that if government based on the arbitrary power of a monarch was wrong, then men's power over women was wrong. Wollstonecraft declared that because women have the power of reason, they deserved equal rights in education, as well as in economic and political life.

During the Enlightenment, ideas were spread through the **salon.** These were elegant gatherings in the homes of the wealthy upper class. They brought writers and artists together with aristocrats, government officials, and the wealthy middle class.

John Wesley, an Anglican minister, tried to make his preaching understandable to the lower classes. His Methodist movement influenced both the English and later the American movement to abolish slavery.

Section Wrap-up

Answer these questions to check your understanding of the entire section.

1. What is laissez-faire?

_____

_____

_____

2. What Enlightenment movement was important to the abolition of slavery?

_____

_____

_____

Persuasive Writing

Using information from the text and your knowledge of life today, argue in favor of Mary Wollstonecraft's position on women's rights or against it. Write your answer on a separate sheet of paper.

_____

_____

_____

_____

_____

_____

_____

_____

The Impact of the Enlightenment

Big Idea

Europe's individual nations were chiefly guided by the self-interest of their rulers. As you read, use a chart like the one below to list the conflicts of the Seven Years' War. Include the countries involved and where the conflicts were fought.

> **Conflicts of the Seven Years' War**

 **Notes**　　**Read to Learn**

Enlightenment and Absolutism (page 318)

Which monarch tried hardest to institute reforms?

_____

_____

_____

_____

The philosophes believed in natural rights for all people. These rights included equality before the law; freedom of religious worship; freedom of speech; freedom of the press; and the rights to assemble, hold property, and pursue happiness. To establish and preserve their natural rights, people needed to be governed by enlightened rulers. Many historians once assumed that a new type of monarchy, **enlightened absolutism,** emerged in the eighteenth century.

Frederick II of Prussia made a few reforms, such as granting limited freedom of speech and press, and greater religious toleration. But he kept Prussia's serfdom and rigid social structure intact.

In Austria, Joseph II made far-reaching reforms, including abolishing serfdom and establishing equality before the law and religious toleration. However, he alienated the nobles and Church by doing so, and his successors undid almost all of Joseph II's reforms.

In Russia, Catherine the Great favored the landed nobility and took strong measures to put down peasant rebellion. She greatly expanded Russia's territory. Monarchs of all three of these nations cared more for power and territory than for reform.

 **Notes** | **Read to Learn**

The Seven Years' War *(page 322)*

Drawing Conclusions

What drive on the part of a monarch set the stage for the Seven Years' War?

_____

_____

_____

_____

The Seven Years' War was a global conflict with shifting alliances. Prussia conquered Austrian Silesia. France allied with Prussia, and Austria allied with Great Britain. Territories were forcibly exchanged in Europe, India, and North America. In 1748 the Treaty of Aix-la-Chapelle ended the war and returned all occupied territories to their original owners, except for Silesia.

Austria's ruler, Maria Theresa, rebuilt her army and then got France and Russia to ally with Austria. The British then allied with the Prussians. The European conflict eventually ended and Maria Theresa had to officially recognize Prussia's control of Silesia.

The struggle between Britain and France went on in other parts of the world and is known as the Great War for Empire. The greatest conflicts of the Seven Years' War took place in North America. The British and French fought for control of the St. Lawrence waterways (in present-day Canada) and for control of the Ohio River valley. Eventually, the British won. In the Treaty of Paris in 1763, the French gave Canada and the lands east of the Mississippi to England, which also got Florida from France's ally, Spain. To make up for the loss of Florida, France gave Spain its Louisiana territory. Great Britain was now the world's greatest colonial power.

Enlightenment and Arts *(page 325)*

Comparing and Contrasting

How were the baroque and rococo styles different?

_____

_____

_____

_____

The ideas of the Enlightenment had an impact on world culture. By the 1730s, a new style, known as **rococo,** had spread over Europe. Unlike the baroque, which stressed grandeur and power, rococo emphasized grace and charm.

Eighteenth-century Europe produced some of the world's most enduring music. Bach, a German composer, is one of the greatest composers of all time. Handel, a German who worked in England, wrote *Messiah*. These two composers perfected the baroque musical style.

Franz Joseph Haydn and Wolfgang Amadeus Mozart, in the latter part of the century, wrote music in the classical style. Mozart was a child prodigy who wrote some of the world's greatest operas.

In the 1700s, European novelists began to choose realistic social themes, as opposed to a focus on heroism and the supernatural.

Section Wrap-up

Answer these questions to check your understanding of the entire section.

1. Which nation was the world's greatest colonial power at the end of the Seven Years' War?

_____

_____

_____

2. What four musical geniuses lived in the eighteenth century?

_____

_____

_____

Descriptive Writing

Describe two imaginary residences—one built in the baroque style— to project power and grandeur—and one built in the rococo style to project grace and charm, using delicate designs, curves, and gold color.

_____

_____

_____

_____

_____

_____

_____

_____

_____

_____

_____

The American Revolution

Big Idea

The American Revolution and the formation of the United States of America seemed to confirm premises of the Enlightenment. As you read, use a chart like the one below to identify key aspects of the government created by the American colonists.

New American Government

 **Notes**

Read to Learn

Britain and the American Revolution (page 330)

Drawing Conclusions

Why was the American Revolution such a gamble?

_____

_____

_____

_____

In 1707 England and Scotland were united into the United Kingdom of Great Britain. Parliament and the monarch shared power, with Parliament gradually becoming more important.

The British government wanted to raise taxes in the colonies to help pay for the war and the colonies' defense. In 1765 Parliament passed the Stamp Act, which imposed a tax on legal documents and newspapers. There was strong opposition, and the act was repealed in 1766. Crisis followed crisis in the 1770s. Fighting erupted in April 1775. The Second Continental Congress approved the Declaration of Independence. The revolution was a big gamble, as Britain was a strong military power with enormous financial resources. The Continental Army was made up of untrained amateurs.

Other nations, seeking revenge on Britain, supplied arms, money, and soldiers to the rebels.

The British decided to end the war in 1781. The Treaty of Paris in 1783, gave Americans control of the territory from the Appalachians to the Mississippi.

Notes | Read to Learn

The Birth of a New Nation *(page 333)*

Analyzing Information

What part of the Constitution guaranteed natural rights to Americans?

_____

_____

_____

_____

After throwing off oppressive rule, the former colonies, now states, feared a strong central government. Thus, their first constitution, the Articles of Confederation, created a government that lacked the power to deal with the nation's problems. In 1787 delegates met again and wrote an entirely new plan, called the Constitution.

The Constitution created a **federal system,** in which the national government and the state governments shared power. Based on Montesquieu's ideas, the national, or federal, government was separated into three branches: the executive (headed by the president), the legislative (the Congress), and the judicial (the courts). Each branch had some power to restrain acts of the other branches.

During negotiations over ratification, the new Congress proposed 12 amendments to the Constitution, and 10 of them were approved by the states. These 10 amendments became known as the Bill of Rights. They guaranteed freedom of religion, speech, press, petition, and assembly. They gave Americans the right to bear arms and to be protected against unreasonable searches and arrests. They guaranteed trial by jury, due process of law, and the protection of property rights.

Many of the rights in the Bill of Rights were similar to the natural rights proposed by the philosophes. Many Europeans saw the American Revolution as the acting out of the Enlightenment's political dreams. The creation of the United States seemed to confirm that a better world could be achieved.

Section Wrap-up

Answer these questions to check your understanding of the entire section.

1. What countries supported the Americans in their revolution against the British?

_____

_____

_____

2. Why did Europeans see the creation of the United States as the acting out of the Enlightenment's political dreams?

_____

_____

_____

Informative Writing

Trace the American Revolution from the Stamp Act to the Treaty of Paris.

_____

_____

_____

_____

_____

_____

_____

_____

_____

_____

_____

The French Revolution Begins

Big Idea

Social inequality and economic problems contributed to the French Revolution. As you read, use a diagram like the one below to list the factors that contributed to the French Revolution.

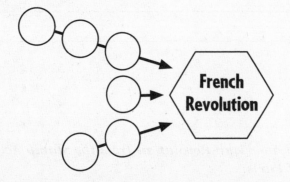

 **Notes** | **Read to Learn**

Background to the Revolution (page 340)

Determining Cause and Effect

Why was Louis XVI forced to call a meeting of the Estates-General?

_____

_____

_____

_____

The French Revolution created both a new political order and a new social order. It is considered a turning point in European history.

Since the Middle Ages, the French population had been legally divided into three status groups, or **estates.** The First Estate held the clergy, the Second Estate held the nobles, and the Third Estate held everyone else. The First and Second Estates controlled most of the wealth of the kingdom but did not pay the *taille,* France's chief tax. The Third Estate contained vastly different people, from wealthy merchants to craftspeople to poor peasants to the **bourgeoisie,** or middle class. They all resented the old rigid social order.

The French aristocracy spent money lavishly during economic decline. Louis XVI was forced to call a meeting of the Estates-General, which contained representatives of all three estates, to raise taxes.

From Estates-General to National Assembly (page 343)

Making Inferences

Why would the king support the old system of voting in the Estates-General?

_____

_____

_____

_____

Louis XVI called a meeting of the Estates-General on May 5, 1789. Most of the Third Estate wanted to set up a constitutional government that would make the clergy and the nobility pay taxes, too. The Third Estate demanded that each deputy have a vote. The king supported the old system, which gave the First and Second Estate the power to outvote the larger Third Estate.

On June 17, 1789, the Third Estate declared that it was the National Assembly and would draft a constitution. Locked out of their meeting place they moved to a nearby indoor tennis court and swore that they would continue meeting until they had a new constitution.

Louis XVI prepared to use force against the Third Estate. After hungry Parisians destroyed the Bastille, in search of arms, the king's authority collapsed in Paris. Revolts then spread all over France. Peasant rebellions became part of a vast panic known as the Great Fear. The peasants were afraid that foreign troops would stop the revolts, so they broke into the houses of the lords to destroy the records of their obligations.

End of the Old Regime (page 345)

Drawing Conclusions

Why did the French Revolution turn more radical?

_____

_____

_____

_____

In reaction to the peasant rebellion, the National Assembly abolished all legal privileges of the nobles and clergy on August 4, 1789. On August 26 it adopted the Declaration of the Rights of Man and the Citizen that proclaimed that all men were free and equal before the law, that appointment to public office should be based on talent, and that no group should be exempt from taxation. It was not clear whether these rights were to include women.

Thousands of Parisian women marched to Versailles. They met with the king and forced him to accept the decrees.

The revolutionaries then decided to weaken the Church, because it had been a supporter of the old system. The National Assembly seized and sold Church lands, and a law was passed requiring that bishops and priests be elected by the people, not appointed by the pope.

The new Constitution of 1791 set up a limited monarchy. A Legislative Assembly would make the laws. However, only males over 25 who paid a certain amount of taxes could vote, and only relatively wealthy people could be deputies. Some people wanted more reform.

European leaders began to fear that revolution would spread to their countries. Austria and Prussia threatened to use force to restore Louis XVI to full power. The Legislative Assembly declared war on Austria in 1792. Angry citizens protested this, and Paris radicals declared themselves a commune—a popularly run city council. They organized a mob attack on the royal palace and Legislative Assembly. They took the king captive and forced the Legislative Assembly to extend the right to vote to all adult males. Many members of the Paris Commune called themselves **sans-culottes,** because they wore long pants instead of the knee-length breeches favored by the nobles. Economic conditions and the threat of foreign intervention had made the revolution more radical.

Section Wrap-up

Answer these questions to check your understanding of the entire section.

1. Before the French Revolution, which group paid all the taxes?

_____

_____

_____

2. Why did France declare war on Austria?

_____

_____

_____

Informative Writing

Trace the conditions and events that led to the Great Fear.

_____

_____

_____

_____

_____

_____

_____

Radical Revolution and Reaction

Big Idea

Political groups controlled the revolution, which many people in France and abroad opposed. As you read, create a diagram like the one below listing actions taken by the National Convention.

Actions taken by the National Convention
1.
2.
3.
4.

Notes

Read to Learn

The Move to Radicalism (page 350)

Drawing Conclusions

Why did some people want the king to be executed?

_____

_____

_____

_____

In August, 1792 the sans-culottes attacked the palace, and the royal family had to seek protection from the Legislative Assembly. The Paris Commune forced the Assembly to call a National Convention to draft a new constitution.

The National Convention began to serve as the ruling body of France. It abolished the monarchy and established the French Republic. Political clubs, such as the Girondins and the Jacobins, formed **factions**—groups that oppose each other. Girondins favored keeping the king alive, while Jacobins wanted him executed to keep him from serving as a rallying point for the republic's opponents. In early 1793, the Convention condemned Louis XVI to death, and he was beheaded on January 21.

A coalition of Austria, Prussia, Spain, Portugal, Britain, and the Dutch Republic took up arms against France. Disputes between political factions blocked the writing of a constitution. The Convention gave broad powers to the Committee of Public Safety, which came to be dominated by Maximilien Robespierre.

The Reign of Terror *(page 353)*

Determining Cause and Effect

Why did the Convention try to de-Christianize France?

_____

_____

_____

_____

For about a year during 1793 and 1794, the Committee of Public Safety took control of the government. It adopted practices that became known as the Reign of Terror. Almost 40,000 people were killed. Revolutionary armies were set up to bring rebellious cities under control.

The Committee of Public Safety held that the violence was only temporary. They took steps to shape what Robespierre called the Republic of Virtue. A law aimed at primary education for all was passed, but not widely implemented. Another law abolished slavery in the French colonies. The Committee tried to control the high prices of essential goods such as food, fuel, and clothing, but with little success.

The National Convention tried to de-Christianize France, because it believed the religion encouraged superstition rather than reason. Churches and cathedrals were closed or given new purposes. Priests were encouraged to marry. Robespierre came to realize that most French people were still Catholic and would not accept de-Christianization.

A Nation in Arms *(page 355)*

Formulating Questions

What are some questions that could be asked about France's raising of such a huge army, and about that army's victories?

_____

_____

As foreign troops gathered on France's borders, the Committee of Public Safety raised the largest army ever seen in Europe. It pushed the invaders back across the Rhine and even conquered the Austrian Netherlands. By summer of 1794, France had largely defeated its foreign enemies. There was less need for the Reign of Terror, but still it continued. But in July, Robespierre himself was guillotined. In August, the release of prisoners began.

Determining Cause and Effect

After the Reign of Terror ended, how did the National Convention change?

_____

_____

_____

With the Terror over, the National Convention moved in a more conservative direction. A new constitution was created. It set up two legislative houses. A lower house drafted laws. An upper house accepted or rejected proposed laws. However, members of both houses were chosen by **electors.** Only those who owned or rented property worth a certain amount could be an elector. Only 30,000 people in the whole nation qualified to be an elector.

The executive power was held by a committee of five called the Directory. The Directory lasted only five years, and was known for its corruption. Eventually, the military gained power. Then one successful and popular general, Napoleon Bonaparte, toppled the Directory in a **coup d'etat**—a sudden overthrow of a government.

Section Wrap-up

Answer these questions to check your understanding of the entire section.

1. What steps did the National Convention take to try to de-Christianize France?

_____

_____

_____

2. Why was the government of the Directory unpopular?

_____

_____

_____

Expository Writing

Explain why the Reign of Terror took place.

_____

_____

_____

_____

_____

The Age of Napoleon

Big Idea

As Napoleon built his empire across Europe, he also spread the revolutionary idea of nationalism. As you read, use a diagram like the one below to list the achievements of Napoleon's rule.

Achievements of Napoleon's Rule

 Notes

 Read to Learn

The Rise of Napoleon (page 360)

Analyzing Information

Why did Napoleon become a hero to the French?

_____

_____

_____

_____

In one sense, Napoleon Bonaparte brought the revolution to an end when he took power. However, he always reminded the French that he had preserved the best parts of the revolution during his reign as emperor. His father came from minor nobility in Italy, but the family was not rich. However, Napoleon was talented and won a scholarship to a famous military school. He devoted himself to reading French philosophers and studying military campaigns. Napoleon rose quickly through the ranks.

At the age of 24, he became a brigadier general. He won battles against the Papal States and the Austrians that gave France control of northern Italy. Napoleon became known for speed, surprise, and decisive action. His troops were devoted to him. In 1797 he returned to France as a hero. He was given an army to invade Britain. Napoleon knew that such an invasion would fail and suggested taking Egypt, an important colony of Britain's, instead. However, the British navy defeated the French naval forces supporting Napoleon's army in Egypt. Seeing certain defeat, Napoleon abandoned his army and returned to Paris. There he took part in the coup d'etat of 1799 that overthrew the Directory. He set up a new government, the **consulate.** In theory, it was a republic, but actually, Napoleon had absolute power. In 1802 Napoleon was made consul for life. In 1804 he crowned himself Emperor Napoleon I.

Notes | Read to Learn

Napoleon's Domestic Policies *(page 362)*

Drawing Conclusions

In what ways was Napoleon a despot?

_____

_____

_____

One of Napoleon's first moves at home was to establish peace with the Catholic Church. This eliminated the Church as an enemy and also gave Napoleon the support of those who had acquired church lands.

Napoleon's most famous achievement was codifying the laws. Before the revolution, France had almost 300 different legal systems. The most important code, the Napoleonic Code, preserved the principles of equality of all citizens before the law, the right of an individual to choose a profession, religious toleration, and abolition of serfdom and feudal obligations. However, under the Napoleonic Code women lost control over their property when they married, they could not testify in court, and they were generally treated as children.

Napoleon created a strong, centralized administration. Public officials and military officers were all promoted on the basis of ability. Careers were opened to men of talent. However, Napoleon was also despotic. He shut down 60 of France's 73 newspapers and banned many books. He insisted that all manuscripts be looked at by the government before publication. Even the mail was opened by government police.

Napoleon's Empire *(page 365)*

Determining Cause and Effect

Why did Napoleon want to sell the Louisiana territory?

_____

_____

_____

_____

In 1803 Napoleon sold the Louisiana territory to the United States for $15 million. This gave him money to fight his enemies. In a series of battles at Ulm, Austerlitz, Jena, and Eylau from 1805 to 1807, Napoleon's Grand Army defeated the Austrian, Prussian, and Russian armies. From 1807 to 1812, Napoleon was the master of Europe. At the core of his empire was an enlarged France. Spain, Holland, the kingdom of Italy, the Swiss Republic, the Grand Duchy of Warsaw, and the Confederation of the Rhine were all dependent states ruled by Napoleon's relatives. Prussia, Austria, Russia, and Sweden were forced to become allies in Napoleon's struggle against Britain.

Also, Napoleon aroused ideas of **nationalism**—the sense of unique identity of a people based on common language, religion, and national symbols—in the conquered countries. They felt united in hating the French, while at the same time, they saw what power national unity had brought France.

Copyright © Glencoe/McGraw-Hill, a division of The McGraw-Hill Companies, Inc.

The Fall of Napoleon (page 366)

Determining Cause and Effect

What happened after Napoleon invaded Russia?

_____

_____

_____

_____

Napoleon's downfall began when he invaded Russia in 1812. The Russian army retreated for hundreds of miles and burned the countryside so the French army could not get food or fuel. Fewer than 40,000 of Napoleon's 600,000 soldiers returned from Russia. Other countries attacked, and Napoleon was defeated and sent into exile on the island of Elba in 1814. The victorious powers restored the monarchy with Louis XVIII as king. The French did not support the monarchy, and when Napoleon escaped, the troops sent to capture him instead supported him. He entered Paris in triumph in 1815. However, at Waterloo in Belgium, Napoleon suffered a bloody defeat at the hands of a British and Prussian army commanded by the Duke of Wellington. Napoleon was exiled to the island of St. Helena.

Section Wrap-up

Answer these questions to check your understanding of the entire section.

1. What were the results of Napoleon's peace-making agreement with the Catholic Church?

_____

_____

_____

2. What general commanded the combined British and Prussian army that finally defeated Napoleon?

_____

_____

_____

Expository Writing

Contrast the impact of the Napoleonic code on male citizens with its impact on women.

_____

_____

_____

_____

_____

_____

The Industrial Revolution

Big Idea

The Industrial Revolution changed the way people lived and worked. As you read, use a table like the one below to name important inventors mentioned in this section and their inventions.

Inventors	Inventions

 **Notes** | **Read to Learn**

The Industrial Revolution in Great Britain (page 378)

Determining Cause and Effect

What effect resulted from each of the causes listed below?

changes in farming

_____

_____

_____

new machines

_____

_____

railroads

_____

_____

_____

The Industrial Revolution began in Great Britain in the 1780s. Changes in farming had increased food production and reduced the need for farm labor, so workers were available for factories. Parliament also passed **enclosure movement** laws, which fenced off common lands and forced many peasants to move to towns, where the factories were.

Britain also had wealthy people with money, or **capital,** to invest. The country had natural resources, such as rivers, iron, and coal. **Entrepreneurs** found new ways to make profits. With growing cities and a vast colonial empire, there were markets at home and abroad.

James Hargreaves invented a spinning jenny. Edmund Cartwright invented a water-powered loom. These new machines made spinning and weaving cotton into cloth much faster. James Watt invented a steam engine and a way for his engine to drive machinery. The new spinning and weaving machines had to be near the source of power: water or steam. Work moved from homes **(cottage industry)** into factories. Children as well as adults worked long hours in the factories.

Better-quality iron was produced through a process called **puddling.** Richard Trevithick built a steam locomotive, and George Stephenson designed wheels that would let it run on a railway. Railroads carried resources to the factories and manufactured goods to markets. Building railroads created new jobs. More people could afford the mass-produced factory products, so business owners built more factories. The economy grew.

 **Notes** | # Read to Learn

The Spread of Industrialization (page 382)

Making Generalizations

Based on the text, what general statement can be made about the role of government in industrial growth?

_____

_____

_____

_____

_____

The Industrial Revolution spread faster to some countries than to others. Most countries did not have as much wealth as Great Britain had. Also, government policies influenced the rate of industrialization.

On the continent of Europe, the first three industrialized areas were Belgium, France, and the German states. Governments helped by providing money for roads, canals, and railroads. By 1850 railroads connected many parts of Europe.

Industrialization also grew quickly in the United States. Because the country was so large, transportation was especially important. Thousands of miles of roads, canals, and railroads were built to connect east and west. Robert Fulton built the first paddle-wheel steamboat in 1807, making river transport easier. The whole country became one large market for goods made in the northeastern United States.

American factory workers typically came from farm families. Most of the textile workers were women and girls. Sometimes whole families would work together in a factory.

Social Impact in Europe (page 383)

Problems and Solutions

If you were a member of Parliament in Britain in the 1800s, what law might you propose to improve conditions for the industrial working class?

_____

_____

_____

_____

_____

Huge social changes resulted from the Industrial Revolution. Between 1750 and 1850, the population of Europe almost doubled. Cities grew and the number of large cities increased. One reason was the increasing food supply. The only major famine in Western Europe was the Irish potato famine of 1840s, caused by a fungus. Many Irish people died, and many more migrated to the United States.

Industrial capitalism was an economic system based on industrial production. It gave rise to new social classes: the industrial middle class and the industrial working class. Someone who ran the factories or developed the markets was a member of the industrial middle class, or *bourgeois*. The industrial working class, who worked in a factory or mine, toiled long hours in dangerous, unhealthy settings. Conditions in textile mills and coal mines were especially harsh.

Poor conditions in cities and factories gave rise to reform movements. The Factory Act of 1833 limited child labor in Britain. Some reformers hoped to replace industrial capitalism with **socialism.** In socialism, the public would own the means of production, such as factories. Early socialists thought this would make society fairer.

Section Wrap-up

Answer these questions to check your understanding of the entire section.

1. Why did spinning and weaving move from homes to factories?

_____

_____

_____

2. List two ways an increase in population contributed to the Industrial Revolution.

_____

_____

_____

Descriptive Writing

Imagine that you are a young man or woman in the 1800s who has left the farm to live and work in the city, taking a job in a factory. Write about your experiences at home and at work. Use as many of the five senses as possible: sight, sound, taste, smell, and touch. Try to use strong, active verbs so that your reader will have a clear sense of the experiences you are describing.

_____

_____

_____

_____

_____

_____

_____

_____

_____

_____

_____

_____

_____

Reaction and Revolution

Big Idea

In 1848 liberals and nationalists rebelled against many of the conservative governments of Europe. As you read, use a chart like the one below to summarize the causes of the revolutions in France in 1830 and 1848.

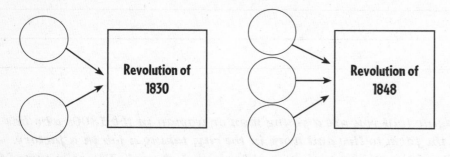

Notes | Read to Learn

The Congress of Vienna (page 388)

Identifying the Main Idea

Paragraph 2 describes Metternich's plan to restore _____ rulers.

Paragraph 3 defines a political philosophy called _____.

Paragraph 4 explains how the leaders tried to establish and maintain a _____ of _____.

The powers that had defeated Napoleon met in September 1814 at Vienna, Austria. There they redrew the map of Europe as part of a final peace settlement.

The most influential leader at the Congress of Vienna was Prince Klemens von Metternich, the foreign minister of Austria. His plan was to restore to power the legitimate rulers, that is, members of the royal families who ruled before Napoleon. He and other leaders followed conservative values.

Conservatism is a political philosophy based on tradition and social stability. Conservatives at that time favored political authority and organized religion. Hating revolutions, they did not value individual rights or representative government.

Leaders at the Congress of Vienna wanted to establish a balance of power in which no one country would dominate Europe. For example, because Russia had gained land, it gave new lands to Austria and Prussia as well. Great Britain, Russia, Prussia, and Austria agreed to meet from time to time to maintain the balance of power. Over time, the leaders of Europe (except Great Britain) adopted a **principle of intervention.** They claimed the right to intervene in other countries after a revolution to restore legitimate rulers to their thrones. On this basis, they crushed revolutions in Spain and Italy.

Notes | Read to Learn

Forces of Change (page 390)

Comparing and Contrasting

How were liberalism and nationalism alike and different?

Alike:

_____

_____

_____

Different:

_____

_____

_____

Liberals and nationalists opposed conservative ideas and the existing political system. **Liberalism** and nationalism were forces for change.

The political philosophy called liberalism grew out of the Enlightenment. Liberals believed that all people should be equal before the law. They wanted freedom of assembly, speech, and the press. Many liberals wanted representative government, separation of church and state, and a constitution or a bill of rights. Liberalism especially attracted wealthy men in the industrial middle class who wanted voting rights for themselves, not a real democracy. Liberalism was similar to republicanism in the belief that a government's power comes from the rule of law and the voting citizens.

Nationalism arose after the French Revolution. Nationalists believed each nationality (group with shared language and customs) should have its own government. German nationalists wanted a united German state. Hungarian nationalists wanted freedom from Austria.

In 1830 liberalism and nationalism led to revolutions in several countries. Belgium won its independence from the Dutch Republic. French liberals overthrew King Charles X and established a constitutional monarchy under his cousin Louis-Philippe.

The Revolutions of 1848 (page 391)

Making Generalizations

Apart from France, what was the outcome of most revolutions in Europe in 1848?

_____

_____

_____

_____

Revolutions occurred in a number of European countries in 1848, starting in France. While the French middle class demanded the right to vote, peasants and workers faced economic hardships. The government of Louis-Philippe refused to make changes. Revolutionaries overthrew the king and set up the Second Republic. A new constitution allowed **universal male suffrage,** meaning all adult men could vote. Napoleon's nephew, Charles Louis Napoleon Bonaparte, was elected president.

News of the revolution in France sparked other movements for change. Many German rulers promised reforms, and elected representatives wrote a united German constitution. However, German rulers did not accept it, and the states did not unite.

The Austrian Empire was a **multinational state**—a state made up of many different nationalities. In 1848 demonstrations broke out in major cities. The Austrian rulers crushed nationalist revolutions by Hungarians and Czechs.

As in Germany, liberals and nationalists in Italy tried to create a unified constitutional state. However, their former rulers (including Austria in the north) succeeded in regaining control.

Section Wrap-up

Answer these questions to check your understanding of the entire section.

1. What were two principal goals of the Congress of Vienna?

_____

_____

_____

2. Explain why radical revolutionaries and members of the working class might not be satisfied with reforms made by the liberals.

_____

_____

_____

Persuasive Writing

Take the position of a European conservative, a liberal, or a nationalist in the period from 1815 to 1848. Write as if you were trying to persuade other people to adopt your position. State what you want to happen and why others should agree. Assemble facts and information to support your point of view. Explain why you consider the opposing viewpoints incorrect. Present arguments to draw undecided readers to your side.

_____

_____

_____

_____

_____

_____

_____

_____

_____

_____

_____

National Unification and the National State

Big Idea

In the mid-1800s, the Germans and Italians created their own nations. However, not all national groups were able to reach that goal. As you read, use a table like the one below to list the changes that took place in the indicated countries during the nineteenth century.

Great Britain	France	Austrian Empire	Russia

Notes Read to Learn

Toward National Unification *(page 394)*

Distinguishing Fact from Opinion

Decide whether each statement is fact or opinion. Write **F** *beside the statements of fact. Write* **O** *beside the statements of opinion.*

_____ *Russia should not have attacked Ottoman territory.*

_____ *The Crimean War broke up the Concert of Europe.*

_____ *Garibaldi was a greater leader than Bismarck was.*

_____ *Prussia had a strong leadership.*

Although the efforts of Italian and German nationalists failed in 1848, by 1871, both Italy and Germany were unified states. This became possible because the Concert of Europe broke down. Relationships changed because of the Crimean War between Russia and the Ottoman Empire (1853–1856). After Russia invaded Ottoman lands, Britain and France declared war on Russia. Austria did not support either side. Without working together, they were not strong enough to keep control.

Italian nationalists hoped to unite under King Victor Emmanuel II of Piedmont, in northern Italy. The king's foreign minister, Cavour, allied with the French and then got Austria to declare war in 1859. In the peace settlement, Piedmont got Lombardy from Austria. Other Italian states then revolted against their rulers and joined Piedmont.

In southern Italy, nationalist Giuseppe Garibaldi raised a volunteer army called the Red Shirts. They took control of much of Italy and turned their conquests over to Piedmont. The new state of Italy was proclaimed in 1861. Rome and other areas were added by 1870.

German nationalists looked to Prussia, known for its **militarism,** for leadership. King William I and his prime minister, Count Otto von Bismarck, built a strong army. Prussia won wars against Austria in 1866 and France in 1870–1871. William I was proclaimed **kaiser** (emperor) of Germany in 1871.

 **Notes** | # Read to Learn

Nationalism and Reform in Europe *(page 398)*

Analyzing Information

What were some strengths and weaknesses of Louis-Napoleon's rule in France?

Strengths:

_____

_____

Weaknesses:

_____

_____

After 1848 Great Britain grew more liberal. The governments of France, Austria, and Russia grew more authoritarian. Britain passed a law in 1832 letting more men vote. Most of the new voters were in the industrial middle class. Other reforms followed. The country was fairly stable during the long reign of Queen Victoria. Irish nationalists protested British control of Ireland, however.

In France, the **plebiscite,** or popular vote, overwhelmingly approved Louis-Napoleon's proposal to restore the empire. He became Emperor Napoleon III in 1852. He expanded the economy and rebuilt the city of Paris. His empire fell after France lost the Franco-Prussian War of 1870.

The Hapsburg rulers of Austria kept firm control over minority nationalities before 1866, when they lost a war with Prussia. Then they agreed to a compromise with Hungarian nationalists. Austria and Hungary became separate, self-governing units under one monarch.

After losing the Crimean War, Russia remained isolated. Czar Alexander II freed, or **emancipated,** the serfs in 1861. His son turned against reform. He also began construction of the Trans-Siberian railway, which improved transportation and communication throughout Russia.

Nationalism in the United States *(page 401)*

Making Inferences

In the 1800s, why might government leaders in the United States have reacted differently to liberal ideas from leaders of countries in Europe?

_____

_____

_____

Liberalism and nationalism were written into the United States Constitution. However, different factions had different ideas about how to interpret those ideals. Federalists wanted a strong central government. Republicans feared a strong central power.

By the middle of the century, the United States was deeply divided over the issue of slavery. The economy in the South depended on cotton plantations, worked chiefly by slave labor. Eli Whitney's invention of the cotton gin, a machine that removed cotton seeds quickly, increased the demand for slave labor. **Abolitionists** in the North thought slavery should be abolished.

After Abraham Lincoln was elected president in 1860, South Carolina voted to withdraw, or **secede,** from the United States. Other southern states did the same in 1861. The states that withdrew from the Union formed a new country, the Confederate States of America.

A bloody civil war between the Union and the Confederacy lasted from 1861 to 1865. The Confederacy was defeated, and the southern states were brought back into the Union. Slavery was ended throughout the United States.

Section Wrap-up

Answer these questions to check your understanding of the entire section.

1. What is a likely reason Great Britain did not experience such revolutionary upheavals as other European countries did?

_____

_____

_____

2. What similar, parallel events occurred in Russia and the United States in the 1860s?

_____

_____

_____

Informative Writing

Write about the unification of Italy. Tell events in the order they occurred. Be sure your narrative answers the questions who, when, where, what, how, and why.

_____

_____

_____

_____

_____

_____

_____

_____

_____

_____

_____

_____

_____

Romanticism and Realism

Big Idea

Artistic movements are influenced by the society around them. Romanticism was in part a reaction to the Industrial Revolution, while advances in science contributed to a new movement called realism. As you read, use a table like the one below to list popular literature from the romantic and realist movements.

Romanticism	Realism

Notes   Read to Learn

Romanticism (page 402)

Formulating Questions

To judge whether a work of art was classical or romantic, one might ask:

Does it pay more attention to reason or to _____?

Does it show more respect for technology or for _____?

Does it draw more inspiration from the present or from the _____?

Romanticism was a new movement in art, music, and literature that began in the late 1700s. It was a reaction to the Enlightenment focus on universalism and reason. Instead, romanticism stressed the unique individual, emotions, and the imagination. Romantics were interested in past times before the Industrial Revolution. Their architecture copied medieval styles. Many romantics rebelled against middle-class conventions. They wore long hair and unusual clothes.

Romantic artists tried to reflect their inner feelings and imagination. They abandoned classical reason for warmth and emotion. The French romantic painter Delacroix showed scenes of popular uprisings and exotic animals. The later music of composer Ludwig van Beethoven had powerful, intense melodies. He reflected romantic ideals when he said, "I must write, for what weighs on my heart, I must express."

Romantic literature shows a similar interest in emotion, the past, and the unfamiliar. *Ivanhoe* by Sir Walter Scott was set in medieval England. Mary Shelley's *Frankenstein* and Edgar Allan Poe's short stories were filled with imaginative horror. Poems by William Wordsworth and William Blake honored nature and the human soul.

New Age of Science (page 405)

Predicting

What effect might faith in science have on popular attitudes toward religion?

_____

_____

_____

_____

_____

The Industrial Revolution brought a new interest in scientific research. By the 1830s, new discoveries had brought practical benefits for much of Europe. Europeans developed a great faith in science.

In biology, Louis Pasteur of France suggested that diseases were caused by germs. That made modern medical advances possible.

In chemistry, Dmitry Mendeleyev of Russia classified all the known chemical elements on the basis of their atomic weights.

In physics, Michael Faraday of Great Britain made an electrical generator. It was the first step toward the use of electrical current.

These new discoveries led Europeans to have a greater faith in science, which undermined religious faith. **Secularization,** or the indifference to or rejection of religion in the affairs of the world, increased in the 1800s.

Charles Darwin's theory of evolution influenced many fields of science. He published *On the Origin of Species by Means of Natural Selection* in 1859 and *The Descent of Man* in 1871. In a principle called **organic evolution,** Darwin argued that every species, including humans, evolved from earlier species. In a process he called **natural selection,** the organisms best suited for survival are the ones that live to reproduce. Many people objected to Darwin's ideas as offending their moral values or religious beliefs.

Realism (page 407)

Comparing and Contrasting

The romantics showed strange, exotic settings. The realists were more interested in

_____.

The romantics showed medieval heroes or great events. The realists preferred to show

_____.

Realism was another movement in art and literature after about 1850. Influenced by developments in science, the realists believed the world should be shown as it really is. They had an interest in everyday life and ordinary people.

Many realists cared about social issues. They wrote novels about the ways social issues affected their characters.

In France, the novelist Gustav Flaubert wrote *Madame Bovary.* It showed the limitations of life in a French small town.

In Great Britain, author Charles Dickens wrote many novels about the life of the poor during the Industrial Revolution. Novels such as *Oliver Twist* and *David Copperfield* show life among the poor in London. Dickens became immensely popular.

Realist artists believed that no subject was too ugly to paint. The most famous was the French realist painter Gustave Courbet. He painted pictures of factory workers and peasants.

Section Wrap-up

Answer these questions to check your understanding of the entire section.

1. The French realist painter Gustave Courbet once said, "I have never seen either angels or goddesses, so I am not interested in painting them." What did he mean?

_____

_____

_____

_____

2. Why did the writings of Charles Darwin arouse so much controversy?

_____

_____

_____

_____

Expository Writing

Form a theory about the Industrial Revolution and scientific discoveries affected trends in art and literature in the 1800s. How did they influence romanticism? How did they influence realism? Write about your theory, illustrating it with specific examples from literature and art.

_____

_____

_____

_____

_____

_____

_____

_____

_____

_____

_____

_____

_____

_____

_____

The Growth of Industrial Prosperity

Big Idea

Industrialization led to dramatic increases in productivity as well as to new political theories and social movements. As you read, complete a diagram like the one below showing the cause and effect relationship between the resources and the products produced.

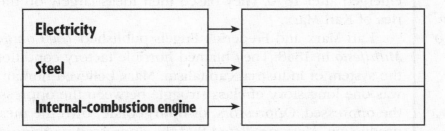

Electricity	→	
Steel	→	
Internal-combustion engine	→	

Notes | **Read to Learn**

The Second Industrial Revolution (page 416)

Synthesizing Information

The Second Industrial Revolution resulted in part from the electrical generator and the internal combustion engine, which provided new sources of _____.

By the late 1800s, a new age of steel, chemicals, electricity, and petroleum—the Second Industrial Revolution—made European economies even more productive. The substitution of steel for iron allowed for smaller, lighter, and faster machines and engines. The Bessemer process made the production of steel cheap and efficient.

The first practical electrical generators were made in the 1870s. Electricity was a valuable new source of energy. It could be carried from place to place on wires. It was easy to convert to other forms of energy such as light, heat, and motion. Electricity gave rise to new inventions such as Thomas Edison's light bulb, Alexander Graham Bell's telephone, and Guglielmo Marconi's radio. Oil and gasoline provided a new source of power for transportation. They were the fuel for the internal combustion engine. Oil-fueled ocean liners, airplanes, and automobiles all used the internal combustion engine.

In the industrialized parts of Western Europe, wages rose after 1870. **Assembly line** production, introduced by Henry Ford in 1913, made **mass production** more efficient. Improved transportation lowered the cost of getting goods to market.

The Working Class *(page 419)*

Detecting Bias

Karl Marx was sympathetic toward the proletariat, or working class. He wrote that society was "more and more splitting up into two great hostile camps, into two great classes directly facing each other: Bourgeoisie and Proletariat."

Based on this quote, what was Marx's bias toward the bourgeoisie?

_____

_____

_____

_____

_____

While industrialization brought some people a higher standard of living, it was also very hard on industrial workers. They worked long hours in terrible conditions and lived in crowded slums. Reformers of that period thought that industrial capitalism was heartless.

Moderate reformers wanted to work within the system. They hoped for shorter hours, better benefits, and safer working conditions.

More radical reformers wanted to replace industrial capitalism with a new system called socialism. Socialist political parties emerged after 1870. They based their ideas largely on the theories of Karl Marx.

Karl Marx and Frederick Engels published *The Communist Manifesto* in 1848. They blamed horrible factory conditions on the system of industrial capitalism. Marx believed human history was one long story of class struggle between the oppressor and the oppressed. Oppressors, or **bourgeoisie,** own the means of production. Marx predicted that the oppressed working class, or **proletariat,** would eventually rebel and form a **dictatorship.** The rebels would take control of the means of production. Economic differences would end, bringing a society without social classes.

In time, working class leaders formed socialist parties based on Marx's ideas. Most important was the German Social Democratic Party (SPD), formed in 1875. By 1912 it was the biggest party in Germany. SPD members of the German parliament passed laws to improve life for the working class. Socialist parties in different countries of Europe joined together to form the Second International. Still, other Marxists, called **revisionists,** rejected the revolutionary approach.

Trade unions, or labor unions, worked for change within the system. Workers would organize a union. Then they would try to get their employers to let union representatives negotiate for the whole group. This process is called collective bargaining.

To pressure employers to negotiate, unions would sometimes strike. Striking workers would stop working until their demands were met. At first, laws in many countries made strikes illegal. Unions in Great Britain won the right to strike in the 1870s.

Section Wrap-up

Answer these questions to check your understanding of the entire section.

1. How did the use of steel contribute to the Second Industrial Revolution?

_____

_____

_____

2. Why was it important to labor unions to be allowed to strike?

_____

_____

_____

Persuasive Writing

Take a position on the opinions of Karl Marx. Clearly state your position and try to persuade your reader to agree. Provide facts and other evidence for your position, and refute any opposing arguments. Conclude by restating your position and summing up the evidence.

_____

_____

_____

_____

_____

_____

_____

_____

_____

_____

_____

_____

_____

_____

The Emergence of Mass Society

Big Idea

The Second Industrial Revolution resulted in an increased urban population, a growing working class, and an increased awareness of women's rights. As you read, complete a chart like the one below summarizing the divisions among the social classes.

Social Classes		
Working	**Middle**	**Wealthy**

Notes   Read to Learn

The New Urban Environment (page 422)

Problems and Solutions

Dams, reservoirs, aqueducts, and tunnels were parts of the solution to the urban need for _____ water.

As workers migrated to cities, urban centers grew and became overcrowded. Between the 1850s and 1890, the percentage of the population that lived in cities increased by half in Great Britain, nearly doubled in France, and more than doubled in Prussia, the largest German state. The city of London, which had 960,000 people in 1800, increased to 6,500,000 by 1900. The population grew even faster because of improvements in public health and sanitation.

Cholera and other diseases spread easily in crowded conditions. Contaminated water carried germs from person to person. For example, cholera ravaged Europe in the 1830s and 1840s.

Citizens and reformers asked government to do something about housing, public health, and sanitation. City governments responded by setting up boards of health. Building inspectors and medical officers inspected the quality of housing.

Cities required that new buildings have running water and internal drainage systems. Dams and reservoirs were constructed to store fresh, clean water. Aqueducts and tunnels carried the water into the cities. Gas heaters in the 1860s, and later electric heaters, enabled many people to take hot baths. Huge underground pipes carried untreated sewage to disposal sites far away from the cities.

 **Notes** | # Read to Learn

Social Structure *(page 424)*

Evaluating Information

Which of these would be the best source of information about the challenges of city life for the working class?

_____ *letters written by a banker who rented out property in the city*

_____ *Diary of a young mother who worked in a textile mill*

While standards of living rose in general after 1871, a large gap remained between rich and poor. Western society was divided into three broad classes.

A wealthy elite with rich bankers, merchants, and industrialists made up only 5 percent of the population but controlled from 30 to 40 percent of the wealth. The middle class included doctors, lawyers, business managers, and members of the civil service who lived comfortable lives. Small shopkeepers, traders, and prosperous farmers formed a lower middle class. Below them were white-collar workers such as bookkeepers and telephone operators. The working classes made up almost 80 percent of Europe's population, including peasants, farm workers, industrial workers, and domestic servants.

After 1870, urban workers began to live more comfortably. Higher wages and lower consumer costs allowed people to buy things other than food and clothing. Labor unions lobbied for improved working conditions.

Women's Experiences *(page 425)*

Drawing Conclusions

What was life like for women in the early 1800s?

_____

_____

_____

_____

Women had few rights in the early 1800s. They were defined mainly by their family roles. Legally and economically, they depended on men. Married women could not hold property in their own name. Home and family remained a full-time job for most married middle-class women. Working-class women typically worked to help support their families, at least until they married.

Feminism, or the movement for women's rights, began during the Enlightenment. Some women claimed that they had a natural right to own property. Some middle-class and upper-middle-class women fought for the right to attend universities or enter occupations dominated by men.

Some, such as Emmeline Pankhurst in Britain, demanded **suffrage,** or the right to vote. However, few nations allowed women to vote before 1914.

Copyright © Glencoe/McGraw-Hill, a division of The McGraw-Hill Companies, Inc.

Education and Leisure *(page 428)*

Based on your knowledge of leisure activities today, what is one lasting effect you can infer that the Second Industrial Revolution had on leisure activities?

_____

_____

Between 1870 and 1914, most Western governments began to pay for primary schools. Boys and girls between age 6 and age 12 were required to go to school. Governments also set up schools to train teachers.

One reason was the white-collar jobs created by the Second Industrial Revolution. These new jobs called for workers who could read, write, add, and subtract. Another reason was the effect of liberalism and nationalism. As more citizens gained the right to vote, they needed to be able to read. By 1900 most adults in Western and Central Europe could read. The increase in **literacy** gave rise to newspapers for a mass reading public.

Besides reading, other new forms of leisure became popular. With the separation of work from home, people thought of leisure as what they did for fun after work. New forms of leisure included dance halls, amusement parks, and organized team sports.

Section Wrap-up

Answer these questions to check your understanding of the entire section.

1. List two reasons European cities grew rapidly in the 1800s.

_____

_____

_____

2. List two reasons governments began to provide primary education for children.

_____

_____

_____

Informative Writing

Write about how the lives of women changed between 1800 and 1914. Organize your account as a narrative. Explain what life was like for women in different times, places, and social classes. Include the reasons for the changes and the effects of the changes.

_____

_____

_____

_____

_____

The National State and Democracy

Big Idea

While democracy triumphed in Western Europe, authoritarianism prevailed in central and eastern Europe, and industrialization swept the United States. International rivalries set the stage for war. As you read, complete a diagram like the one below listing the countries in each alliance.

Triple Alliance 1882

Triple Entente 1907

Notes

Read to Learn

Western Europe and Political Democracy *(page 432)*

Comparing and Contrasting

How were the political party systems in Great Britain and France different and alike?

Great Britain

_____

France

_____

Both

_____

Growing prosperity after 1850 contributed to the expansion of democracy in Western Europe. Countries passed laws allowing all adult males to vote. Prime ministers began to answer to a group elected by the people, such as a parliament, instead of to the king. This principle was known as **ministerial responsibility.** Mass political parties formed and looked for ways to appeal to voters.

Great Britain had a working two-party parliamentary democracy, made up of the Liberal Party and the Conservative Party. Extending the right to vote led to social reforms. At first, working-class voters supported the Liberal Party. Then they formed trade unions with more radical goals and turned their support to the new Labour Party, which formed in 1900.

In France, the Third Republic gained a constitution in 1875. It had a president, a prime minister, and a two-house legislature. High-ranking officials elected the upper house. All adult males got to vote for members of the lower house, the Chamber of Deputies. The prime minister was responsible to the Chamber of Deputies. Because the country had a dozen political parties, he had to form a coalition in order to stay in power.

Central and Eastern Europe: The Old Order (page 434)

Synthesizing Information

In the major countries of Central and Eastern Europe in the late 1800s, the individual with the most political power was the _____.

Germany, Austria-Hungary, and Russia were less industrialized than Western Europe. Fewer people could read. Voters had little say in what happened. Emperors and elites kept the real power.

Germany had a two-house legislature under the constitution of 1871. However, ministers were responsible to the emperor instead of to the legislature. Emperor William II, Chancellor Bismarck, and the wealthy elite did not let democracy take hold. The dual monarchy of Austria-Hungary (1867) had a constitution, but Emperor Francis Joseph largely ignored it. He issued decrees when parliament was not in session and kept personal control over the government. Nicholas II in Russia was committed to maintaining the absolute power of the czar, or emperor. Industrialization gave rise to socialist parties, but Czar Nicholas repressed them. The czar created a legislature called the **Duma** but limited its power.

The United States (page 435)

Identifying the Main Idea

By 1900 the United States was the _____ country in the world and had started to gain a global _____.

After recovering from the American Civil War, the United States became an industrial world power. The Second Industrial Revolution brought economic expansion. American steel and iron production was the best in the world. The United States was the richest country in the world, but wealth was very concentrated. The richest 9 percent of the people owned 71 percent of the wealth.

In the late 1800s, the United States began to expand abroad. Americans started a colony in the Samoan Islands in the Pacific. By 1887 American settlers controlled the Hawaiian sugar industry and annexed the Hawaiian Islands. By winning the Spanish-American War in 1898, the United States gained Puerto Rico, Guam, and the Philippines.

International Rivalries (page 436)

In 1871 Germany emerged as the most powerful state in Europe. Otto von Bismarck was afraid that France would form an alliance against Germany. For protection against France, he made a defensive alliance with Austria-Hungary in 1879. Italy joined the alliance in 1882. It was called the Triple Alliance. Bismarck also arranged a treaty with Russia and tried to stay on good terms with Great Britain.

Emperor William II fired Bismarck in 1890 and took personal control of German foreign policy. He dropped the treaty with Russia. Almost at the same time, France formed an alliance

Analyzing Information

Why did the formation of defensive alliances among European powers make a major war more likely?

_____

_____

_____

with Russia. By 1907 Britain joined the alliance with France and Russia. That alliance was called the Triple Entente. Europe was divided into two opposing camps.

Crises in the Balkans set the stage for World War I. Austria and Russia competed for influence in the Balkans. In 1908 Austria-Hungary annexed Bosnia and Herzegovina. That angered the Serbians, who had hoped to combine the southern Slavs into one strong state. Russia threatened to attack Austria. However, Emperor William II of Germany spoke in support of Austria, and Russia backed down.

Wars broke out among the Balkan states in 1912 and 1913. Austria considered Serbia a threat to the empire of Austria-Hungary. Russia was determined to defend the Slavs and not to back down again. Because both Russia and Austria-Hungary had powerful allies, war could easily explode.

Section Wrap-up

Answer these questions to check your understanding of the entire section.

1. Why did Emperor William II of Germany fire Chancellor Bismarck?

_____

_____

_____

2. What overseas territories did the United States acquire by 1900?

_____

_____

_____

Expository Writing

Explain why the Balkans were so critical to the relationships among larger European powers in the early 1900s. Make a general statement and support it with specific factual information. Describe the issues in the Balkans in that time period and the positions of the major powers involved.

_____

_____

_____

_____

_____

_____

Toward the Modern Consciousness

Big Idea

Radical change in the economic and social structure of the West was matched by equally dramatic artistic, intellectual, and political changes. As you read, complete a chart like the one below that lists an artist and a characteristic of the art movement indicated.

Impressionism		
Post-Impressionism		
Cubism		
Abstract painting		

Notes   Read to Learn

The Culture of Modernity (page 438)

Evaluating Information

If you wanted to know what the French countryside looked like in the late 1800s, which paintings would provide the most accurate information?

___ *Impressionist*

___ *Post-Impressionist*

___ *Cubist*

___ *Abstract*

Between 1870 and 1910, many writers and artists rebelled against traditional styles. The changes they produced are called **modernism.** Naturalist writers addressed social problems realistically. Symbolist writers thought the only reality was the human mind; art should reflect the mind, not comment on society.

Impressionist painters such as Claude Monet went outside to paint nature directly. Monet captured the interplay of light, water, and sky. Starting in France in the 1880s, Post-Impressionists Paul Cezanne and Vincent van Gogh used color to express moods and feelings.

After photography, painters no longer felt a need to paint realistically. Pablo Picasso created a style called cubism. He used geometric designs and looked at the human body from many angles. Starting about 1910, abstract painters such as Wassily Kandinsky avoided visual reality completely. Kandinsky used only line and color.

Architects made functional buildings and skyscrapers, free of ornamentation. Frank Lloyd Wright designed homes with geometric lines. In music, Igor Stravinsky used strong expressive rhythms.

 **Notes** | **Read to Learn**

Uncertainty Grows (page 440)

Identifying the Main Idea

New ideas in science challenged the Newtonian belief that physical reality worked like a _____.

Scientific discoveries changed how people thought about themselves and the world. Westerners in the 1800s thought science gave solid information about the physical world. Following the ideas of Isaac Newton, they thought the physical world worked like a giant machine.

Science brought greater uncertainty after about 1900. The French scientist Marie Curie discovered that the element radium gave off energy, or radiation. This energy came from inside the atom; so atoms must not be hard material bodies but small, active worlds.

Albert Einstein published his special theory of relativity in 1905. He wrote that space and time are not absolute but are relative to the observer. He concluded that matter was another form of energy.

Sigmund Freud, a doctor from Vienna, changed ideas about the human mind. He published *The Interpretation of Dreams* in 1900. Freud believed that past experiences and internal forces strongly influence human behavior, even when people are not aware of them. He invented a method called **psychoanalysis** to help people become aware of their repressed experiences and thoughts.

Extreme Nationalism (page 442)

Distinguishing Fact from Opinion

"War is a biological necessity of the first important, . . . since without it an unhealthy development will follow, which excludes every advancement of the race, and therefore all real civilization."
—F. von Bernhardi

Does this quotation represent fact or opinion? _____

Nationalism became more intense in the late 1800s. For some people, this meant that their nation was more important than any other.

Some writers tried to justify the dominance of Western nations by using ideas from Charles Darwin. They applied Darwin's theory of natural selection to human societies. This was called **Social Darwinism.** The British philosopher Herbert Spencer argued that social progress came from survival of the fittest. Some thought this meant that the weak should die and the strong should not help them.

Extreme nationalists used Social Darwinism to justify acts of violence against people who did not share their language and traditions. They believed that war was the best way to achieve survival of the fittest.

Anti-Semitism, or prejudice against Jews, was common. New parties in Germany and Austria-Hungary won votes by blaming problems on the Jews. In Russia, many Jews were killed in **pogroms,** or massacres.

Jewish nationalists called **Zionists** dreamed of a Jewish homeland to be established in Palestine. Many Jews moved to Palestine or the United States to escape persecution in Europe.

Answer these questions to check your understanding of the entire section.

1. What important scientific discovery was made by Marie Curie?

_____

_____

_____

2. How did anti-Semitism affect politics in Germany and Austria-Hungary?

_____

_____

_____

Form a theory about how new ideas in science and psychology might have influenced new developments in art in the late 1800s and early 1900s. Consider how a change in people's image of the natural world might affect what they choose to portray in their art. Support and illustrate your theory with specific individuals, ideas, and types of art.

_____

_____

_____

_____

_____

_____

_____

_____

_____

_____

_____

_____

_____

Colonial Rule in Southeast Asia

Big Idea

Through the new imperialism, Westerners controlled vast territories, exploited native populations and opened markets for European products. As you read, make a chart showing which countries controlled what parts of Southeast Asia.

Spain (until 1898)	
Netherlands	
United States (after 1898)	
France	
Great Britain	

 **Notes**

Read to Learn

The New Imperialism (page 450)

Detecting Bias

"The path of progress is strewn with the wrecks of nations . . . Yet these dead people are, in truth, the stepping stones on which mankind has arisen to the higher intellectual and deeper emotional life of today."

This British quote may be biased because the British had been _____ *in recent wars.*

In the 1880s, European states began to scramble for overseas territory. In this "new imperialism," they wanted direct control over large areas. One reason was economic. European countries saw Asian and African societies as a source of raw materials such as oil, tin, and rubber. They also saw those societies as a market for manufactured goods.

Nationalism was another motive. Colonies were a source of national prestige. European nations competed with one another to see who could have the most colonies or the best colonies.

Imperialism was also tied to Social Darwinism and **racism.** Social Darwinists believed that in the struggle between nations, the fit are victorious over the unfit. Racists believed that race determines a person's traits and abilities. They considered some races superior to others.

Some Europeans took a more religious and humanitarian approach to imperialism. They believed Europeans had a moral responsibility to civilize primitive people. They called this responsibility the "white man's burden." To some, this meant spreading Christianity. To others, it meant bringing the benefits of Western democracy and capitalism to non-Western societies.

Colonial Takeover (page 452)

Determining Cause and Effect

What caused control of the Philippines to pass from Spain to the United States?

_____

What caused guerrillas led by Emilio Aguinaldo to fight against the United States?

_____

Competition for overseas territories increased European involvement in Southeast Asia. By 1900 almost the whole area was under European rule. Only Thailand (then called Siam) managed to keep its independence. In 1819 the British founded the colony of Singapore. Singapore soon became a major stopping point for steamships going to or from China. Afraid the British would try to take over Vietnam, the French made that country a French **protectorate**—a political unit that depends on another government for its protection. France also extended power over nearby countries. It united the whole area as French Indochina.

After the Spanish-American War, the United States made the Philippines an American colony. Emilio Aguinaldo led an independence movement in the Philippines. After several years of war, the United States defeated the Filipino guerrillas.

Colonial Regimes (page 454)

Comparing and Contrasting

How were indirect rule and direct rule alike and different?

Alike:

_____

Different—
Indirect rule:

_____

Direct rule:

_____

European countries governed their new colonial empires either by indirect rule or direct rule. In **indirect rule,** the colonial power cooperated with local political elites. Where local rulers resisted foreign conquest, the colonial powers removed them from power. In these cases, the colonial power brought people from the home country to govern the colony. This was called **direct rule.**

The colonial powers used their colonies to provide raw materials and buy European products. In many colonies, this led to plantation agriculture. Peasants on the plantations worked at poverty levels. Colonial rule did bring some progress, such as the construction of roads and railroads.

Formulating Questions

To understand the causes of a colonial resistance movement, one might ask:

Did _____ agriculture under colonial rule make life hard for peasants?

Many people in Southwest Asia were not happy about colonial rule. The earliest resistance came from the existing ruling class. Some resistance came in the form of peasant revolts. Under colonial rule, peasants were often driven off the land to make way for plantation agriculture.

A new kind of resistance began after 1900. It was based on the force of nationalism. The leaders were members of a new, educated, urban middle class. Colonial rule had created this new class of merchants, clerks, students, and professionals.

At first, many of the leaders of these movements did not demand national independence. They simply tried to defend their people's economic interests or religious beliefs. Not until the 1930s, however, did these resistance movements begin to demand independence as a nation.

Section Wrap-up

Answer these questions to check your understanding of the entire section.

1. What were two interpretations of the "white man's burden"?

_____

_____

_____

2. Why did colonial powers establish plantations in their colonies?

_____

_____

_____

**Informative Writing**

Tell the story of the extension of European power over the societies of Southeast Asia. Use a story plan made up of four elements: time, place, colonial power, and events. Discuss what happened, when it happened, why it happened, how it happened, and what parties were involved.

_____

_____

_____

_____

_____

_____

Empire Building in Africa

Big Idea

Almost all of Africa was under European rule by 1900. As you read, make a chart like the one below showing which countries controlled what parts of Africa.

Western Power	Area of Africa
Belgium	
Britain	
France	
Germany	

Notes   Read to Learn

West Africa and North Africa (page 456)

Making Inferences

Italy was the only European state to lose a battle to an African state. What can one infer from this about Italy's motives for taking Tripoli as a colony?

_____

_____

_____

Between 1880 and 1900, almost all of Africa came under European rule. Such products as peanuts, timber, and palm oil drew Europeans to West Africa. The British started settlements along the coast to protect their trade interests. Britain **annexed**—incorporated another country within an existing state—part of the Gold Coast in 1874 and established a protectorate over Nigeria. France added much of West Africa to its empire by 1900. Germany controlled Togo, Cameroon, German Southwest Africa, and German East Africa.

In Egypt, an army officer named Muhammad Ali seized power from the Ottomans in 1805 and established a separate Egyptian state. He introduced modern reforms including public schools. In 1869 the French entrepreneur Ferdinand de Lesseps completed the Suez Canal, connecting the Mediterranean and Red Seas. The British bought Egypt's share in the canal in 1875. In 1914 Egypt became a British protectorate. The British also wanted to control the Sudan, south of Egypt. A Muslim cleric known as the Mahdi started a revolt in 1881. Britain did not secure control of the Sudan until 1898.

France started colonies in Algeria, Tunisia, and Morocco. Italy tried to take over Ethiopia but lost to Ethiopian forces in 1896. Later Italy seized Turkish Tripoli and renamed it Libya.

Notes | Read to Learn

Central and East Africa (page 459)

Problems and Solutions

Bismarck acquired colonies in East Africa as a solution to which problem?

_____

_____

European explorers aroused popular interest in the jungles of Central Africa. David Livingstone and Henry Stanley explored Africa for decades. When the British did not accept Stanley's suggestion to send settlers to the Congo River, Stanley approached King Leopold II of Belgium. Leopold rushed in with enthusiasm to settle lands along the Congo River. France then occupied parts of Central Africa farther north.

Under popular pressure to build an empire, the German chancellor Otto von Bismarck said, "All this colonial business is a sham, but we need it for the elections." The Berlin conference met in 1884 and 1885 to settle conflicting claims in East Africa. The conference awarded colonies to both Britain and Germany. Portugal received a clear claim on Mozambique.

South Africa (page 460)

Synthesizing Information

The United States and the Union of South Africa were similar in being self-governing states run by the descendants of settlers from

_____.

Europeans had a strong and fast-growing presence in South Africa. Cecil Rhodes, the British founder of diamond and oil companies, dreamed of British colonies all the way from Egypt to Cape Colony, connected by a railroad. The Boers were descendants of original Dutch settlers who believed in white superiority and had placed many **indigenous** peoples, those native to the region, on reservations. When diamonds were discovered in Boer territory, the British settlers flocked there. The result was a war between the British and the Dutch Boers, starting in 1899. After the British won the Boer War in 1902, they combined Cape Colony, Orange Free State, and Transvaal into a self-governing Union of South Africa. Only whites were allowed to vote.

Effects of Imperialism (page 461)

Analyzing Information

What were the advantages and disadvantages of how Britain and France ruled in Africa?

_____

_____

By 1914 only two independent states remained in Africa: Ethiopia and Liberia. All the rest of the continent was divided up among Great Britain, France, Germany, Belgium, Italy, Spain, and Portugal.

The British governed chiefly by indirect rule. This system did not disrupt local customs. British administrators made all the decisions, and the old elite were responsible for enforcing them.

Most other European colonial powers governed their colonies in Africa through direct rule. In the French colonies, the government of France appointed a French governor-general. The French ideal was to assimilate African subjects into French culture rather than to preserve native traditions.

Section Wrap-up

Answer these questions to check your understanding of the entire section.

1. The Red Sea was connected with the Indian Ocean. Why did Great Britain particularly care about control of the Suez Canal?

_____

_____

_____

2. What was the cause of the Boer War? What was the outcome?

_____

_____

_____

Descriptive Writing

Pretend that you are a journalist traveling with Henry Stanley during his search for David Livingstone. Write a description of your travel through the tropic rain forest and finding Livingstone on the shore of Lake Tanganyika. Use as many of the five senses as possible to communicate your experience to newspaper readers back home.

_____

_____

_____

_____

_____

_____

_____

_____

_____

_____

_____

_____

_____

_____

British Rule in India

Big Idea

The British brought stability to India but destroyed native industries and degraded Indians. As you read, use a chart like the one below to identify some causes and effects of British influence on India.

Cause	Effect
1. British textiles	
2. cotton crops	
3. school system	
4. railroad, telegraph, telephone services	

Notes | Read to Learn

The Sepoy Mutiny (page 466)

Predicting

When people are ordered to do something that deeply offends their religion, they may be expected to

_____.

During the 1700s, British power in India increased. The power of the Moguls declined. The British government authorized the British East India Company to take an active role in Indian affairs. The British East India Company hired Indian soldiers, called **sepoys.**

Sepoys rebelled in 1857. They had just been issued a new kind of rifle. A rumor started that the cartridges, which soldiers had to bite, were greased with pig and cow fat. This offended both Hindus and Muslims. When a group of sepoys refused to bite the cartridges, the British put them in prison. Other sepoys rebelled.

The rebellion spread. Both sides committed atrocities. Indians killed 200 women and children in a building in Kanpur. The British killed many Indians as well. Within a year, Indian troops loyal to the British crushed the rebellion.

As a result of the uprising, the British Parliament transferred the rule of India from the East India Company to the British government. In 1876 Queen Victoria took the title Empress of India. She called India the jewel in her crown. Another result of the uprising was the beginning of nationalist feeling in India.

British Colonial Rule (page 468)

Drawing Conclusions

From the description of the school system the British set up in India, one can conclude that the schools were primarily designed to meet the needs of the

_____

_____.

After the Sepoy Mutiny, the British government began to rule India through a **viceroy**—a governor—and a civil service staff. The British administration brought order and relatively honest, efficient government. A school system, using the English language, was set up to train upper-class Indian children for civil and military service.

The British built roads, canals, universities, and medical centers. A postal service was introduced, and a rail network across India was constructed.

British rule also harmed the people of India in several ways. British manufactured goods destroyed local industries. Local officials, sent by the British to collect taxes, abused their authority. Because the British encouraged farmers to switch from food production to growing cotton, the food supply could not keep up with the growing population. Millions died of starvation.

Indian Nationalists (page 469)

Synthesizing Information

In both Africa and India, many leaders of the nationalist and independence movements had a

_____

education.

The British presence in India led to an Indian independence movement.

Early nationalists pressed for reform, not independence. However, the pace of reform was slow. Many Indian nationalists, who were English-educated, decided they could not count on the British to make changes voluntarily. In 1885 a small group met in Mumbai (then called Bombay) and formed the Indian National Congress (INC). The INC called for a share in the governing process.

Mohandas Gandhi became active in the independence movement. He began a movement based on nonviolent resistance. Its aim was to force the British to improve the lot of the poor and to grant independence to India. After many years, Gandhi's movement led to Indian independence.

Colonial Indian Culture *(page 470)*

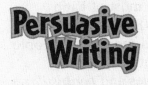

Identifying the Main Idea

Read the paragraph about newspapers. Write a sentence that expresses the main idea of the paragraph.

_____

_____

The relationship between India and the British led to a cultural awakening. A British college was established in Calcutta in the early 1800s. A local publishing house was opened. It printed a variety of textbooks. Newspapers were printed in the regional languages of India. Nationalists used newspapers to arouse mass support for nationalist causes.

The most famous Indian author was Rabindranath Tagore. A great writer and poet, he won the Nobel Prize in literature in 1913. He set to music the Bengali poem that became the anthem of Indian nationalism. He set up a school that became an international university.

Section Wrap-up

Answer these questions to check your understanding of the entire section.

1. What was the immediate cause of the Sepoy Mutiny?

_____

_____

_____

2. List two goals of Gandhi's movement based on nonviolent resistance.

_____

_____

_____

Persuasive Writing

Imagine that you were a member of the British Parliament or the British colonial administration during the period of British colonial rule in India. Make one policy recommendation for the British government related to India. Clearly state your recommendation as though in a speech or letter. Support your recommendation with arguments and specific facts related to Indian history, economics, or culture.

_____

_____

_____

_____

Nation Building in Latin America

Big Idea

Latin American countries gained their independence but became economically dependent on Western powers. As you read, create a Venn diagram comparing and contrasting colonial rule in Africa and in Latin America.

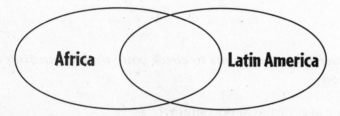

Africa   **Latin America**

 **Notes** | **Read to Learn**

Nationalist Revolts (page 472)

Determining Cause and Effect

The American Revolution inspired Latin Americans to revolt against Spanish or Portuguese rule.

Cause:

_____

_____

Effect:

_____

_____

New political ideas from the successful American Revolution influenced **creole** elites—descendants of Europeans permanently living in Latin America. They controlled land and business, but resented the **peninsulares**—Spanish and Portuguese officials—who treated them poorly and drained the Americas of their wealth.

Napoleon's wars weakened the authority of Spain and Portugal in their colonies, and a series of revolts allowed most of Latin America to become independent. In Mexico in 1810, a priest named Miguel Hidalgo led Native Americans and **mestizos**—people of mixed European and Native American descent—in a revolt against Spanish rule, but the uprising failed. Creoles and *peninsulares* declared Mexico independent in 1821, keeping power for themselves. Initially a monarchy, Mexico became a republic in 1823.

Two members of the creole elite led revolutions throughout South America. They were José de San Martín of Argentina and Simón Bolívar of Venezuela. Between 1810 and 1824, forces led by San Martín or Bolívar overthrew Spanish rule in Argentina, Bolivia, Chile, Colombia, Paraguay, Peru, Uruguay, and Venezuela. Brazil became independent in 1822 and Central America in 1823. United States president James Monroe warned European powers not to try to restore European control. This was called the Monroe Doctrine.

Nation Building *(page 475)*

Problems and Solutions

How did settlers in Texas solve the problem of corrupt government under Santa Anna?

_____

_____

_____

Unclear boundaries led to wars among the new republics in Latin America. Transportation and communication were difficult. There was little sense of national unity.

The new republics had little experience in self-government. Strong leaders called **caudillos** came into power. For example, Antonio López de Santa Anna ruled Mexico 11 times from 1833 to 1855. He misused money and stopped reforms. In the Mexican state of Texas, settlers from the United States revolted against Santa Anna's rule. Texas became independent in 1836 and joined the United States in 1845. The United States conquered other Mexican territory by 1848 in the War with Mexico. The next strong Mexican leader was Benito Juárez. He brought many reforms: religious toleration, public schooling, and land for the poor.

Latin American countries had political independence, but became economically dependent on Great Britain and later on the United States. The United States pursued "dollar diplomacy," extending its influence by investing in Latin American development. Foreign investors built transportation and communication systems. National economies came to depend on **cash crops** such as sugar and coffee, produced for export. The landed elites continued to dominate society and government. Most people remained very poor.

Change in Latin America *(page 477)*

Predicting

If U.S. Marines stayed in a Latin American country for decades, how would the people of that country be likely to respond?

_____

_____

After 1870 Latin American governments wrote constitutions. They took ideas from the United States and democracies of Europe. However, the elites kept power by limiting the right to vote.

As the United States became a world power about 1900, it intervened in Latin America. The Spanish-American War of 1898 gave the United States control over Cuba and Puerto Rico. After helping Panama break away from Colombia in 1903, the United States built the Panama Canal from coast to coast. U.S. forces were sent to various Latin American countries to protect U.S. commercial interests.

Mexico had another revolution. The conservative dictator Porfirio Díaz ruled Mexico between 1877 and 1911. Wages declined and most rural people had no land. A liberal landowner, Francisco Madero, forced Díaz from power in 1911. A wider revolution followed. Bandits led by Pancho Villa swept the countryside. Emiliano Zapata led peasants to demand and enforce land reform. A new constitution in 1917 set up a presidential government, land reform, and limits on foreign investors.

Answer these questions to check your understanding of the entire section.

1. How did the United States extend its influence in Latin America in the 1800s?

_____

_____

_____

2. What was the Monroe Doctrine?

_____

_____

_____

Explain the importance of social class to the revolutions of Latin America and the governments that followed. Give specific examples of the role different social classes played in particular events. Start and finish with a general statement that gives an overview of the role of social class in Latin American history in that period.

_____

_____

_____

_____

_____

_____

_____

_____

_____

_____

_____

_____

_____

_____

The Decline of the Qing Dynasty

Big Idea

As the Qing dynasty declined, Western nations increased their economic involvement with China. As you read, create a chart like the one below to compare the Tai Ping and Boxer Rebellions.

	Tai Ping	Boxer
Reforms Demanded		
Method Used		
Outcomes		

Notes

Read to Learn

Causes of Decline (page 488)

Drawing Conclusions

From the events leading up to the Opium War, one can conclude that the British who determined polity in relation to China cared more about _____ than about _____.

The Qing dynasty of the Manchus was at its height in 1800. Soon after that, however, the dynasty went into decline. Some problems were internal: corruption, peasant unrest, and incompetence. The government did not want to make reforms.

Other problems came from Western powers. To limit foreign influence, the Qing rulers allowed European merchants in only one place: Guangzhou, or Canton. The Indian cotton the British exported to China was not enough to cover the cost of their imports. They added another export: opium, an addictive drug. The Chinese government protested. In the resulting Opium War of 1839–1842, the British won the island of Hong Kong and wider trading privileges. Europeans living in China were not subject to China's laws, a practice known as **extraterritoriality.** China later legalized the opium trade.

Peasants revolted in the Tai Ping Rebellion of 1850–64. Their leader called for giving land to all peasants, treating women as equals, outlawing alcohol and tobacco, and eliminating private property. Europeans and local warlords helped the Qing dynasty restore order. The weakened dynasty finally started to listen to reformers. They called for a policy of **"self-strengthening,"** adopting Western technology but keeping Confucian values. They built industries but did not introduce democracy.

Notes | Read to Learn

The Advance of Imperialism (page 492)

Making Generalizations

In general, under what conditions was foreign influence strongest in China?

_____

_____

_____

The weakness of the Qing dynasty enabled other nations to gain power in China. Britain, France, Germany, Russia, and Japan signed agreements with local warlords. These agreements gave each nation a **sphere of influence,** where only that nation was allowed to trade.

Russia forced China to give up some lands in the north. When Russia took control of Manchuria, Japan felt threatened and signed an alliance with Britain.

Japan made inroads into Korea, which China ruled. China and Japan went to war over Korea in 1894. Japan won the war, gaining Taiwan.

In 1897 Chinese rioters killed two German missionaries. That formed an excuse for Germany to demand land on the Shandong Peninsula. After China agreed, other European powers made more demands.

China was in an internal crisis. The young emperor Guang Xu announced One Hundred Days of reform in 1898. He tried to modernize and westernize Chinese institutions. His aunt, Empress Dowager Ci Xi, put him in prison and stopped his reforms.

Responses to Imperialism (page 494)

Detecting Bias

The behavior of the Boxers showed their bias _____ Chinese traditions and _____ foreign influences.

Great Britain and the United States feared that other countries would overrun China if the dynasty collapsed. Britain had a sphere of influence in China, but the United States did not. Acquiring Hawaii and the Philippines increased American interests in the Pacific.

In 1899 United States secretary of state John Hay proposed an **Open Door policy.** Under such a policy, all countries would have equal trading privileges in China. The policy did not end spheres of influence, but it made it easier for other countries to do business there. It also reduced worries among the other imperialist powers that any one power would try to dominate trade in China.

The Open Door Policy came too late to prevent the Boxer Rebellion. "Boxers" were members of the Society of Harmonious Fists. They were upset by foreign influences and the foreign takeover of Chinese lands. In 1900 they roamed the countryside, killing foreign missionaries and Chinese converts to Christianity. They also killed foreign businessmen and a German diplomat. Response was immediate and overwhelming. An allied army from six imperialist nations restored order. They made the Chinese government pay **indemnity,** or payment for damages, and demanded still more privileges.

Section Wrap-up

Answer these questions to check your understanding of the entire section.

1. "Balance of trade" refers to the relations between a country's imports and exports. A country that exports more than it imports has a favorable balance of trade. One that imports more than it exports has an unfavorable balance of trade. Use this concept to explain why the British insisted on bringing illegal opium into China.

   _____

   _____

   _____

2. How did the Tai Ping Rebellion increase the power of local warlords?

   _____

   _____

   _____

Persuasive Writing

Take a position on the Open Door Policy. Was it a good or a bad idea? Write to persuade readers to agree with your opinion. State your position clearly. Present facts and information to support your point of view.

_____

_____

_____

_____

_____

_____

_____

_____

_____

_____

_____

_____

_____

_____

_____

_____

Revolution in China

Big Idea

Reforms led to a revolution in China, and the arrival of Westerners brought changes to its culture and economy. As you read, create a chart like the one below listing the reforms requested by Sun Yat-Sen and those implemented by Empress Dowager Ci Xi.

Sun Yat-sen's Proposals	Empress Dowager Ci Xi's Reform

Read to Learn

The Fall of the Qing *(page 496)*

Formulating Questions

Which question would best guide research about the influence of Sun Yat-sen?

_____ *Who were his followers and allies?*

_____ *How was he regarded in Russia?*

_____ *What were his favorite leisure activities?*

Empress Dowager Ci Xi had resisted suggestions for reform. After the Boxer Rebellion, however, she introduced reforms. They included a Western-style school system and **provincial,** or local, legislative assemblies. In 1910 China held elections for a national assembly. However, the pace of reform was too slow for the emerging new urban middle class.

One radical was Sun Yat-sen. He formed the Revive China Society. He believed China needed a strong national government, which the Qing dynasty could not provide. He hoped to bring democracy in three stages: a military takeover, one-party rule, and finally a constitutional democracy. In 1905 he united radical groups from across China into an alliance. It later became the Nationalist Party. He called for a republic based on equality. His principles included nationalism, democracy, and the right to earn a livelihood.

In 1911 while Sun Yat-sen was traveling abroad, his followers revolted. The government was too weak to react, and the Qing dynasty collapsed. The rebels asked an army general, Yuan, to serve as president. They asked him to allow the election of a legislature.

The Westernized middle class that supported Sun Yat-sen was small. Few peasants supported him. General Yuan ruled as a dictator and tried to start a new dynasty. China fell into civil war.

Cultural Changes (page 499)

Analyzing Information

"Before my eyes are many miserable scenes, the suffering of others and myself forces my hands to move. I become a machine for writing."
—Ba Jin

According to the quotation above, Ba Jin _____ because he has to.

Traditional Chinese culture was based on the ideas of Confucius. In the early 1900s, those ideas came into tension with new Western ideas. This was especially true in the cities. Traditional culture remained more popular in the countryside and among Chinese conservatives.

Trade and industry were growing in China, and a national market arose for such **commodities**—agricultural, mined, and mass-produced marketable goods—as oil, copper, salt, tea, and porcelain. Foreign investments were making the Chinese economy more modern. Westerners introduced modern transportation and communication. They created a market for Chinese exports. They brought China into the world economy.

On the other hand, these changes caused problems for China. Imperialism destroyed local industries. Profits went back to the imperialist countries instead of staying in China.

During World War I, foreign investment in China dropped temporarily. Chinese entrepreneurs started new businesses. Shanghai and other major cities developed an urban middle class. An industrial working class grew as well.

Daily life in the cities had changed much since 1800. Ideas from Europe and the United States influenced the educated, wealthy elite and middle class. Radical reformers wanted to get rid of traditional culture. They introduced Western books, paintings, music, and ideas.

Chinese writers copied Western writers in describing life realistically. They wrote about the Westernized Chinese middle class. *Midnight* by novelist Mao Dun described the changing customs of the urban elite in Shanghai. Ba Jin wrote three books—*Family, Spring,* and *Autumn*—about the loss of traditional ways as younger family members break away.

Section Wrap-up

Answer these questions to check your understanding of the entire section.

1. List three stages by which Sun Yat-sen hoped to move China from Qing rule to democracy.

_____

_____

_____

2. What themes did the Chinese novelists Mao Dun and Ba Jin feature in their novels?

_____

_____

_____

Expository Writing

Explain the causes and effects of the growth of a new, educated middle class in Shanghai and in other cities of China. Start and end with an overview of the changes you will describe. Organize your information to make it clear to the reader.

_____

_____

_____

_____

_____

_____

_____

_____

_____

_____

_____

_____

_____

Rise of Modern Japan

Big Idea

Western intervention opened Japan to trade, and the interaction between Japan and Western nations led to a modern industrial Japanese society. As you read, create a table like the one below listing the promises in the Charter Oath of 1868 and the provisions of the Meiji constitution of 1890.

Charter Oath	Constitution

Notes

Read to Learn

Japan Responds to Foreign Pressure (page 502)

Determining Cause and Effect

Perry brought warships into Edo Bay. What was the cause of this event? What was the effect?

Cause:

_____

_____

Effect:

_____

_____

By 1800 the Tokugawa shogunate had ruled Japan for 200 years. The Tokugawa followed a policy of isolation. Japan had formal relations with only one other country, Korea. It allowed no foreign merchants except Dutch and Chinese traders at Nagasaki.

Western nations wanted to end Japan's isolation. In 1853 Matthew Perry brought four American warships into Edo Bay (now Tokyo Bay). He brought a letter from United States president Millard Fillmore. The president asked Japan to open relations with the United States. About six months later, Perry returned with a larger fleet. Under military pressure, Japan agreed to make **concessions** and open several ports to Western traders. Diplomatic relations began between Japan and Western nations.

Samurai warriors in southern Japan did not want Japan to interact with foreigners. In 1863 rebellious groups made the shogun promise to end relations with the West. When they fired on Western ships, however, the ships returned fire and destroyed their fortifications.

The incident strengthened the samurai resistance. When the shogun did not take a stronger position against the West, the samurai attacked the shogun's palace at Kyōto. His forces collapsed. That ended the shogunate system and restored the power of the emperor.

Notes | Read to Learn

The Meiji Restoration (page 504)

Comparing and Contrasting

In the Meiji Restoration, how were the Liberals and the Progressives alike and different?

Alike:

_____

_____

Different:

_____

_____

The new leaders put an end to the old order. The new leaders made the young emperor Mutsuhito the symbol of the new era. He called his reign the Meiji, or "Enlightened Rule." This period is called the Meiji Restoration.

The new leaders stripped the daimyo—the local nobles—of their titles to their land. Instead, they were named governors of the territories formerly under their control, now known as **prefectures.**

Two main factions emerged in the legislative assembly—the Liberals and the Progressives. The Liberals wanted political reform based on the Western democracies. An elected parliament would hold the supreme authority. The Progressives wanted to give the executive branch more control. They wanted power shared between the executive and legislative branches.

In the end, the Progressives won. The Meiji constitution was adopted in 1889. Based on the constitution of Germany, it gave most authority to the executive branch. Real power lay with the prime minister and cabinet, chosen by the Meiji leaders.

The Meiji leaders introduced economic changes. The Meiji leaders wanted a "rich country and a strong state." They encouraged industry by providing subsidies, training, improved transportation and communications, and education in applied science.

Joining the Imperialists (page 507)

Making Inferences

Why were the Western powers stunned by Japan's victory over Russia?

_____

_____

Japan wanted colonies too. Japanese expansion began in 1874. In that year, Japan seized the Ryukyu Islands from China. In 1876 Japan's navy made Korea open Korean ports to Japanese trade. Defeating China in war in 1894 brought Japan the Chinese island of Taiwan (then called Formosa). In 1904 Japan launched a surprise attack on the Russian naval base at Port Arthur. When Russia sent its Baltic fleet to the Pacific, the Japanese navy defeated it. The Western powers were stunned by Japan's victory over Russia. Japan was now a world power.

Copyright © Glencoe/McGraw-Hill, a division of The McGraw-Hill Companies, Inc.

152   Chapter 15, Section 3

Culture in an Era of Transition *(page 509)*

The main idea is that Japanese _____ *was heavily influenced by Western* _____ *during the Meiji Restoration.*

Western culture greatly influenced Japanese culture during the Meiji Restoration. Japanese authors began to write novels that followed the French tradition of realism. The Japanese invited technicians, engineers, architects, and artists from Europe and the United States to teach their skills in Japan. In time, a reaction set in. Many Japanese artists began to return to older techniques. Japanese artists looked for forms of expression that were new but truly Japanese. Some tried to combine Japanese and foreign techniques.

Section Wrap-up

Answer these questions to check your understanding of the entire section.

1. How did the Meiji leaders promote industrial growth?

_____

_____

_____

2. List two reasons Japan wanted territories overseas.

_____

_____

_____

Informative Writing

Write an account of the Meiji Restoration, including its causes and effects. Describe events generally in the order in which they happened. Include the four story elements of time, place, people, and events. Write the story so that it flows smoothly, without displaying emotion or interjecting your opinion.

_____

_____

_____

_____

_____

_____

_____

The Road to World War I

Big Idea

Militarism, alliances, imperialism, and nationalism contributed to the start of World War I. As you read, create a diagram like the one below to identify the factors that led to World War I.

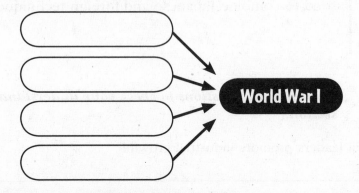

World War I

Notes

Read to Learn

Causes of the War (page 522)

Predicting

The rapid growth of European armies increased the likelihood that if a war began, the war would be

_____.

The late 1800s were a period of intense nationalism and imperialist expansion. European nation-states competed with one another. They formed defensive alliances in case their rivals got too strong. Germany, Austria-Hungary, and Italy formed the Triple Alliance in 1882. France, Great Britain, and Russia created the Triple Entente in 1907. Crises in the Balkans and elsewhere tested those alliances. The crises left European states angry at one another and eager for revenge.

Not all national groups had their own states. The Slavs in the Balkans and the Austro-Hungarian Empire, the Irish in the British Empire, and the Poles in the Russian Empire dreamed of having their own states.

Another source of conflict was the growth of socialist labor movements. They used strikes that sometimes became violent. Some conservative leaders responded to suppress internal disorder. Industrialization aided ship and weapon building. European armies doubled in size between 1890 and 1914. Most countries had a military draft, or **conscription.** (The United States and Britain did not.) Militarism was growing. As armies grew, so did the influence of military leaders. They drew up complex plans to use in case of war. When war broke out in 1914, political leaders had to follow the plans.

The Outbreak of War (page 524)

Determining Cause and Effect

What caused Germany to declare war on Russia?

_____

_____

Serbia wanted to form a large, independent Slavic state in the Balkans. Russia, a Slavic nation, favored the idea. Austria-Hungary, which had many Slavic minorities, was opposed. A secret society called the Black Hand was willing to use violence to help create a large Serbian kingdom.

In 1914 Archduke Francis Ferdinand was the heir to the throne of Austria-Hungary. He and his wife visited Sarajevo, Bosnia, a part of Austria-Hungary in the Balkans. Bosnia had many Serbs. On June 28, 1914, a Bosnian Serb shot and killed Archduke Francis Ferdinand and his wife. The shooter was a member of the Black Hand.

Austrian leaders did not know whether the government of Serbia was involved. They wanted to attack Serbia. Afraid that Russia would help Serbia defend itself, the Austrians asked Germany for support. Emperor William II of Germany promised to support Austria in case of a war between Austria and Russia. On July 28, Austria-Hungary declared war on Serbia.

Czar Nicholas II of Russia ordered the Russian army to get ready for a war (**mobilize**) against Austria-Hungary. Army leaders told the czar their plan was for a war against Austria-Hungary and Germany; they could not follow only part of their plan. The czar agreed to mobilize against both empires. Germany then declared war on Russia.

German officers had a plan too. Their plan was for a war against Russia and France. The plan was to attack France first, through Belgium, and then move against the other. They were not willing to change their plan, so Germany declared war on France.

On August 4, Great Britain declared war on Germany for violating Belgian neutrality. All the great powers of Europe were at war.

Section Wrap-up

Answer these questions to check your understanding of the entire section.

1. List three examples of European minority groups in multinational empires that wanted their own national state.

   _____

   _____

   _____

2. What was the German military plan for a war with Russia?

   _____

   _____

   _____

Expository Writing

How were militarism, nationalism, and alliances among European powers contributing causes of World War I? Give specific illustrations for each point. Consider both the events that triggered the war and the expansion of a local incident into a conflict among many powerful countries.

_____

_____

_____

_____

_____

_____

_____

_____

_____

_____

_____

World War I

Big Idea

The stalemate at the Western Front led to a widening of World War I, and governments expanded their powers to accommodate the war. As you read, identify which country belongs to the allies and the Central Powers. What country changed allegiance? What country withdrew from the war?

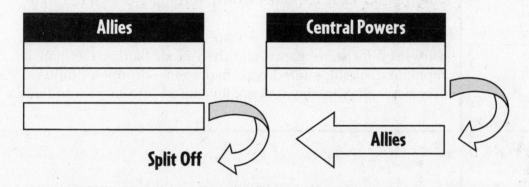

 **Notes** | **Read to Learn**

1914 to 1915: Illusions and Stalemate *(page 526)*

Comparing and Contrasting

How was war on the Western Front different from and similar to the war on the Eastern Front?
Western Front:

_____

_____

Eastern Front:

_____

_____

Both:

_____

_____

Before 1914 many political leaders thought diplomacy could prevent war. On the Western front, the German plan was to capture France quickly. French soldiers, rushing to the front in taxicabs from Paris, stopped the Germans before they reached Paris. The German advance ended with the First Battle of the Marne in September 1914. Both sides dug trenches for shelter. Soon trenches reached from the English Channel to Switzerland. Neither side could make the other move. Deadly trench warfare continued for four years.

War on the Eastern Front was very different. Troops moved quickly. Russian troops moved into eastern Germany. The Germans stopped them at the battles of Tannenberg in August and Masurian Lakes in September. Italy left the Triple Alliance and joined the former Triple Entente of France, Britain, and Russia. Russia had early victories over Austria-Hungary, but Germany helped Austria push the Russians back. Millions of Russians were killed, captured, or wounded. Together, Germany, Austria-Hungary, and Bulgaria attacked Serbia. Serbia had to drop out of the war.

Notes | Read to Learn

The Great Slaughter (page 528)

Analyzing Information

Military leaders were unused to trench warfare. How did that fact affect their decisions?

_____

_____

_____

Many more soldiers died in World War I than in earlier European wars of the 1700s or 1800s. One reason was **trench warfare.** Military leaders were not used to trench warfare. Sometimes they would attack to try to break through enemy lines. The defending troops in their trenches could easily shoot the men running toward them. At Verdun, in France, 700,000 men were killed over a period of 10 months. Each side tried to wear the other down, turning World War I into a **war of attrition.**

Air warfare was a new feature of World War I. Airplanes were used for surveillance and then in air battles. German zeppelins—airships filled with hydrogen—dropped bombs over England. Shooting a zeppelin caused it to burst into flames.

A World War (page 530)

Distinguishing Fact from Opinion

Label each of these newspaper headlines "F" or "O" to indicate whether it expresses a fact or an opinion.

___ *"Lusitania Sunk"*

___ *"Sinking of Lusitania Illegal and Immoral"*

As the war went on and on, more countries became involved. The Ottoman Empire and Bulgaria allied with Austria-Hungary and Germany. They became known as the Central Powers. Russia, Britain, and France (called the Allies) declared war on the Ottomans.

The Ottoman Empire controlled much of the Middle East. A British officer known as Lawrence of Arabia urged Arab princes to revolt against the Ottomans. British troops from Egypt, India, Australia, and New Zealand defeated the Ottoman Empire in 1918.

The United States tried to remain neutral, but when a German submarine sank the British ship *Lusitania,* Americans aboard the ship were killed. This incident caused the United States to enter the war.

The Impact of Total War (page 531)

Evaluating Information

Rank these sources by their value in providing information about what life was like for women during World War I.

The war affected the lives of everyone in the warring countries. To mobilize so many resources and people, governments assumed greater powers. They drafted millions of young men. They set up price, wage, and rent controls. They rationed food supplies and materials. They took over transportation systems and industries. European nations set up **planned economies** directed by government agencies. World War I had become a **total war,** requiring a complete mobilization of resources and people.

_____ **A small-town newspaper article about local women**

_____ **Letters from women who had war-related jobs**

_____ **Government propaganda encouraging women to work in weapons factories**

As the war went on, public enthusiasm waned. Governments used **propaganda** to influence public opinion. They also used force. Even in democracies, governments permitted less freedom of expression than in peacetime. Newspapers were censored. In Britain, under the Defence of the Realm Act, protesters could be arrested as traitors.

World War I created new roles for women. Because so many men were away at war, many of their jobs were given to women. When the men came home after the war, women lost their jobs to men. The social role of women had changed, however.

Section Wrap-up

Answer these questions to check your understanding of the entire section.

1. Why were zeppelins relatively unsatisfactory as air fighting machines?

_____

_____

_____

2. Who was Lawrence of Arabia?

_____

_____

_____

Descriptive Writing

Write a description of trench warfare as it might have been experienced by the soldiers in the trenches. Guide your reader to feel that he or she is sharing the experience. Create vivid images that involve as many of the five senses as possible. Use strong, active verbs to draw the reader into your description.

_____

_____

_____

_____

_____

The Russian Revolution

Big Idea

The fall of the czarist regime and the Russian Revolution put the Communists in power in Russia. As you read, use a chart like the one below to identify the factors and events that led to Lenin coming to power in 1917.

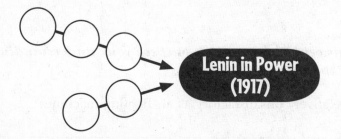

Lenin in Power (1917)

 **Notes**	**Read to Learn**

Background to Revolution (page 536)

Making Inferences

The German word for city is burg. *The Russian word for city is* grad. *What can you infer about why the city of St. Petersburg was renamed Petrograd in 1914?*

_____

_____

_____

Russia was not ready for the challenges of World War I. Czar Nicholas II took personal charge of the army, though he did not have military skills. Millions of Russian soldiers were killed or wounded. Meanwhile, the czar's wife, Alexandra, came under the influence of a man named Grigori Rasputin. He seemed to have magical powers to stop her son's uncontrolled bleeding. While the czar was away at war, Rasputin influenced government decisions through Alexandra.

Economic disasters on the home front added to public unrest. In early 1917, the Russian government started to ration bread. Mothers working in the factories did not have enough to feed their children. At the beginning of March, working-class women held strikes in Petrograd (formerly St. Petersburg). They demanded "Peace and Bread." Other workers joined them. A general strike shut down all the factories in Petrograd.

Many soldiers in Petrograd refused to shoot at the crowd. Instead, they joined the demonstrators. The Duma, or legislative body, set up a provisional (temporary) government. No longer supported by the aristocrats or the army, the czar resigned. Alexander Kerensky headed the provisional government. He made the mistake of deciding to keep Russia in the war. That angered the workers and peasants. **Soviets,** or councils representing workers and soldiers, sprang up all over Russia.

Notes

Read to Learn

Formulating Questions

Which question would best help lead to an understanding of the events of November 16, 1917?

___ *How old was the Winter Palace?*

___ *Who was using the Winter Palace?*

___ *What was the architecture of the Winter Palace?*

The Bolsheviks began as a small group within a Russian party that followed the ideas of Karl Marx. Their leader was a radical known as V. I. Lenin. Lenin was out of the country when the provisional government took power in March 1917. German leaders, at war with Russia, wanted to cause problems in Russia. Hoping Lenin would cause trouble, they shipped him back to Russia in April 1917.

Lenin believed that only violent revolution could end the capitalist system. The Bolsheviks promised to end the war, redistribute land, and put committees of workers in charge of factories. They promised to transfer power from the provisional government to the soviets. By the end of October, Bolsheviks made up a slight majority in the soviets of Moscow and Petrograd.

Leon Trotsky was the head of the Petrograd soviet. He was a dedicated revolutionary. On November 6, Bolsheviks seized the Winter Palace, headquarters of the provisional government. The provisional government quickly collapsed.

A Congress of Soviets from all over Russia was meeting at the time. Publicly, power passed from the provisional government to the Council of Soviets. Real power remained with Lenin. He ended the war with Germany in March 1918 by the Treaty of Brest-Litovsk. However, Russia sank into civil war.

Liberals, moderate socialists, and czarists opposed the new Bolshevik, or Communist, government. Many liberals wanted a constitutional monarchy. Many socialists wanted gradual reform and democracy.

The Allies were very concerned about the Communist takeover. They also wanted to bring Russia back into the war. They sent aid to the anti-Communist forces in Russia. From 1918 to 1921 civil war raged between the Communists, or Reds, and their opponents, or Whites.

The Communists had several advantages. Unlike their opponents, they had a unified goal and were able to translate their beliefs into practical instruments of power—such as their policy of **war communism,** which ensured the Red Army had supplies They had a strong leader in Leon Trotsky, commissar of war. They also used terrorist techniques through their secret police, the Cheka. Finally, because foreign armies were helping the anti-Communist forces, the Communists could appeal to Russian patriotism. By 1921 the Communists were in total command of Russia. It was a centralized, one-party state.

Section Wrap-up

Answer these questions to check your understanding of the entire section.

1. How did the provisional government and the Bolsheviks differ in relation to World War I?

_____

_____

_____

2. How did Rasputin gain influence over Russian government decisions?

_____

_____

_____

Informative Writing

Write an account of the Russian revolution from 1917 (or before) to 1921. Present the facts as they happened, without inserting your opinion. Be sure your account answers the questions who, what, when, where, why, and how.

_____

_____

_____

_____

_____

_____

_____

_____

_____

_____

_____

_____

End of World War I

Big Idea

After the defeat of the Germans, peace settlements brought political and territorial changes to Europe and created bitterness and resentment in some nations. As you read, use a chart like the one below to identify the national interests of each country as it participated in the Paris Peace Conference.

France	Britain	United States

Notes

Read to Learn

The Last Year of the War (page 542)

Identifying the Main Idea

In 1918 the stalemate was broken and the arrival of

_____

enabled the Allies to win the war.

After Russia withdrew from the war in 1918, Germany no longer had to fight on two fronts. General Erich von Ludendorff guided German military operations. Free to concentrate on the Western Front, Ludendorff hoped to win the war with one big final push into France. German troops attacked in March 1918. By April they were within 50 miles (80 kilometers) of Paris. American troops arrived in time to help stop them. French, Moroccan, and American troops defeated German troops at the Second Battle of the Marne on July 18. The Allies went on to win the Second Battle of the Somme on August 8.

A million American troops poured into France in 1918. The Allies began a steady advance toward Germany. On September 29, 1918, Ludendorff informed German leaders that the war was lost. He advised them to make peace. The Allies refused to make peace with the government of Emperor William II. German sailors, workers, and soldiers rebelled across northern Germany. The emperor left the country, and the Social Democrats announced a new democratic republic. On November 11, 1918, they signed an **armistice,** or an agreement to stop fighting.

Read to Learn

The Peace Settlements (page 544)

Problems and Solutions

France suffered greatly from German attacks during the war. The French were afraid Germany might attack again in the future.

Which provisions of the peace settlement were intended to solve this problem?

_____

_____

_____

_____

In January 1919, representatives of 27 Allied nations met in Paris to work out a final settlement. They did not all have the same interests. When the war had started, both sides fought for territorial gains. Some countries had been promised territory in return for joining the war.

President Woodrow Wilson of the United States saw the war differently. He described it as a fight between democracy (the Allies) and absolutism (the Central Powers). Before the end of the war, he described his ideas for a peace settlement in a speech to the United States Congress. These ideas were Wilson's Fourteen Points. They included reducing military forces and weapons; letting each people choose their own government; reaching peace agreements openly; and creating a League of Nations to guarantee the rights of all nations. Wilson's ideas were popular with the Allies. National interests also affected their decisions. David Lloyd George, prime minister of Great Britain, had won election by promising to make the Germans pay for the war. Georges Clemenceau, premier of France, wanted revenge and national security—protection against future German attacks.

The final peace settlement consisted of five separate treaties with Germany, Austria, Hungary, Bulgaria, and Turkey. Most important was the Treaty of Versailles, signed with Germany on June 28, 1918. It declared that Germany and Austria were responsible for starting the war. It ordered Germany to pay the Allies **reparations** for all the damage the war had caused. It required Germany to reduce its army and navy and eliminate its air force. Germany lost territory in the west to France and in the east to a new Polish state. To protect France from future attacks, German land along the Rhine River became a demilitarized zone, with no weapons or defenses.

The peace treaties broke up the empires of Central and Eastern Europe. Austria-Hungary and the Ottoman Empire ceased to exist. Germany and Russia lost much territory. New nation-states were created: Finland, Latvia, Estonia, Lithuania, Poland, Czechoslovakia, Austria, and Hungary. In the Balkans, Serbia achieved its dream of a larger union of southern Slavs; Serbs, Croats, and Slovenes were combined in a new state called Yugoslavia.

The settlement left problems that would lead to later conflicts. Because national groups lived in overlapping areas, the new states had ethnic minorities. The Allies broke their promise to Arab states that had been part of the Ottoman Empire; instead of independence, they were placed under French and British rule as **mandates.**

1. What change in 1918 encouraged Ludendorff to think that Germany could win the war with one final push into France?

_____

_____

_____

2. Which feature of the peace settlements caused resentment among the Arab states?

_____

_____

_____

Persuasive Writing

State an opinion about one or more provisions of the peace settlement at the end of World War I. Present your opinion as though you were a participant in the peace conference in Paris, trying to persuade the other Allied representatives of your point of view. Support your opinion with information and arguments. Include responses to counter-arguments, showing why those who disagree with you are wrong.

_____

_____

_____

_____

_____

_____

_____

_____

_____

_____

_____

_____

The Futile Search for Stability

Big Idea

Peace and prosperity were short-lived after World War I as a global depression weakened Western democracies. As you read, use a table like the one below to compare France's Popular Front with the New Deal in the United States.

Popular Front	New Deal

Notes **Read to Learn**

Uneasy Peace, Uncertain Security (page 554)

Predicting

Was the Kellogg-Briand Pact likely to prevent war?

Circle YES or NO.

Why or why not?

_____

_____

_____

The peace settlement at the end of World War I left many nations unhappy. The League of Nations was not strong enough to settle disputes and keep the peace. One problem was that the United States was not a member. The Senate refused to ratify the Treaty of Versailles, wanting to stay out of European affairs.

France demanded strict enforcement of the Treaty of Versailles, including high German reparations. After making its first payment in 1921, Germany experienced a financial crisis and said it could not pay any more. France sent troops into the German industrial area of the Ruhr Valley. German workers went on strike.

Germany printed more paper money to pay workers' wages. As a result, German money lost its value, and prices went up. Inflation was out of control. Workers carried their weekly pay home in wheelbarrows. An international plan was adopted to make reparations more reasonable. Briefly in the later 1920s, Europe enjoyed prosperity and cooperation. Germany and France signed the Treaty of Locarno in 1925. It guaranteed Germany's new western borders with France and Belgium. Sixty-three nations signed the Kellogg-Briand Pact of 1928, promising not to make war. The pact did not provide a way to enforce this.

 **Notes** | # Read to Learn

The Great Depression *(page 556)*

Determining Cause and Effect

In the late 1920s, agricultural overproduction caused

_____.

A crisis in the United States stock markets caused Americans

to _____,
with the result that European banks collapsed. A final result of both those factors was

_____.

A **depression** is a period of low economic activity and high unemployment. A global depression brought an end to the period of prosperity. One cause was a series of downturns in the late 1920s. Farm prices dropped because of overproduction. The other cause was a crisis in the United States stock market. Americans withdrew their investments from Europe, causing European banks to collapse.

In 1932 about 30 percent of German workers and nearly 25 percent of British workers were unemployed. Governments responded by lowering wages and raising tariffs. Those measures made the crisis worse.

Governments assumed more power to try to deal with the crisis. The economic crisis changed how people thought about government and the economy. Workers and intellectuals showed interest in Karl Marx, who had predicted that overproduction would destroy capitalism.

Desperate people were willing to give leaders with simple solutions dictatorial powers.

Democratic States *(page 558)*

Making Generalizations

In times of crisis, such as war or depression, the involvement of governments in the economy tends to

_____.

World War I increased democracy in the short run. Women in several countries won the right to vote. Republics replaced former empires but struggled for economic stability.

Germany's new Weimar Republic battled runaway inflation and social problems. Families lost their life savings. Many Germans blamed the Weimar Republic during the depression.

In France, the Great Depression brought political instability. In 1936 a coalition of Communists, Socialists, and Radicals formed the Popular Front. Its program for workers included **collective bargaining**, a 40-hour workweek, paid vacation, and a minimum wage.

British leaders ignored the ideas of economist John Maynard Keynes, who advised government to stimulate demand by giving people work even if it meant the government engaged in **deficit spending**, or going into debt. Other economists disagreed, however, and thought that depressions should be left to resolve themselves.

In the United States, Franklin Delano Roosevelt's New Deal encouraged government intervention in the economy. It included public works and social security.

Section Wrap-up

Answer these questions to check your understanding of the entire section.

1. Why did the United States Senate refuse to ratify the Treaty of Versailles and join the League of Nations?

   _____

   _____

   _____

2. Describe the ideas of John Maynard Keynes for how to bring about an economic recovery.

   _____

   _____

   _____

Expository Writing

Analyze the relationship between economics and politics in the 1920s and 1930s. Form a theory or generalization about the relationships, and support it with specific illustrations. Consider cause and effect. Also consider any differences among countries. Your theory or generalization may address these differences.

_____

_____

_____

_____

_____

_____

_____

_____

_____

_____

_____

The Rise of Dictatorial Regimes

Big Idea

By 1939 many European countries had adopted dictatorial regimes that
aimed to control every aspect of their citizens' lives for state goals. As you
read, use a web diagram like the one below to list methods Mussolini used
to create a Fascist dictatorship.

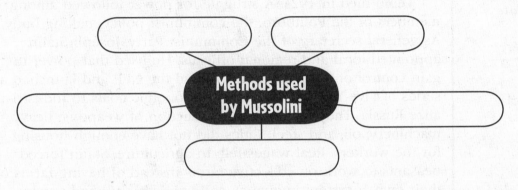

Methods used by Mussolini

Notes

Read to Learn

The Rise of Dictators (page 560)

Distinguishing Fact from Opinion

Mussolini called women's roles as homemakers and mothers "their natural and fundamental mission in life." Was this statement

FACT or OPINION?

(Circle one.)

Democracy in Europe after World War I was short-lived. By the late 1930s France and Britain were the only major democracies in Europe. A new form of dictatorship was the **totalitarian state,** led by one leader and one party. Totalitarian governments aimed to control every aspect of their citizens' lives. Individual rights were less important than the good of the state, as defined by the government.

One form of totalitarianism is **fascism.** Fascism glorifies the state above the individual. In Italy in the early 1920s, Benito Mussolini set up the first fascist movement in Europe. Italy had severe economic problems after World War I. Inflation grew and workers held strikes. The middle class began to fear a communist takeover.

Mussolini's Blackshirts attacked socialist offices and newspapers. They used violence to break up strikes. In 1922 Mussolini threatened to march on Rome unless his Fascists were given power. King Victor Emmanuel III gave in and made Mussolini prime minister.

The Fascists outlawed other parties and established a secret police. Fascist youth groups promoted military activities and values.

A New Era in the USSR (page 563)

Drawing Conclusions

From the information about the changes Stalin introduced, one can conclude that Stalin's rule overall was

_____

for Russia.

During Russia's civil war, Lenin controlled industries. He took grain from peasants to feed the army. By 1921, people were starving. Lenin adopted a New Economic Policy (NEP). It let individuals sell farm produce and run small businesses. The government kept control of heavy industry, mines, and banks. The NEP prevented total disaster. In 1922 the Communists created the Union of Soviet Socialist Republics (USSR or Soviet Union).

Lenin died in 1924. A struggle for power followed among members of the Politburo, the communist policy-making body. As general secretary of the Communist Party, Joseph Stalin appointed local and regional officials. He used that power to gain control of the party. Stalin ended the NEP and launched a series of Five-Year Plans. They set economic goals to industrialize Russia. They emphasized production of weapons, heavy machinery, oil, and steel. Cities did not have enough housing for the workers. Real wages fell. In agriculture, Stalin forced peasants to work on collective farms instead of having farms of their own, a system known as **collectivization.** Food production fell. To keep personal control, Stalin arrested and executed Bolsheviks from the pre-Stalin era.

Authoritarian States in the West (page 566)

Formulating Questions

To determine whether an authoritarian state is also totalitarian, one might ask:

1. _____
_____
_____
_____?

2. _____
_____
_____
_____?

The settlement at the end of World War I created new republics in Eastern Europe. However, they had little experience of self-rule. Many peasants could not read, and large landowners dominated the land. Leaders feared communist unrest and ethnic conflict. They installed authoritarian governments to preserve the old order. While authoritarian, these governments were not totalitarian.

In Central and Eastern Europe, only Czechoslovakia remained a democracy. It had a large middle class and tradition of liberalism.

Spain was another state where authoritarianism replaced democracy. The Second Republic was created in 1931. It lasted barely over five years. Francisco Franco, a military general, led an army revolt against the democratic government in 1936. Spain fell into civil war.

Foreign involvements complicated the war. Italy and Germany sent Franco weapons, money, and soldiers. The republican government got help from the Soviet Union and 40,000 foreign volunteers. Franco's forces won in 1939. Franco set up a dictatorship that favored large landowners, businesspeople, and the Catholic Church.

Answer these questions to check your understanding of the entire section.

1. How did the Blackshirts change Italy?

_____

_____

_____

2. List the main provisions of Lenin's New Economic Policy.

_____

_____

_____

Write about the political history of Spain in the 1930s. Tell events in the general order in which they happened. Discuss what happened, when it happened, why it happened, how it happened, and who was involved. Do not show approval or disapproval. Simply present the facts in an objective way.

_____

_____

_____

_____

_____

_____

_____

_____

_____

_____

_____

Chapter 17, Section 3 (Pages 568–573)

Hitler and Nazi Germany

Big Idea

Hitler's totalitarian state was widely accepted, but German Jews and minorities were persecuted. As you read, use a chart like the one below to list anti-Semitic policies enforced by the Nazi Party.

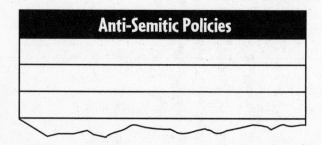

Anti-Semitic Policies

 **Notes**   # Read to Learn

Hitler and His Views *(page 568)*

Problems and Solutions

Hitler wanted power over the government of Germany. After the Beer Hall Putsch failed, he saw that he could achieve that goal through an uprising. How did Hitler solve his problem?

_____

_____

_____

Adolf Hitler was born in Austria in 1889. He formed his basic beliefs of racism, anti-Semitism, nationalism, and Social Darwinism while in Vienna.

He joined a small, nationalist party in Munich in 1919. It soon became the National Socialist German Workers' Party, or **Nazi** (from the German word *Nazional*) for short. The party had an armed force called the SA, the Storm Troops, or Brownshirts. In 1923 he led an unsuccessful revolt called the Beer Hall Putsch. In jail, he wrote his ideas in the book *Mein Kampf (My Struggle)*.

Hitler decided to bring the Nazi Party to power through legal means. He built its membership nationwide. He appealed to national pride, honor, and militarism. Germans suffering from the Great Depression wanted a strong leader. The Nazis became the majority party.

In 1933 President Hindenburg agreed to appoint Hitler chancellor of Germany. The Reichstag, or legislature, authorized the government to ignore the constitution. The Nazis took complete control. They removed Jews from government jobs. They put their opponents into large prisons called **concentration camps.** When Hindenburg died in 1934, they abolished the office of president. Hitler was sole dictator.

The Nazi State, 1933–1939 (page 570)

Copyright © Glencoe/McGraw-Hill, a division of The McGraw-Hill Companies, Inc.

Analyzing Information

People in Germany called Hitler their Führer, or "leader." What does this say about how Germans saw their relationship to Hitler?

_____

_____

_____

Hitler wanted to build a totalitarian state. He believed—incorrectly—that Germans and Scandinavians were descended from ancient Greeks and Romans, whom he called the **Aryan** race (Indo-Europeans). The Germans had ruled an empire (Reich) twice before: the Holy Roman Empire and the German Empire of 1871–1918. He planned to establish a new German empire, the Third Reich.

All the people of Germany would have to help. "The time of personal happiness is over," Hitler stated. The Nazis organized groups to involve people in their goals. They used terror and repression. The *Schutzstaffeln* ("Guard Squadrons"), or SS, ran the police. They used concentration camps, execution squads, and death camps. The goal was to make the Aryans the master race.

Hitler put people back to work and ended the depression. Some new jobs were in construction projects and public works. Even more important, the government put many people to work building weapons. One reason many people accepted Hitler and the Nazis was that they succeeded in ending unemployment.

Mass demonstrations and party rallies raised popular enthusiasm. The Nazis also controlled churches, schools, and universities. Youth organizations taught Nazi ideals. The Nazis considered women important as the ones who would bear Aryan children to continue the race. Women could be social workers or nurses, but they were not allowed to hold jobs in industry or traditionally male professions.

Anti-Semitism was part of Nazi beliefs from the beginning. Once in power, the Nazis enforced anti-Semitic policies. In 1935 in Nuremberg, they announced new laws called the Nuremberg laws. Anyone with even one Jewish grandparent was defined as a Jew. Jews were no longer German citizens. They had no civil rights and could not marry non-Jews. They could not hold certain jobs. Later, they were required to wear yellow stars and carry identification cards saying they were Jewish.

The night of November 9, 1938, brought a violent rampage known as *Kristallnacht,* "night of shattered glass." Nazis killed Jews, burned synagogues, and destroyed Jewish businesses. Jews were required to clean up the mess.

More restrictions on Jews were introduced. The SS encouraged them to leave Germany. Those who did so were fortunate, compared to those who stayed.

Section Wrap-up

Answer these questions to check your understanding of the entire section.

1. List two activities of the Nazi government illustrate that it was a totalitarian state.

_____

_____

_____

2. How was Hitler successful in ending the Great Depression in Germany?

_____

_____

_____

Persuasive Writing

What policies do you think the United States should have followed in relation to Nazi Germany in the 1903s? Take a position. Use information to support your position. Try to convince your reader to agree with your position.

_____

_____

_____

_____

_____

_____

_____

_____

_____

_____

_____

Cultural and Intellectual Trends

Big Idea

The destruction of World War I and the turmoil of the Great Depression
profoundly affected the work of artists and intellectuals. As you read, use
a table like the one below to list literature works by Hesse and Joyce.
Describe the techniques used in each work.

Literary Works	Techniques

 **Notes**

Read to Learn

Mass Culture and Leisure (page 576)

Determining Cause and Effect

What was a cause of widespread ownership of radios in Germany?

Cause:

_____

_____

What was an effect of widespread ownership of radios in Germany?

Effect:

_____

_____

New inventions changed mass communications. From 1920
to 1922, broadcasting facilities were built in Japan, Europe, and
the United States. Mass production of radios began.

Governments used radio broadcasting and movies for propaganda. Germans heard Hitler's fiery speeches over the radio.
The Nazis encouraged production of cheap radios sold on the
installment plan. The German propaganda minister Joseph
Goebbels called movies one of the "most modern and scientific
means of influencing the masses."

Leisure changed after World War I. Mass production made
consumer goods more available. People had more income or
could buy on credit. The eight-hour day became common for
workers, allowing free time for leisure activities. Professional
sports became popular. People of all social classes traveled to
holiday resorts by train, bus, or car.

Totalitarian states used mass leisure as another way to control people. The Nazi program "Strength through Joy" filled the
time of working people with concerts, films, sporting events,
and cheap vacations.

Arts and Science (page 578)

Synthesizing Information

In the 1920s the new physics, the psychology of Freud, and the experience of world war all contributed to making people feel

_____.

After four years of war, many Europeans felt a sense of despair. The Great Depression and the growth of fascist movements increased the sense of hopelessness. The future seemed uncertain.

Artistic trends after 1918 continued trends that had begun before the war. Abstract art became more popular. Even before the war, artists were exploring the absurd and the unconscious. World War I increased the feeling that the world did not make sense.

The Dada movement was based on the idea that life has no purpose. Dada artists tried to reflect the insanity of life in their art. For example, **photomontage,** or a picture made from multiple photographs, was used by Dada artist Hannah Höch to comment on women's roles. Artists of the **surrealism** movement portrayed the unconscious: fantasies, dreams, and nightmares. The paintings of Spanish surrealist Salvador Dalí showed objects in strange new relationships. Some people wanted art to be more realistic. This was especially true in Nazi Germany. The Nazis favored art that showed the Germans as strong, healthy, and heroic.

Literature reflected the interest in the unconscious. "Stream of consciousness" was a technique that showed characters' thoughts. The most famous example is *Ulysses* by the Irish writer James Joyce. The German writer Herman Hesse wrote about spiritual loneliness in modern society. His novels *Siddhartha* and *Steppenwolf* show the influence of Buddhist religion and Freudian psychology. He won the Nobel Prize for literature in 1946.

Science built on the changes that began with Albert Einstein's theory of relativity. Isaac Newton's mechanical view of nature was breaking down. In 1927 German physicist Werner Heisenberg announced his **uncertainty principle,** based on the unpredictable behavior of subatomic particles. He said that all physical laws are based on uncertainty. The new science fit with the sense of uncertainty that affected art and literature in that period.

1. How did "Strength through Joy" serve the purposes of the Nazi government?

_____

_____

_____

2. List two nonrealistic artistic trends of the 1920s.

_____

_____

_____

Write a description of a family weekend in the 1920s. Include at least three leisure activities discussed in this section, such as listening to the news on the radio, attending a movie or sports event, or going to the beach. Use active verbs. Make your description vivid enough for the reader to feel that he or she is there. Remember differences between the 1920s and earlier or later periods. Reflect the distinctive character of the 1920s in your description.

_____

_____

_____

_____

_____

_____

_____

_____

_____

_____

_____

Nationalism in the Middle East

Big Idea

After World War I, the quest for national self-determination led to the creation of Turkey, Iran, and Saudi Arabia. In the same period, the Balfour Declaration supported the creation of a national Jewish homeland in Palestine. As you read, make a venn diagram like the one below comparing and contrasting the national policies of Atatürk and Reza Shah Pahlavi.

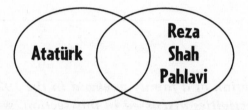

	Read to Learn

Decline and Fall of the Ottoman Empire *(page 586)*

Britain, France, and Russia protested the killing of Armenians. Put together what you know about the event and the time period. Why did Britain, France, and Russia not intervene to stop the killing?

_____

_____

_____

The Ottoman Empire had been steadily declining since the late 1700s. In 1876 reformers adopted a constitution, but the sultan suspended it. A group called the Young Turks restored the constitution in 1908 and deposed the sultan the next year. However, they lacked broad popular support.

The Ottomans allied with Germany in World War I. Britain encouraged Arab nationalist activities in Arab areas under Ottoman rule. Arabia declared its independence in 1916. British troops from Egypt seized Palestine.

Christian Armenians were a minority in the Ottoman Empire. In 1915 the government began killing Armenian men and making Armenian women and children leave the empire, often dying along the way. About 1.4 million Armenians died in the **genocide,** or the mass murder of a particular group of people (also called **ethnic cleansing**).

At the end of the war, the remains of the Ottoman Empire collapsed. Britain and France divided the former Ottoman territory. Only the area of present-day Turkey remained under Ottoman control. The Turkish war hero Mustafa Kemal led calls for a Turkish republic. In 1923 the Ottoman Empire had come to an end.

Middle East Changes *(page 589)*

Comparing and Contrasting

Compare and contrast Arab expectations for the settlement after World War I and what actually happened.

Arab expectations:

_____

_____

_____

What actually happened:

_____

_____

_____

Something the expectations and reality both had in common:

_____

_____

_____

President Kemal became known as Atatürk, or "father Turk." He tried to transform Turkey into a modern democracy. The Turkish language was now written in the Roman alphabet instead of Arabic. Turkish citizens had to adopt family names. Popular education was introduced. Factories were established to modernize the economy.

Atatürk tried to break the power of Islam and make Turkey a secular state. The caliphate was abolished in 1924. Men were forbidden to wear the fez (brimless cap). Women were forbidden to wear the veil. Women received new rights, including the right to vote in 1934.

In Persia, the Qajar dynasty had ruled from 1794 to 1925. It was not very successful in solving its internal problems. The dynasty asked the Russians and British to help protect it from its own people. The foreign presence increased after the discovery of oil in 1908. That upset Persian nationalists. In 1921 an officer named Reza led an army revolt. In 1925 he became shah, or king, with the name Reza Shah Pahlavi. He tried to modernize Persia (called Iran from 1935). He created a modern school system and forbade women to wear the veil.

Arabs within the old Ottoman Empire were not a nation, but they shared a common language, religion, and culture. World War I freed them from Ottoman rule. However, instead of self-governing states, they became mandates under the League of Nations. France ruled the mandates of Syria and Lebanon. Britain ruled Iraq, Palestine, and Jordan. Arabs retained a sense of Arab nationalism.

In the early 1920s, a reform leader named Ibn Sa'ūd united the Arabs in the northern part of the Arabian peninsula. He established the kingdom of Saudi Arabia in 1932. At first, it was very poor. However, the discovery of oil brought Western investors and hope for wealth.

Palestine became an area of tension between Arabs and Jews. Jews had lived there in ancient Israel and Judah but had been forced into exile. Muslim Arabs made up about 80 percent of the population. Starting in the 1890s, the Zionist movement worked to establish Palestine as a Jewish state. The nationalism of Jews and Arabs came into conflict.

During World War I, the British government issued the Balfour Declaration in support of a Jewish homeland. After the Nazis began anti-Semitic policies in Germany in the 1930s, many Jews fled to Palestine. Violence between Jews and Arabs flared. Britain tried to stop Jewish migration to Palestine, which made matters worse.

Answer these questions to check your understanding of the entire section.

1. Why did Persian nationalists rebel against the Qajar dynasty?

_____

_____

_____

2. How did British policy regarding Jews in Palestine change between World War I and the late 1930s?

_____

_____

_____

Expository Writing

Analyze the causes and effects of the breakup of the Ottoman Empire. Choose a clear way to organize your writing so that the reader can easily follow your analysis.

_____

_____

_____

_____

_____

_____

_____

_____

_____

_____

Chapter 18, Section 2 (Pages 592–599)
Nationalism in Africa and Asia

Big Idea

Nationalism led the people of Africa and Asia to seek independence. As
you read, use a table like the one below to contrast the backgrounds and
values of Gandhi and Nehru.

Mohandas Gandhi	Jawaharlal Nehru

 **Notes**

Read to Learn

African Independence Movements *(page 592)*

*How was there a
gap between Western
ideals and Western
practice?*

Ideals:

_____

_____

Practice:

_____

_____

A new generation of Western-educated leaders in Africa
called for independence. Black Africans had fought in World
War I in the French and British armies. They had learned
Western ideas of freedom and nationalism. After the war, they
decided to seek reform. In Nigeria after World War I, educated
Africans joined with the traditional king of Lagos in opposing
British rule. Civil engineer Herbert Macaulay and the editor
of the *Lagos Weekly Record* ran an editorial campaign against
the colonial government. Forces in Libya carried on a guerrilla
revolt against the Italians.

In Kenya, land had been taken from black Africans and
given to white settlers. Protest organizations emerged in the
1920s. They included the Kikuyu Association and the Young
Kikuyu Association. Government authorities shot into a
protesting crowd, killing at least 20 people.

Many of the young Africans had been educated abroad and
were influenced by the ideas of W.E.B. Du Bois and Marcus
Garvey's **Pan-Africanism** movement, which stressed the need
for the unity of all Africans. Jomo Kenyatta of Kenya wrote that
British rule was destroying traditional culture. Léopold Senghor
started an independence movement in Senegal.

Chapter 18, Section 2

181

**Notes** | # Read to Learn

Revolution in Asia (page 595)

Drawing Conclusions

Although the Comintern was an international organization, the country of

_____

probably had the greatest influence on its policies and activities.

Before World War I, Asian intellectuals had little interest in the ideas of Karl Marx because most of Asia was agricultural. That changed after Lenin's Bolsheviks showed that a revolutionary party could change a system that was not fully industrialized.

Lenin adopted a new approach to spreading communist ideas. The Communist International, or Comintern, was formed in 1919 to promote revolution worldwide. Agents were trained in Moscow. Then they were sent to their home countries to form Marxist parties. In some countries, such as China, the Communists cooperated with nationalist parties to oppose Western imperialism. In French Indochina, Moscow-trained Ho Chi Minh organized the Communists of Vietnam in the 1920s.

Indian Independence (page 596)

Comparing and Contrasting

How did Gandhi's and Nehru's approaches to independence differ?

_____

_____

_____

_____

_____

_____

People in India called Mohandas Gandhi "Great Soul," or Mahatma. He used the nonviolent method of **civil disobedience,** or refusal to obey unjust laws. Britain responded by passing the Government of India Act in 1935. This expanded the role of Indians in governing. Instead of an advisory council, India had a two-house parliament with some elected members.

The Indian National Congress (INC) pushed for independence. Gandhi advised Indians not to pay taxes or buy goods made in England. Britain increased the salt tax and prohibited Indians from harvesting their own salt. In 1930 Gandhi led a march to the sea to gather salt illegally. He and other INC members were arrested.

The members of the independence movement split, some identifying with Gandhi and some with Jawaharlal Nehru. Nehru's approach was secular, Western, and modern, while Gandhi's was religious, Indian, and traditional. The Muslim League, led by Mohammed Ali Jinnah, believed in the creation of a separate Muslim state of Pakistan.

A Militarist Japan (page 598)

Making Generalizations

Two common economic reasons for imperialism

Huge financial and industrial corporations called *zaibatsu* dominated the Japanese economy. By 1937 the four largest zaibatsu were Mitsui, Mitsubishi, Sumitomo, and Yasuda. Together, they controlled 21 percent of the banking industry, 26 percent of mining, 35 percent of shipbuilding, and over 60 percent of paper manufacturing and insurance.

are that the home country wants:

1. a source of

_____

for its industries, and

2. _____
for its industrial products.

The Great Depression's problems brought calls for traditionalism, separation from the West, and new territory to provide raw materials for manufacturing. In the late 1920s, a militant group within the ruling party gained control. Army officers invaded Manchuria in 1931. The government disapproved, but the conquest had popular support. Soon supporters of militarism and expansionism dominated the government. Japanese society was put on wartime status.

Section Wrap-up

Answer these questions to check your understanding of the entire section.

1. How were communist ideas spread in Asia?

_____

_____

_____

2. Explain the role of *zaibatsu* in the Japanese economy.

_____

_____

_____

Persuasive Writing

Pretend that you write for a newspaper in either Nigeria or India. Write an editorial making the case for independence from British rule. Include facts that support your case. Try to present your case in a way that might persuade people in Britain as well as the people of your society.

_____

_____

_____

_____

_____

_____

_____

_____

_____

Chapter 18, Section 3

(Pages 600–605)

Revolutionary Chaos in China

Big Idea

During the 1920s, two men, Chiang Kai-shek and Mao Zedong, struggled to lead a new Chinese state. As you read, make a cluster diagram like the one below showing the Confucian values that Chiang Kai-shek used to bring modern Western ideas into a culturally conservative population.

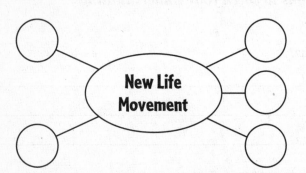

New Life Movement

Notes | Read to Learn

Nationalists and Communists (page 600)

Determining Cause and Effect

What two shared goals caused the Nationalist and Communist parties to work together for a few years?

1. _____

_____

2. _____

_____

Which event of 1927 caused the Communists to go into hiding?

_____

_____

By 1920, two political parties emerged as rivals for leadership: the Nationalists of Sun Yat-sen and the Chinese Communists. In 1923 the two parties formed an alliance to drive Western imperialists out of China and subdue the warlords. In 1926 they formed a revolutionary army, known as the Northern Expedition, to march north and seize control over China. General Chiang Kai-shek, head of the Nationalist party after Sun's death in 1925, did not trust the Communists. In the Shanghai Massacre of April 1927, he killed thousands of Communists. The rest went into hiding. Chiang founded a Chinese republic at Nanjing.

After the Shanghai Massacre, Chinese Communist leaders secretly spread Communist Party ideas to working class people of Shanghai. A Communist organizer named Mao Zedong led some party members south into the mountains of Jiangxi Province. He promoted Communist ideas to poverty-stricken peasants.

In 1934 Chiang's troops surrounded the Communist base at Jiangxi. Mao's smaller People's Liberation Army used **guerrilla tactics,** which are unexpected methods like sabotage and deception, to break through Chiang's forces to march north to the last surviving Communist base in China. Combating Chiang's army and facing cold and starvation along the way, only 9,000 of the original 90,000 Communist troops survived the year-long trek known as the Long March.

184 Chapter 18, Section 3

The New China (page 603)

Detecting Bias

Sun Yat-sen wrote: "China . . . needs a republican government just as a boy needs school. As a schoolboy must have good teachers and helpful friends, so the Chinese people, being for the first time under republican rule, must have a farsighted revolutionary government for their training." Sun thought rule by the _____ Party could best provide such training.

Chiang Kai-shek shared Sun Yat-sen's idea that China should become a republic. Like Sun, he believed the Chinese people were not ready for self-rule. They would learn during a period of dictatorial one-party rule. During that period, the Nationalists would carry out land reform and build a modern industrial state.

China was suffering from years of civil war. The peasants were still very poor. Most of them could not read or write. They were culturally conservative. Peasants made up 80 percent of the population of China. In the cities, a westernized middle class had begun to form. Most of the support for Chang Kai-shek's new government came from the urban middle class. His supporters had little in common with the peasants.

Chiang tried to combine modern Western ideas with the traditional values of Confucius: hard work, obedience, and integrity. He and his wife set up a "New Life Movement." It aimed to promote traditional Confucian ethics. It rejected the excessive individualism and greed of Western capitalism.

He had some success. He built and repaired highways and railroads. New Chinese-owned factories opened. Foreign powers gave up many of their leases. Chiang established a national bank. He improved the educational system.

He was less successful in other ways. His land-reform program had little effect. Because most of his support came from the middle class, he did not work hard to help the poor. Chiang did not press for programs that would lead to a **redistribution of wealth** from the rich minority to the poor majority. Afraid of the Communists, he did not allow free political expression. That lost him the support of intellectuals and political moderates.

Section Wrap-up

Answer these questions to check your understanding of the entire section.

1. What was the Northern Expedition of 1926?

_____

_____

_____

2. What was the base of support for Chiang Kai-shek's Nationalist government in China?

_____

_____

_____

Descriptive Writing

Describe the Long March of 1934–1935. Give your reader a sense of the hardships along the way as the group moved on foot through mountains, marshes, rivers, and deserts, fighting the Nationalist army. Include information about the origin of the Long March, its destination, and possible motives for participating. Provide sensory detail.

_____

_____

_____

_____

_____

_____

_____

_____

_____

_____

_____

_____

Nationalism in Latin America

Big Idea

In Latin America, the Great Depression made politics unstable, and in many cases, military dictatorships were the result. As you read, make a chart like the one below listing the main exports of Latin America.

Country	Exports

Notes | Read to Learn

The Latin American Economy (page 608)

Problems and Solutions

Analyze the creation of Latin American government-run industries during the Great Depression in terms of problem and solution.

Problem:

_____

_____

Solution:

_____

_____

At the beginning of the 1900s, the Latin American economy depended on the export of foods and raw materials. Argentina exported beef and wheat; Chile, nitrates and copper; Brazil, coffee and cotton; the Caribbean nations, sugar; and Central America, bananas.

Beginning in the 1920s, the United States began to replace Great Britain as the main investor in Latin America. For example, the United Fruit Company owned land, packing plants, and railroads in Central America. American companies controlled copper mining in Chile and Peru, and the oil industries in Mexico, Peru, and Bolivia.

Many Latin Americans resented U.S. control of Latin American industries. U.S. businesses sometimes used their profits to keep ruthless dictators in power. In Venezuela, U.S. oil companies had close ties to dictator Juan Vicente Gómez.

In 1933 U.S. President Franklin Roosevelt announced a Good Neighbor policy, rejecting the use of military force in Latin America. The last United States Marines left Haiti in 1934.

The Great Depression was a disaster for Latin American economies. Demand for their exports dropped. Lacking money to buy imports, governments invested in manufacturing. Government-run industries produced steel in Chile and Brazil, and oil in Argentina and Mexico.

Authoritarian Rule (page 610)

Identifying the Main Idea

In some large Latin American countries during the Great Depression,

_____

brought to power new rulers who can be described as

_____.

Although most countries of Latin America were republics, they were run by a small elite of church leaders, military leaders, and large landowners. New military dictatorships formed in the early 1930s. An oligarchy of large landowners controlled Argentina. An **oligarchy** is a government controlled by a select group of people. A middle-class leader was elected president in 1916. Both the landowners and the middle class feared labor unrest. A revolt in 1930 tried to restore the old export economy. The Group of United Officers (GOU) overthrew the regime in 1943. One of them, Juan Perón, was elected president in 1946.

In Brazil, the army had overthrown the monarchy in 1889 and set up a republic. The power of large landowners weakened when the Great Depression hurt coffee prices. A coup made Getúlio Vargas president (1930–1945). He passed laws to help workers and built industry. He took dictatorial power and used secret police to silence his opponents.

Mexico was neither authoritarian nor a true democracy. The Mexican revolution had helped the masses and created a stable political order. The Institutional Revolutionary Party (PRI) ran the government. President Lázaro Cárdenas (1934–1940) redistributed land to peasants and nationalized the Mexican oil industry.

Culture in Latin America (page 613)

Making Inferences

Which people in Latin America and the United States might be most likely to object to Diego Rivera's paintings?

_____

_____

_____

Artistic movements from Europe influenced Latin America in the early 1900s. Modern art became popular in the cities. Latin American artists went abroad and brought back modern techniques. They adapted the European styles to their own native roots.

Modern artists who created abstract art included Roberto Matta from Chile and Carlos Merida from Guatemala. Gunther Gerzso is considered Mexico's most significant abstract artist of the twentieth century.

Many artists and writers used their work to promote a new national spirit. An example was the Mexican artist Diego Rivera. He had studied in Europe. He was particularly influenced by fresco painting in Italy. After his return to Mexico, he painted large murals on walls. Rivera tried to create a national art that would show Mexico's legends, festivals, and folk customs. His work carried a political and social message. He did not want people to forget the Mexican Revolution, which had overthrown the large landowners and the foreign interests that supported them.

Section Wrap-up

Answer these questions to check your understanding of the entire section.

1. What was the Good Neighbor policy of President Franklin D. Roosevelt?

_____

_____

_____

2. List two cases of revolts or coups that changed regimes in Latin America between 1920 and 1940.

_____

_____

_____

Expository Writing

How did economics influence politics and government in Latin America in the 1920s and 1930s? Make one or more general statements and support them with historical information. Consider such economic factors as social classes, exports, foreign investment, industrialization, and the influence of the Great Depression.

_____

_____

_____

_____

_____

_____

_____

_____

_____

_____

_____

_____

Paths to War

Big Idea

The ambitions of Japan and Germany paved the way for the outbreak of World War II. As you read, create a chart like the one below listing examples of Japanese aggression and German aggression prior to the outbreak of World War II

Japanese Aggression	German Aggression

Notes | Read to Learn

The German Path to War *(page 620)*

Distinguishing Fact from Opinion

After the Munich conference of 1938, Prime Minister Chamberlain reported that the agreement meant "peace for our time."

What FACT influenced Chamberlain's view?

_____

_____

What OPINION affected Chamberlain's view?

_____

_____

Adolph Hitler believed Germans needed more land. In 1935 he announced a new air force and a military draft. The next year, he sent troops into the **demilitarized** Rhineland. All these steps violated the Treaty of Versailles. Distracted by the Great Depression, other countries did not interfere. Britain tried **appeasement,** or meeting Germany's demands.

Benito Mussolini, leader of Fascist Italy, grew closer to Hitler after Italy invaded Ethiopia in 1935. In 1936 Germany formed alliances with Italy (the Rome-Berlin Axis) and Japan (the Anti-Comintern Pact). Italy and Germany helped General Francisco Franco in the Spanish Civil War. In the *Anschluss,* or union, of 1938, Hitler joined Austria to Germany.

In September 1938, Hitler demanded that Germany be given the Sudetenland, part of Czechoslovakia. At a conference in Munich, Britain and France agreed. Hitler said he would make no more demands. British prime minister Neville Chamberlain believed him.

In March 1939, Hitler occupied more Czech territory. He demanded the Polish port of Danzig. Britain offered to protect Poland in case of war. To prevent a British-French-Soviet alliance, Hitler signed a pact with Joseph Stalin, head of the Soviet Union. Hitler invaded Poland on September 1, 1939. Britain and France declared war on Germany.

The Japanese Path to War *(page 623)*

Problems and Solutions

What problem did Japan try to solve by conquering territory on mainland Asia?

_____

_____

Japan needed natural resources. That gave Japan a motive to seize other countries. Japan controlled a railway in Manchuria. On the night of September 18, 1931, Japanese soldiers blew up part of a railway. The soldiers were disguised as Chinese soldiers. Their purpose was to give Japan an excuse to blame China and occupy Manchuria. Japan conquered Manchuria easily. It had many people and resources. A year after the explosion, Japan formed Manchuria into a separate state called Manchukuo. After this conquest, Japan's army became committed to an expansionist policy—a policy of enlarging the Japanese Empire.

The League of Nations sent investigators. When the investigators' report condemned the Japanese action, Japan withdrew from the League. The United States did not recognize the Japanese takeover of Manchuria but was unwilling to threaten force. As more countries condemned Japan's actions, Japanese citizens became more supportive of their army and its policies.

Japanese expansion continued over the next several years. Japan established control over the eastern part of Inner Mongolia and parts of northern China. The Japanese army determined Japanese foreign policy. Neither the emperor nor the government had any control over the army. By the mid-1930s, the army and its supporters controlled the government of Japan.

Chiang Kai-shek, leader of China, tried to avoid a war with Japan. He considered the Communists to be a greater threat. When clashes broke out between Chinese and Japanese troops, he practiced a policy of appeasement. The Japanese army moved south into China. Protests occurred in several Chinese cities. In December 1936, Chiang stopped fighting the Communists to focus on the Japanese. Chinese and Japanese forces clashed in 1937. Japan seized the Chinese capital of Nanjing in December 1937. Tens of thousands of Japanese civilians were killed in what became known as the Rape of Nanjing. Chiang's government fled but fought on.

Japanese military leaders hoped to establish a new order in Asia. Japan would teach Manchuria and China how to modernize. Japan also cooperated with Nazi Germany in the hope that both countries would attack the Soviet Union and divide its resources. When Hitler signed a nonaggression pact with Stalin, Japan turned its attention south instead. In the summer of 1940, Japan demanded the right to mineral resources in French Indochina. The United States objected. Japan bought oil and scrap iron from the United States. The United States threatened to apply economic **sanctions,** which would cut off badly needed materials. Japan decided to launch a surprise attack on the United States and Southeast Asia at the same time.

Chapter 19, Section 1

Section Wrap-up

Answer these questions to check your understanding of the entire section.

1. Describe an incident in relation to Japan that showed the weakness of the League of Nations.

_____

_____

_____

2. How and why did Chiang Kai-shek change his response to Japan?

_____

_____

_____

Informative Writing

Write the story of Hitler's military and diplomatic activity from 1935 through September 1, 1939, and the response of other European powers. Use a story plan made up of four elements: time, place, people, and events. Present the facts in a way that flows smoothly, without showing emotion or inserting your opinion.

_____

_____

_____

_____

_____

_____

_____

_____

_____

_____

_____

_____

The Course of World War II

Big Idea

Allied perseverance, effective military operations, and Axis miscalculations brought the devastation of World War II to an end. As you read, create a chart like the one below listing key events during World War II and their effect on the outcome of the war.

Event	Effect

Notes

Read to Learn

Europe at War (page 628)

Comparing and Contrasting

Compare and contrast the British and French relationships to Germany in 1940.

Both:

_____

_____

British:

_____

_____

French:

_____

_____

Hitler's attack on Poland stunned Europe. His **blitzkrieg,** or lighting war, used columns of tanks, supported by airplanes. Germany and the Soviet Union divided Poland. After a quiet winter, Germany attacked Denmark and Norway in April 1940, then the Netherlands, Belgium, and France. Germany had simply gone around France's heavily armed Maginot Line, dividing the allied armies.

France signed an armistice on June 22. German troops occupied about three-fifths of France. The rest of France, known as Vichy France, had an authoritarian regime led by Marshal Pétain, under German control.

Germany now controlled central and western Europe, except Britain. Although American **isolationists** wanted to stay neutral, and **neutrality** acts passed in the 1930s prevented the U.S. from becoming involved in European wars, the United States provided Britain with food, ships, airplanes, and weapons. The German air force launched an attack on Britain in August 1940. Starting with military targets, they soon switched to bombing British cities. The British air force fought back bravely.

Hitler took control over the Balkans. In June 1941, he invaded the Soviet Union. That winter the Soviets stopped the German advance. It was the first time in the war that German armies were stopped.

Read to Learn

Japan at War *(page 631)*

Synthesizing Information

Both Japan and Germany misjudged the United States in thinking that

_____

_____

On December 7, 1941, Japanese airplanes bombed the United States naval base at Pearl Harbor in Hawaii. Japan soon seized a number of Pacific islands. By spring 1942, Japan controlled almost all of Southeast Asia and much of the Western Pacific.

Japanese leaders thought their strike at Pearl Harbor would destroy the American fleet in the Pacific. Instead, the attack unified Americans. The isolationist insistence on staying out of the war faded. In response to the attack on Pearl Harbor, the United States declared war on Japan.

Four days after Pearl Harbor, Hitler declared war on the United States. He thought the United States would be too busy fighting in the Pacific to cause him problems in Europe.

The Allies Advance *(page 632)*

Drawing Conclusions

A natural condition that helped to prevent German forces from conquering the Soviet Union was the

_____

The entry of the United States into the war created a new coalition, the Grand Alliance between Great Britain, the United States, and the Soviet Union. They agreed to stress military operations and overlook their political differences.

The war went well for Germany through mid-1942. By May 1943, however, British and American forces defeated Germany and Italian troops in North Africa. Germany captured the Crimea and went on to attack Stalingrad. The Soviet Union fought back successfully in the winter of 1942–1943 by cutting off German supply lines in the frigid winter conditions.

The turning point in the Pacific came when American forces won the Battle of Midway Island in June 1942. United States forces moved toward the Philippines. They also recaptured some Japanese-held islands by "island hopping," or taking some islands and skipping others.

Last Years of the War *(page 634)*

Predicting

The United States and Britain cooperated with the Soviet Union to defeat Germany. Would you expect this cooperation

By spring 1943, the Allies were winning. On June 6, 1944 (D-Day), the Allies invaded the French coast along the English Channel. Within three months, the Allies landed 2 million men and 500,000 vehicles. They pushed inland against the Germans. After breaking through German defensive lines, Allied troops moved south and east. They liberated Paris by the end of August. In March 1945, they crossed the Rhine River and advanced into Germany.

to continue after the war?

Circle YES or NO.

Explain your choice.

_____

_____

_____

The Allied and Soviet armies met at the Elbe River in northern Germany at the end of April 1945. The Soviets began a steady advance westward. Hitler committed suicide on April 30, two days after Italian **partisans,** or resistance fighters, shot Mussolini. Germany surrendered on May 7, 1945.

Fighting continued in Asia and the Pacific. U.S. President Harry S. Truman decided to drop atomic bombs on the Japanese cities of Hiroshima and Nagasaki to end the war rapidly. Japan surrendered on August 14.

Section Wrap-up

Answer these questions to check your understanding of the entire section.

1. How did the U.S. become indirectly involved in the war despite the neutrality acts that prevented its involvement in European wars?

_____

_____

_____

2. Why did Hitler declare war on the United States?

_____

_____

_____

Persuasive Writing

Do you think President Truman should or should not have dropped the atomic bombs on Hiroshima and Nagasaki? Take a stand. Use information to support your position. Respond to any arguments that people who disagree with you would be likely to make. Try to persuade your reader to agree with your point of view.

_____

_____

_____

_____

_____

_____

_____

The New Order and the Holocaust

Big Idea

Millions of people were forced to labor for the German and Japanese war machines. The Holocaust claimed the lives of 6 million Jews. As you read, use a Venn diagram like the one below to compare and contrast the New Order of Germany and the New Order of Japan.

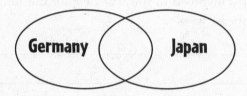

 **Notes**   **Read to Learn**

The New Order in Europe (page 638)

Identifying the Main Idea

In addition to relocating many non-Germans from their homelands, Germany used non-Germans as

_____

during World War II.

In 1942 Nazi rule stretched across Europe from the English Channel to the outskirts of Moscow. Some of this territory, such as western Poland, was annexed directly to Germany. Most of occupied Europe was run by German officials with help from local collaborators.

The Nazis saw land in the east as living space for German expansion. They thought the native Slavs in those areas were racially inferior. They planned to move Slavs out and replace them with Germans. Soon after conquering Poland, the Germans started putting their resettlement plans into effect. SS leader Heinrich Himmler was in charge. One million Poles were forced from their homes and relocated to southern Poland. Two million ethnic Germans had been settled in Poland by 1942.

Hitler had bigger plans for after the war. He planned to remove Poles, Ukrainians, and Russians from their lands and make them work as slaves. German peasants would settle on the abandoned lands. Himmler predicted that 30 million Slavs might die to achieve this. Seven million foreign workers were laboring in Germany by the summer of 1944. Another 7 million did forced labor for the Nazis on farms, industries, and military camps. The brutal recruitment of foreign workers increased resistance to the Nazi occupation.

Read to Learn

The Holocaust (page 640)

Detecting Bias

Himmler said about education in Eastern Europe, "I do not consider an ability to read as necessary." This statement reflects his bias that the people of Eastern Europe

_____

_____.

Hitler believed the Germans, or Aryans, were a superior race. He believed the Jews were to blame for Germany's defeat in World War I and for the Depression. The Nazis decided the Final Solution was **genocide,** or the physical extermination of all the Jews.

The SS created special strike forces called *Einsatzgruppen* to carry out this plan. They forced Polish Jews into ghettos in Polish cities. Ghettos were crowded and unsanitary, with little food. The *Einsatzgruppen* followed the army into the Soviet Union. They gathered Jews in villages, shot them, and buried them in mass graves.

To speed up the process, the Nazis built death camps. They shipped Jews by railroad cars from Nazi-occupied areas to Poland. Auschwitz was the largest of six death camps in Poland. About 30 percent of the arrivals at Auschwitz were sent to labor camps. The rest were killed in gas chambers. The Nazi's killing of 5 to 6 million Jews is called the Holocaust. **Collaborators** even helped the Nazis hunt down Jews. The Nazis also killed at least another 9 to 10 million people, including Roma (Gypsies), Slavs, and Soviet prisoners of war.

The New Order in Asia (page 643)

Evaluating Information

Which of these would provide the most accurate information about Japanese policy in Southeast Asia?

____ *memoir of a local nationalist leader*

____ *propaganda by government of Japan*

____ *anti-Japanese editorial in Autralia*

The Japanese conquest of Southeast Asia forced millions of native people to work for the Japanese war machine. Japan had conquered areas under the slogan "Asia for the Asiatics." Japan promised to free colonial areas from Western rule. In fact, Japanese military authorities kept power in each territory.

Japan used these areas as a source of raw materials such as tin, oil, and rubber. Native people in each territory were recruited to work in local military units or public works projects. In some cases, these policies brought severe hardships. In Vietnam, for example, Japanese officials took rice from people by force and sold it abroad. Over a million Vietnamese people died as a result.

At first, many Southeast Asian nationalists agreed to cooperate with Japan against their former Western rulers. Later, it became clear that Japanese policies were only intended to help Japan. Like the Germans, Japanese military forces showed little respect for local people or customs. They used labor forces composed of local workers and prisoners of war. Many nationalists did not like what their new Japanese rulers were doing. Some turned against the Japanese.

Section Wrap-up

Answer these questions to check your understanding of the entire section.

1. Why did the Nazis move people from western Poland into southern Poland?

_____

_____

_____

2. List four groups killed by the Nazis.

_____

_____

_____

Describe life in a Polish ghetto in the 1940s. Convey the sights, sounds, smells, and feelings that must have been common among the residents of the ghetto. Try to draw your reader into the experience you are describing. You may want to present your description as a diary entry by a teenager living in the ghetto.

_____

_____

_____

_____

_____

_____

_____

_____

_____

_____

_____

_____

Home Front and Aftermath of the War

Big Idea

After World War II, a new set of Cold War problems faced the international community. As you read, create a chart like the one below comparing and contrasting the impact of World War II on the lives of civilians.

Country	Impact on Lives of Civilians
Soviet Union	
United States	
Japan	
Germany	

Notes

Read to Learn

The Mobilization of Four Nations (page 644)

Evaluating Information

". . . But it is impossible for me to [tell if they are loyal] with the inscrutable Orientals, and particularly the Japanese."

—California governor
This quote could be a useful source of information about:

____ *Japanese loyalty*

____ *racial prejudice*

____ *Italian Americans*

World War II was a total war that required extensive **mobilization,** or assembling and preparing for war. Civilians made sacrifices to support the war effort. The Soviet Union had shortages of food and housing. Women worked in factories, dug antitank ditches, and fought as snipers and on bomber crews.

U.S. war production soared. Over a million African Americans moved from the rural South to northern cities for jobs. Japanese Americans on the West Coast were moved to camps surrounded by barbed wire.

During the first two years of the war, Germany did not decrease production of consumer goods or build up its armaments. Instead, German soldiers took what they needed from defeated countries. This changed in 1942, however, and Germany's economy was mobilized. Some German women assumed the jobs of men who had been called to war.

Prices, wages, labor, and resources were controlled in Japan. Japan used Chinese and Korean workers rather than women. Late in the war, Japan sent young pilots, called **kamikaze,** or "divine wind," on suicide missions.

The Bombing of Cities (page 648)

Making Generalizations

In general, is the bombing of civilians an effective way to destroy enemy morale in wartime? Circle one:

YES   NO

What evidence supports your answer?

_____

_____

_____

Nearly 20 million civilians died in the war, many of them children. Bombing of cities in Britain, Germany, and Japan destroyed buildings and killed thousands of civilians.

The first sustained bombing of civilians began in September 1940. The German air force bombed London nightly for months. The British called these air raids the **blitz.** The blitz spread to other British cities and towns. It did great damage, but British morale stayed high.

Nevertheless, the British hoped to break German morale by bombing German cities. A thousand bombers attacked the German city of Cologne on May 31, 1942. The firestorms from the bombing of Dresden from February 13 to 15, 1945, may have killed as many as 100,000 inhabitants. Bombs did not destroy Germany's morale or industry, but the destruction of transportation systems and fuel supplies made it hard for new materials to reach the military.

Loss of its air force exposed Japan to bombing late in the war. Cities were built of materials that burned easily. Bombs destroyed many industries and one-fourth of Japanese homes. Most severe were the atomic bombs dropped on Hiroshima and Nagasaki in August 1945.

Peace and a New War (page 650)

Analyzing Information

In a speech in 1946, Winston Churchill said that "an iron curtain has descended across the continent," dividing Europe into two hostile camps. What two camps did he mean?

1._____

2._____

A period of political tensions, known as the **Cold War,** followed the Allied victory in World War II.

Stalin, Roosevelt, and Churchill met at Tehran in November 1943 to decide the future course of the war. They planned for American and British forces to invade through France in the spring of 1944. Soviet forces would liberate Eastern Europe and meet British-American forces in Germany. The three agreed to divide Germany after the war.

They met again at Yalta in southern Russia in February 1945. Churchill and Roosevelt faced the prospect of 11 million Soviet soldiers occupying Eastern and Central Europe. Stalin promised free elections for Poland. Churchill and Stalin agreed to Roosevelt's proposal for a United Nations.

Roosevelt's successor, Harry S. Truman, met with Churchill and Stalin at Potsdam in July 1945. Truman demanded free elections in Eastern Europe. Stalin, whose troops occupied Eastern Europe, refused because he wanted a buffer zone of Soviet-friendly states.

Section Wrap-up

Answer these questions to check your understanding of the entire section.

1. Why did the industrial employment of women increase in several countries during World War II?

_____

_____

_____

2. What was the blitz?

_____

_____

_____

Expository Writing

Analyze the effects of the Tehran, Yalta, and Potsdam conferences. How did the conferences influence the outcome of World War II? What groundwork—positive and negative—did they lay for world events after the war? Select and apply a clear organizational structure to break the topic into smaller and simpler categories.

_____

_____

_____

_____

_____

_____

_____

_____

_____

_____

_____

_____

Development of the Cold War

Big Idea

A period of conflict known as the Cold War developed between the United States and the Soviet Union after 1945, dividing Europe. As you read, use a table like the one below to list the American presidents who held office during this period and the major Cold War events that took place during their administrations.

President	Major Event

Notes

Read to Learn

Confrontation of the Superpowers (page 664)

Making Inferences

What is a probable reason that the Soviet Union lifted the blockade of Berlin after the Berlin Airlift?

_____

_____

_____

_____

For security reasons, the Soviet Union insisted on keeping control over the countries it occupied in Eastern Europe, making them politically dependent **satellite states**.

Communist and anti-Communist forces fought to control Greece. President Harry S. Truman asked Congress in 1947 for aid to Greece and Turkey. The Truman Doctrine was to help people resisting Communist expansion. The American **policy of containment** was to keep communism from spreading.

U.S. secretary of state George Marshall believed economic problems exposed countries to communism. He proposed economic aid to help rebuild war-torn Europe. This was the European Recovery Program, usually called the Marshall Plan.

Germany and Berlin were divided into four occupied zones. The United States, Britain, and France agreed to unite their zones as West Germany. The Soviet Union objected and put a blockade around West Berlin so that no food could get in. Nobody wanted a war. American and British planes flew supplies into Berlin, known as the Berlin Airlift. In 1949 the blockade was lifted, and separate governments were set up for West and East Germany.

Notes | Read to Learn

The Cold War Spreads *(page 667)*

Synthesizing Information

In 1957 the Soviet Union sent a space satellite called Sputnik I to orbit the Earth.

Put this information together with what you know about the arms race. Why did the launch of Sputnik I increase American fears?

_____

_____

_____

_____

American fears about the spread of communism increased. In 1949 Communists gained control of China, and the Soviet Union exploded its first atomic bomb. The United States and the Soviet Union engaged in an **arms race,** in which both countries built up their armies and weapons. They developed the hydrogen bomb and intercontinental ballistic missiles (ICBMs). They believed nuclear weapons provided **deterrence,** meaning that the weapons prevented war. A nuclear war would be too destructive for either country to risk.

The search for security during the Cold War led to new defensive military alliances. In 1949 ten countries of Western Europe, the United States, and Canada, formed the North Atlantic Treaty Organization (NATO). The Soviet Union formed a military alliance in 1955 with Albania, Bulgaria, Czechoslovakia, East Germany, Hungary, Poland, and Romania. This was called the Warsaw Pact.

The Communist government of North Korea tried to take over South Korea in 1950, confirming American fears of Communist expansion. The United States extended its military alliances around the world. The Southeast Asia Treaty Organization (SEATO) was with Thailand, the Philippines, and others. In the Central Treaty Organization (CENTO) were Turkey, Iraq, Iran, Pakistan, Britain, and the United States.

Nikita Khrushchev became the leader of the Soviet Union in 1955. He wanted to stop East Germans from escaping into West Berlin. In 1961 the East German government began building a wall to separate East Berlin from West Berlin. Eventually, it became a massive barrier guarded by barbed wire, floodlights, machine guns, and dog patrols.

In 1959 rebels led by Fidel Castro set up a socialist government in Cuba, with Soviet support. U.S. president John F. Kennedy approved a plan in 1961 for Cuban exiles to invade the Bay of Pigs in Cuba, hoping to trigger a revolt. The plan failed. In 1962 Khrushchev began to place nuclear missiles in Cuba. (The United States had nuclear missiles in Turkey, near the Soviet Union.) Kennedy decided to blockade Cuba to keep the missiles from getting there. After tense hours, Khrushchev and Kennedy reached an agreement. The missiles would be removed, and the United States would promise not to invade Cuba.

The Communists of North Vietnam tried to take over South Vietnam. According to the **domino theory,** if that area fell to communism, other Asian countries would also fall. President Lyndon Johnson sent more U.S. troops to Vietnam starting in 1964. As the war expanded, many Americans protested. President Richard Nixon withdrew troops in 1973. Communist North Vietnam soon absorbed South Vietnam.

Section Wrap-up

Answer these questions to check your understanding of the entire section.

1. How was the Marshall Plan intended to help prevent the spread of communism?

_____

_____

_____

2. The possibility of nuclear war between the Soviet Union and the United States was perhaps highest during the Cuban Missile Crisis of 1962. What made that incident so risky?

_____

_____

_____

Write about the Berlin Wall as though you were a resident of either East Berlin or West Berlin at the time it was built. Describe the background, the construction, and the resulting barrier as it might affect the everyday life of someone living nearby. Describe the sights, sounds, and smells associated with the wall. Use strong, active verbs. Try to give your reader the feeling of sharing your experience.

_____

_____

_____

_____

_____

_____

_____

_____

_____

_____

_____

The Soviet Union and Eastern Europe

Big Idea

The Soviet Union faced revolts and protests in its attempts to gain and maintain control over Eastern Europe. As you read, use a diagram like the one below to identify how the Soviet Union carried out Communist policies.

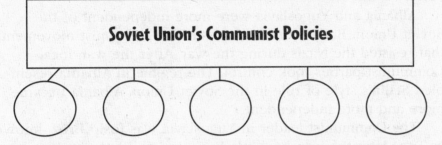

Soviet Union's Communist Policies

Notes | Read to Learn

Postwar Soviet Leaders (page 674)

Comparing and Contrasting

How were Stalin and Khrushchev different and alike?

Stalin

_____

_____

Khrushchev

_____

_____

Both

_____

_____

World War II devastated the Soviet Union. To recover, Stalin returned to his policies of the 1930s. Soviet workers produced goods for export in order to pay for importing machines and technology. The result was a spectacular increase in **heavy industry**—the manufacture of machines and equipment for factories and mines. However, a shortage of consumer goods and housing meant that workers got little in return.

Stalin exercised sole power. He distrusted everybody. He ordered all literary and scientific work to fit Soviet political needs.

After Stalin's death in 1953, Nikita Khrushchev emerged as the Soviet leader. In a program of **de-Stalinization,** he took steps to undo some of the worst features of Stalin's rule. In 1956 he condemned Stalin for his "administrative violence, mass repression, and terror."

Khrushchev loosened government controls on literature. He allowed the publication of *One Day in the Life of Ivan Denisovich* by Aleksandr Solzhenitsyn, set in a prison camp in Siberia. Production of consumer goods increased, and industrial growth declined. Khrushchev was forced out of office in 1964.

 **Notes** **Read to Learn**

Eastern Europe *(page 676)*

Formulating Questions

What are two questions one might ask to determine whether or not a Communist state in Eastern Europe was a satellite of the Soviet Union?

1. _____
_____
_____
_____ ?

2. _____
_____
_____
_____ ?

At the end of World War II, Soviet military forces occupied all of Eastern Europe and much of the Balkans. All the occupied states came under Soviet control. Between 1945 and 1947, Soviet-controlled governments became firmly established in East Germany, Bulgaria, Romania, Poland, and Hungary.

The process took longer in Czechoslovakia, which had a strong tradition of democracy and a multiparty system. The Soviets seized control of the government of Czechoslovakia in 1948. They dissolved all political parties except the Communist Party.

Albania and Yugoslavia were more independent of the Soviet Union. Both countries had strong Communist movements that resisted the Nazis during the war. After the war, local Communist parties took control. The regime in Albania resembled Stalin's style of rule in the Soviet Union. Albania became more and more independent.

The Communist leader in Yugoslavia was Josip Broz, known as Tito. After the war, he made Yugoslavia an independent Communist state. Tito refused to give in to Stalin's demands. Tito gained popular support for insisting on national independence. He ruled Yugoslavia until he died in 1980. Although Yugoslavia had a Communist government, it was not a Soviet satellite state.

Between 1948 and Stalin's death in 1953, the Soviet satellite states in Eastern Europe followed Stalin's example. They adopted five-year plans with an emphasis on heavy industry. They collectivized agriculture, eliminated all political parties except the Communists, and set up secret police.

Communism did not develop deep roots in Eastern Europe. People resented Soviet domination. After Stalin died, some countries made changes. However, they could not escape Soviet control. The Polish Communist Party adopted reforms in 1956 but promised to stay in the Warsaw Pact.

In Hungary, the leader Imre Nagy declared independence on November 1, 1956. He promised free elections. Three days later, the Soviet Army attacked Budapest. The Soviets reestablished control.

Writers led a peaceful rebellion in Czechoslovakia in 1968. Party secretary Alexander Dubcek introduced reforms. The "Prague Spring" was short-lived. The Soviet army invaded in August 1968 and crushed the reform movement.

Section Wrap-up

Answer these questions to check your understanding of the entire section.

1. How did the Soviet Union first acquire power over many states of Eastern Europe?

_____

_____

_____

2. How did governments of the satellite states imitate Stalin's policies between 1948 and 1953?

_____

_____

_____

Informative Writing

Write the story of Soviet control over the satellite states of Eastern Europe, from the beginning through 1968. Use a story plan made up of four elements—time, place, people, and events. Discuss what happened, when, why, how, and who was involved. Present the facts objectively, without showing approval or disapproval.

_____

_____

_____

_____

_____

_____

_____

_____

_____

_____

_____

_____

_____

_____

Western Europe and North America

Big Idea

Post-World War II societies rebuilt their economies and communities, but not without upheaval and change. As you read, use a table like the one below to list programs instituted by Great Britain, the United States, and Canada to promote social welfare.

Great Britain	United States	Canada

Read to Learn

Western Europe: New Unity (page 678)

Identifying the Main Idea

Most countries of Western Europe experienced economic _____ in the period after World War II and into the 1950s and 1960s.

Most of Western Europe recovered after World War II. The Marshall Plan brought economic aid from the United States. France faced a crisis in Algeria in 1958. Charles de Gaulle drafted a constitution for the Fifth Republic. With de Gaulle as president, France became a nuclear and industrial power. Student protests and a general strike in 1968 led de Gaulle to resign in April 1969.

The chancellor of West Germany from 1949 to 1963 was Konrad Adenauer, leader of the Christian Democratic Union. West Germany experienced an "economic miracle." Employment was so high that Germany brought in "guest" workers from other countries.

In Britain, the Labour Party set up a modern **welfare state,** providing services and a basic living standard. The government provided insurance and health care for all. British colonies won their independence. Six countries formed the European Economic Community (EEC), also known as the Common Market, in 1957. The EEC grew into an important trading **bloc** (a group of nations with a common purpose).

Notes | Read to Learn

The U.S. after the War (page 681)

Distinguishing Fact from Opinion

President Truman's attorney general warned that Communists were "everywhere—in factories, offices, butcher stores, on street corners, in private businesses."
Is the statement quoted above fact or opinion?
(circle one)
FACT   OPINION

In the United States, an economic boom followed World War II. Consumer goods were available. Labor unions achieved growth in **real wages,** the actual purchasing power of income.

The Cold War and the Korean War increased fears of communism. Senator Joseph McCarthy set off a "Red Scare" by saying hundreds of Communists were in high government positions and the army.

John F. Kennedy, elected president in 1960, was killed in 1963. Lyndon Johnson succeeded him. Johnson pursued programs of health care for the elderly, antipoverty measures, federal assistance for education, and civil rights. The Reverend Martin Luther King, Jr., led a growing **civil rights movement** for racial equality. New laws were passed to end segregation and discrimination against African Americans.

In the later 1960s, Americans became divided over race riots and antiwar protests. The election of Richard Nixon as president in 1968 began a conservative shift in American politics.

Canada adopted a national pension plan and national health insurance.

Changing Values (page 683)

Determining Cause and Effect

Three causes of the consumer society were:
1. a rise in real
_____;
2. availability of consumer
_____
such as television sets; and
3. ability to buy on
_____.

Advances in technology and the struggle for rights brought changes in society after World War II. Computers, televisions, and jet planes changed the pace of life. The social structure was also changing. A new group of managers and technicians joined the middle class. The number of white-collar workers increased, and the number of industrial workers declined. More people moved from rural areas to cities.

A marked increase in real wages let industrial workers buy consumer goods previously limited to the middle class. Buying on credit became common. Workers could now afford appliances and automobiles. Some called it the **consumer society,** focused on buying goods.

Women made important gains during the two World Wars. They won the right to vote in many countries. For a time after 1945, women returned to traditional roles. The birth rate rose, causing a "baby boom." By the end of the 1950s, families were smaller, and more women returned to the workforce. Still, they earned less than men. Simone de Beauvoir's book *The Second Sex* influenced the **women's liberation movement,** or feminism.

The number of university students increased sharply. Many were dissatisfied. Student protests in Europe reached a peak in 1968.

Answer these questions to check your understanding of the entire section.

1. Name two individuals who led European economic recovery in the 1950s and 1960s.

_____

_____

_____

2. Why did Germany start to accept guest workers from other countries, such as Italy, Spain, Greece, Turkey, and Yugoslavia?

_____

_____

_____

Form a theory, or model, about the relationship between economic prosperity and the government's role in meeting people's needs. Does the welfare state grow when needs are greatest or when society has the most resources to help the less fortunate members of society? Provide historical information to support your theory. Explain what additional kinds of data might help in testing your theory.

_____

_____

_____

_____

_____

_____

_____

_____

_____

_____

_____

_____

_____

_____

Decline of the Soviet Union

Big Idea

One of the largest empires in the world ended when the Soviet Union broke up in 1991. As you read, create a chart like the one below comparing the policies of Brezhnev and Gorbachev.

	Leonid Brezhnev	Mikhail Gorbachev
Foreign Policy		
Economic Policy		
Military Policy		
Personal Policy		

Notes | Read to Learn

The Soviet Union Under Stress (page 694)

Determining Cause and Effect

Determine the cause-and-effect relationship among the following three events. Write **C** *beside the cause(s). Write* **E** *beside the effect(s).*

_____ *Americans withdraw from the Moscow Olympics.*

_____ *Soviets invade Afghanistan to try to restore pro-Soviet regime.*

_____ *Americans stop shipping grain to the Soviet Union.*

After Nikita Khrushchev was removed from office, Alexei Kosygin and Leonid Brezhnev replaced him. Brezhnev emerged as the dominant leader in the 1970s. He benefited from **détente,** improved relations between the United States and the Soviet Union. Tensions between the superpowers relaxed. They signed treaties to limit nuclear arms. Soviet leaders relaxed their authoritarian rule. Brezhnev allowed Western styles of music, dress, and art. However, he still punished **dissidents,** those who spoke out against the regime.

His economic policies still emphasized heavy industry. The central government was huge and inefficient. The ruling class was corrupt. Farmers liked working private plots rather than collective farming.

By the 1970s, détente allowed American grain and consumer goods to be sold to the Soviet Union. However, détente collapsed in 1979, when the Soviet Union invaded Afghanistan. The Soviet Union wanted to restore a pro-Soviet regime in Afghanistan.

The United States viewed this as an act of expansion. It withdrew from the 1980 Olympics in Moscow and stopped shipping grain to the Soviet Union. U.S. president Ronald Reagan, elected in 1980, called the Soviet Union an evil empire. He aided the Afghan rebels. A new arms race began.

 **Notes** | # Read to Learn

Gorbachev and Reform *(page 696)*

Problems and Solutions

In both the United States and the Soviet Union, the arms race took needed money away from domestic problems. What did the United States and the Soviet Union do in 1987 to help solve that problem?

_____

_____

_____

_____

By 1980 the Soviet economy was in trouble. Mikhail Gorbachev, a reform leader, was chosen as Communist Party secretary in 1985. He wanted radical reforms based on **perestroika,** or restructuring.

He wanted a market economy more responsive to consumers. He introduced a policy of glasnost, or "openness." In 1988 he set up a new Soviet parliament with elected members, the Congress of People's Deputies. Its meeting in 1989 was the first such meetings in Russia since 1918. Gorbachev became the first and only president of the Soviet Union.

The Cold War ended when Gorbachev came to power. In 1987 he agreed with the United States to eliminate intermediate-range nuclear weapons. Both countries wanted to spend less money on weapons. Gorbachev also stopped military support for Communist governments in Eastern Europe. That allowed a number of peaceful revolutions.

Nationalist movements resurfaced in parts of the Soviet Union. Antireform Soviet leaders tried to take control in 1991. Boris Yeltsin, president of the Russian Republic, led resistance to the coup. Soviet republics declared independence, and the Soviet Union ceased to exist.

The New Russia *(page 698)*

Predicting

Do you think that military force will persuade the people of Chechnya to be content as part of Russia and drop their demands for independence?

(circle one)
YES   NO

Why or why not?

_____

_____

_____

_____

Gorbachev resigned on December 25, 1991. He turned his responsibilities over to Boris Yeltsin, president of Russia. Yeltsin intended to introduce a free market economy as quickly as possible. A rise in organized crime made problems worse.

Another problem was in Chechnya, part of southern Russia. People in Chechnya wanted to be independent. Yeltsin used force against the Chechen rebels to keep them in Russia.

At the end of 1999, Yeltsin resigned. Vladimir Putin was elected president of Russia in 2000. He had been an officer of the KGB, the former Soviet security agency and secret police. Putin introduced more reforms to boost economic growth. He allowed people to buy and sell land freely. He reduced taxes. The export of oil and natural gas helped the Russian economy. Some felt that Putin was increasing state control and reducing freedoms such as freedom of the press.

Russia continued to face challenges. Alcoholism and organized crime remained high. Chechen terrorists killed about 500 people in Russia between 2002 and 2004. Chechen rebels seized a school in 2004. When Russian troops moved in, hundreds died, including children.

Answer these questions to check your understanding of the entire section.

1. Describe the structure of government of the Soviet Union from 1988 to 1991.

_____

_____

_____

2. List two problems faced by the Russian government under Yeltsin's leadership in the 1990s.

_____

_____

_____

Persuasive Writing

In your opinion, which challenges are most important for the leaders of Russia to address, and how should the leaders address those challenges? Use information and facts to support your opinion. State your point of view clearly and try to persuade your readers to agree with you.

_____

_____

_____

_____

_____

_____

_____

_____

_____

_____

_____

_____

_____

_____

_____

Eastern Europe

Big Idea

Popular revolutions helped end Communist regimes in Eastern Europe. As you read, use a chart like the one below to list reasons for and the results of revolution.

Country	Reasons for Revolution	Results of Revolution
Poland		
Czechoslovakia		
Romania		
East Germany		
Yugoslavia		

 **Notes**

Read to Learn

Revolutions in Eastern Europe *(page 700)*

Synthesizing Information

Between 1988 and 1990, _____ governments fell from power and democracies were installed throughout Eastern Europe.

Without the backing of the Soviet Union, Communist regimes in Eastern Europe soon fell. In Poland, Lech Walesa organized a national trade union called Solidarity in 1980. It had support from workers and the Catholic Church, led by the first Polish pope. In 1988 the Polish regime agreed to the first free parliamentary elections in Eastern Europe in 40 years. A noncommunist government was elected. Walesa became president.

Czech intellectuals remained in opposition after Soviet troops crushed a Czech reform movement in 1968. Demonstrations in 1988 and 1989 drew huge crowds. The Communist government collapsed in December 1989. Václav Havel, a writer, became president. Ethnic tensions led to a peaceful split into the Czech Republic and Slovakia.

Romanian Communist leader Nicolae Ceauşescu used secret police to crush dissent. In December 1989, the secret police shot thousands of peaceful demonstrators. The army refused to support any more repression. Ceauşescu and his wife were arrested and executed. Former Communists ruled for a time but lost power in 1996.

After mass demonstrations in 1989, East Germany opened its border with West Germany. People tore down the Berlin Wall. Germany reunited as one country on October 3, 1990.

Read to Learn

The Disintegration of Yugoslavia *(page 703)*

Making Generalizations

The decline or removal of close Communist control allowed for a revival of _____ feelings and tensions, resulting in the breakup of some countries into smaller independent nations.

Yugoslavia was a federation of southern Slavic republics and provinces. It was under Communist rule but was never a Soviet satellite state. The Communist Party of Yugoslavia collapsed by 1990. Ethnic tensions and nationalism posed new challenges.

Some republics of Yugoslavia wanted to become independent. The leader of Serbia was Slobodan Milošević. He resisted calls by non-Serbian areas for independence. First, he wanted to redraw the borders among parts of the federation to form a new Greater Serbia.

Slovenia and Croatia declared their independence in June 1991. That September, the Yugoslavian army (dominated by Serbs) attacked Croatia. They captured one-third of Croatia's territory before a cease-fire ended the conflict.

The Serbs next attacked Bosnia-Herzegovina. They acquired 70 percent of Bosnian territory. Many Bosnians were Muslims. The Serbs followed a policy of removing Muslims by killing them or forcing them from their homes. Such a policy is called **ethnic cleansing.** By 1995 there were 250,000 Bosnians killed and 2 million homeless.

NATO air attacks helped Bosnia and Croatia regain some of their lost territory. The Serbs finally signed a peace treaty dividing Bosnia into a Serb republic and a Muslim-Croat federation. NATO troops tried to keep peace along the border between them.

In 1998 a new war broke out over Kosovo. Kosovo had been an **autonomous** (self-governing) province within Yugoslavia until 1989, when Milošević took away its autonomy. Groups of ethnic Albanians in Kosovo formed the Kosovo Liberation Army (KLA). They fought against Serbian rule. Serb forces tried to crush the KLA by killing ethnic Albanians.

The United States and NATO tried to stop the killing. The Albanians in Kosovo regained their autonomy in 1999. The rule of Milošević ended in Serbia in 2000. He was later arrested and put on trial for killing civilians in Kosovo.

Yugoslavia ended in 2004. It was officially renamed Serbia and Montenegro. The people of Montenegro voted for independence in 2006. All six republics that had formed Yugoslavia in 1918 were now independent nations.

Section Wrap-up

Answer these questions to check your understanding of the entire section.

1. Other than Yugoslavia, which Eastern European country's removal of Communist dictators involved the most bloodshed? Describe the bloodshed that took place in that country.

_____

_____

_____

2. Why did NATO send bomber planes and ground troops into Yugoslavia?

_____

_____

_____

Descriptive Writing

Pretend that you are a journalist covering wartime events in either Bosnia or Kosovo during the 1990s. Describe what you see and experience in a way that will help your readers to share the experience. Write vividly. Use strong verbs. Include as many of the five senses as possible.

_____

_____

_____

_____

_____

_____

_____

_____

_____

_____

_____

_____

_____

_____

Europe and North America

Big Idea

Postwar Western societies rebuilt their communities, but shifting social structures led to upheaval and change. As you read, use a Venn diagram like the one below to compare and contrast economic policies of Thatcherism and those of the Reagan Revolution.

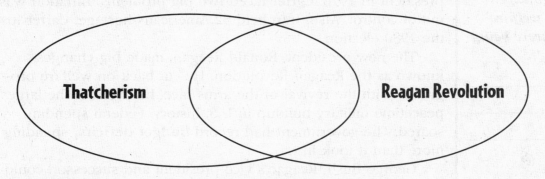

Thatcherism   Reagan Revolution

Notes

Read to Learn

Winds of Change in Western Europe (page 704)

Drawing Conclusions

What economic benefit would countries of Europe gain by adopting a common currency?

_____

_____

_____

_____

Western Europe had almost full employment in the 1950s, 1960s, and early 1970s. An economic downturn began about the mid-1970s, and inflation and unemployment rose.

More nations joined the European Community. In 1994 it became the European Union (EU) and in 2002 created a common European currency, the euro.

France shifted toward socialism under President François Mitterrand in the 1980s. The economy continued to decline. Conservatives regained control in the 1990s.

In 1969 the Social Democrats became the leading party in West Germany. Chancellor Willy Brandt received the Nobel Peace Prize for increasing contacts between West and East Germany. Conservatives gained power in the 1980s. German reunification in 1990 made Germany the leading power in Europe. It brought economic problems and extremist attacks on foreigners.

In Britain, Catholic-Protestant conflict raged in Northern Ireland. Conservative prime minister Margaret Thatcher broke the power of labor unions and tried to end social welfare. Her economic policy was called **Thatcherism.** Antitax riots in 1990 led Thatcher to resign.

Notes

Read to Learn

The U.S. and Canada (page 707)

Analyzing Information

When Reagan was president in the 1980s, why did budget deficits increase even though expenditures on welfare programs were being cut?

_____

_____

_____

In the United States, white southern Democrats began switching to the Republican Party. President Richard Nixon used illegal methods to gain information about his political opponents. This led to the Watergate scandal. Nixon resigned on August 9, 1974.

Vice President Gerald Ford succeeded him in office. Jimmy Carter, a Democrat and former governor of Georgia, was elected president in 1976. Carter faced two big problems. Inflation was out of control. Also, Iran held 52 Americans hostage. Carter lost the 1980 election.

The new president, Ronald Reagan, made big changes, known as the Reagan Revolution. He cut back on welfare programs. With the revival of the arms race, he oversaw the largest peacetime military buildup in U.S. history. Federal spending soared. The government had record **budget deficits,** spending more than it took in.

George Bush, Reagan's vice president and successor, could not reverse the economic downturn. He lost the presidential election of 1992 to Bill Clinton. Clinton claimed to be a new, more conservative kind of Democrat. A sexual scandal led to his impeachment (formal charges of misconduct), but he was not removed from office. His problems helped George W. Bush, son of former president George Bush, win the presidency in 2000 in a very close election.

On September 11, 2001, terrorists hijacked four commercial jets in the United States. Three were flown into buildings: the two World Trade Center towers in New York City and the Pentagon in Arlington, Virginia. Almost 3,000 people were killed. Heroic passengers crashed the fourth plane before it could fly into yet another building.

The attacks were carried out by the Islamic terrorist group al-Qaeda, under the direction of Osama bin Laden. Bin Laden trained al-Qaeda terrorists in Afghanistan. That country was governed by a militant Islamic group, the Taliban, which allowed al-Qaeda activity. The United States responded to the terrorist attacks by leading a coalition in a war against Afghanistan. The Taliban was removed from power. The United States introduced new airport security measures and established a Department of Homeland Security. Bush later involved the United States in an unpopular war in Iraq.

Canada joined the United States and Mexico in the North American Free Trade Agreement in 1993. In 1995, voters in the French-speaking province of Quebec narrowly defeated a proposal to withdraw from Canada.

Answer these questions to check your understanding of the entire section.

1. Which European national leader won the Nobel Peace Prize, and why?

_____

_____

_____

2. List two actions the United States took in response to the al-Qaeda attacks of September 11, 2001.

_____

_____

_____

Informative Writing

Trace United States political history from the early 1970s to the early 2000s. Do not let your opinions show or influence your account. Include major events during each presidency and factors influencing the outcome of presidential elections. Tell events in the approximate order in which they took place.

_____

_____

_____

_____

_____

_____

_____

_____

_____

_____

_____

_____

_____

Western Society and Culture

Big Idea

Trends in contemporary Western society include rapid changes in science and technology, changes in family structures and population trends, increased religious diversity, and a shared popular culture among nations. As you read, complete a chart like the one below to list the issues and outcomes for the women's movement since 1970.

Issues	Outcomes

 **Notes**   **Read to Learn**

The Quickening Pace of Change (page 710)

Distinguishing Fact from Opinion

Beside each of the statements below, write F if it is a statement of fact. Write O if it is a statement of opinion.

____ *Abortion became a controversial issue in the United States.*

____ *The United States Supreme Court legalized abortion in 1973.*

____ *Abortion will become more common in the future.*

Since 1970 the pace of material change has quickened and produced a global economy. Science and technology have changed people's lives dramatically. By funding weapons projects during World War II, governments set a new model for scientific research. Complex projects took teams of scientists and huge, expensive laboratories. An example is the space race. An American landed on the moon in 1969.

Concerns arose about technology and the environment. Chemical fertilizers interfered with the balance of nature. Organic farming and genetically modified foods are controversial.

Marriage rates fell and divorce rates increased. The average age of marriage went up slightly. The birthrate fell. More women went to college and joined the workforce.

"Consciousness-raising" groups drew attention to **gender stereotyping,** restricting a person's activities by gender. In 1963 the United States passed the Equal Pay Act, requiring women to get the same pay as men for doing the same work. Norway and Denmark adopted **gender parity** policies in the 1970s, requiring that women make up a certain number of candidates or of those elected to office.

 **Notes** | **Read to Learn**

Culture and Identity (page 713)

Making Generalizations

In general, communications technology

_____

the globalization of culture.

The United States dominated the art world after World War II. New York City became the artistic center of the Western world. Abstract expressionists conveyed emotion and feeling. By the 1980s, postmodern styles emerged. **Postmodernism** is a revival of traditional elements and techniques. Postmodern artists often create works that include elements of film, performance, and sculpture.

Movies, music, and spectator sports have become part of **popular culture**—entertainment created for a mass audience, for a profit. Radio, television, and film have spread American pop culture around the world. Europeans watch American television shows and become familiar with the brand names of American products. They also learn American attitudes about family, work, and money.

Sports have become big business and are sometimes a part of politics. A Palestinian terrorist group took 11 Israeli athletes hostage at the 1972 Olympic Games in Munich, Germany. After the United States refused to send athletes to the 1980 Olympics in Moscow, the Soviet Union refused to take part in the Los Angeles Olympics in 1984.

Some people worried that the dominance of American pop culture weakened their own national traditions. They called this domination **cultural imperialism.** A law in France reserved at least 40 percent of radio time for French-language music. At the same time, Western music was influenced by music from other cultures, such as reggae and Latin pop.

Migration from former colonies increased religious diversity in Europe. Millions of immigrants from Africa established Muslim communities in France, Germany, and Great Britain. Some Europeans considered non-Christians a threat to their traditional culture. An evangelical Protestant revival grew in the United States. Conservative Christian groups became a larger force in American politics.

Many minorities in Europe and North America want to preserve their culture. In 1995 a small majority in the French-speaking province of Quebec voted to remain in Canada. Basque extremists used terror to pursue independence for the Basque region of Spain and France. In Northern Ireland, on "Bloody Sunday" in 1972, British troops fired into a crowd of Catholic protesters. Thousands died before Catholics and Protestants signed the Good Friday Agreement in April 1998.

Section Wrap-up

Answer these questions to check your understanding of the entire section.

1. List three ways families changed after 1970.

_____

_____

_____

2. Define popular culture and give two examples.

_____

_____

_____

Persuasive Writing

An issue in France has been whether or not to forbid Muslim girls to wear head scarves in school. People who want to ban the practice say the scarves are distracting and draw attention to religious differences. People who oppose the ban say the girls should be free to follow their religion. Take a position on this issue. Answer the arguments of those who disagree. Try to persuade your reader to share your opinion.

_____

_____

_____

_____

_____

_____

_____

_____

_____

_____

_____

_____

_____

_____

General Trends in Latin America

Big Idea

Economic instability led some Latin American countries to move toward democracy, while the United State intervened to protect its interests. As you read, use a diagram like the one below to identify social and political challenges in Latin America since 1945.

 **Notes**   **Read to Learn**

Economic and Political Developments *(page 724)*

Making Generalizations

In general, economic

———————

tend(s) to create pressure for governments to change.

In response to the Great Depression, Latin American countries had developed manufacturing industries to provide the goods they could no longer afford to import. They depended on the United States, Europe, and Japan for advanced technology. It was hard to find markets abroad to sell their manufactured products.

Economic problems led to political instability. In the 1960s, military regimes in Chile, Brazil, and Argentina returned to export-import economies financed by foreigners. They encouraged **multinational corporations** (companies with divisions in more than two countries) to come to Latin America. That made the countries still more dependent on foreigners. They borrowed huge amounts of money in the 1970s. Wages fell. Unemployment and inflation rose sharply.

With the debt crisis in the 1980s came a movement toward democracy. Countries had to make reforms to get new loans. Some military leaders did not want to deal with the problems. Several countries established democratic regimes by the mid-1990s.

The new democracies were insecure. Globalization and foreign debt continued to cause economic stress. Several Latin American countries elected authoritarian figures in the 1990s; however, in the 2000s some countries elected populist leaders.

 **Notes** | **Read to Learn**

Latin American Society *(page 726)*

Changes in population made economic problems worse. The population of Latin America grew very fast. It more than tripled between 1950 and 2000. This change brought a rapid rise in the size of cities. More than 75 percent of Latin America's people now live in cities. Fifty cities in Latin America and the Caribbean had more than a million people by 2000. These are examples of megacities. A **megacity** is a huge city that has grown too fast for urban services to keep up. Many megacities have slums and shantytowns. Crime and corruption from the international drug trade are common.

The gap between rich and poor is huge in Latin America. Landholding elites own huge estates; urban elites own large businesses. Peasants and the urban poor struggle to survive.

Women's roles have changed in Latin America. Some women work in industry and as teachers, professors, doctors, and lawyers.

The U.S. and Latin America *(page 726)*

Making Inferences

Why did the United States continue to interfere in Latin America?

_____

_____

_____

_____

The United States often intervened in Latin America to help U.S. business interests. Sometimes this meant backing dictators.

President Franklin D. Roosevelt announced his Good Neighbor policy in the 1930s. He said that the United States would not send troops to Latin America. In 1948 the nations of the Americas formed the Organization of American States (OAS). It passed a resolution to end military action by one nation in the affairs of another. It encouraged regional cooperation.

However, the U.S. did not end its interference in Latin America. President John F. Kennedy's Alliance for Progress encouraged social reform and economic development in Latin America, but this program failed. When Cuba started guerilla wars in other Latin American countries, the U.S. sent aid to anti-Communist regimes. In the 1980s and 1990s, the U.S. returned to a policy of direct intervention in Latin America, taking action in countries including Grenada, Panama, and Haiti.

Latin American Culture *(page 728)*

A new form of literature called **magic realism** developed in Latin America in the 1940s. It combines realistic events with dreamlike or fantasy backgrounds. Writers use elements of magic to comment on a national or social situation. An important example is the novel *One Hundred Years of Solitude*. The author, Gabriel García Márquez of Colombia, won the Nobel Prize in literature in 1982.

Identifying the Main Idea

Authors of magic realism combine

_____

and

_____.

The first Latin American winner of the Nobel Prize in Literature was Gabriela Mistral, a poet from Chile. Other important writers include the novelists Jorge Edwards from Chile and Julio Cortázar from Argentina.

International styles influenced Latin American art and architecture after World War II. Perhaps the most striking modern architecture is in Brasília, the capital of Brazil. The chief architect was Oscar Niemeyer from Brazil. He was already known internationally as one of the two architects who designed the United Nations building in New York City.

Section Wrap-up

Answer these questions to check your understanding of the entire section.

1. What made Latin American countries economically dependent on foreigners?

_____

_____

2. Why has the United States sometimes supported dictators in Latin America?

_____

_____

Descriptive Writing

Describe a typical megacity of Latin America. (You do not have to select a particular city. Write about the features that megacities have in common.) Create vivid images of the sights, sounds, and smells. Consider the various parts of the city and the different classes of people who live there.

_____

_____

_____

_____

_____

_____

_____

_____

_____

_____

Mexico, Cuba, and Central America

Big Idea

Mexico and Central America faced political and economic crises after World War II, making national progress difficult. As you read, use a table like the one below to identify the political and economic challenges faced by El Salvador, Nicaragua, Panama, and Guatemala after 1945.

El Salvador	Nicaragua	Panama	Guatemala

Notes

Read to Learn

Mexico (page 730)

Detecting Bias

Many Americans have strong opinions about NAFTA. Write + if the bias is positive or – if it is negative below.

_____ *NAFTA increases export opportunities.*

_____ *NAFTA takes away American jobs.*

_____ *NAFTA lets consumers buy goods at lower prices.*

_____ *NAFTA lets companies avoid environmental laws.*

The Mexican Revolution in the early 1900s created a fairly stable political order. The Institutional Revolutionary Party (PRI) dominated politics. Every six years, Mexicans elected the PRI candidate as president. Wages rose in the 1950s and 1960s.

In 1968 police fired on student demonstrators, killing hundreds. PRI leaders grew concerned. The next two presidents made political reforms. They allowed more freedom of debate. New parties formed.

Large oil reserves were discovered in Mexico in the late 1970s. The government came to depend on money from selling oil abroad. When world oil prices dropped in the mid-1980s, Mexico could no longer make payments on its foreign debt. The government had to change its economic policies. One new policy was **privatization,** or selling government-owned companies to private businesses.

The next president, Carlos Salinas de Gortari, sped up privatization to help pay Mexico's debts. He worked with leaders of the United States and Canada to form the North American Free Trade Agreement (NAFTA). Problems continued. Support for the PRI dropped. In 2000 Mexico elected Vicente Fox, its first non-PRI president in over 70 years.

The Cuban Revolution (page 732)

Making Inferences

Based on the information provided here about Ché Guevara, one can infer that his political views were probably

_____.

The dictator Fulgencio Batista controlled Cuba for a quarter century, starting in 1934. Opposition arose in the 1950s, led by Fidel Castro. He became a revolutionary while studying law at the University of Havana. In 1953 he and his brother Raúl led an attack on an army camp. It failed, and the brothers spent time in prison.

Next, the Castro brothers joined a rebel band in the mountains of Mexico. They produced propaganda. The Batista regime collapsed. Castro's group took control of Cuba in 1959.

Castro's regime received aid from the Soviet Union. Worried, the United States declared a **trade embargo,** stopping all trade with Cuba. A failed U.S. attempt to overthrow Castro's government with the Bay of Pigs invasion caused Cuba to grow closer to the Soviet Union. The Soviet Union placed nuclear missiles in Cuba (the Cuban Missile Crisis). Castro tried to spark revolutions in other parts of Latin America. His ally Ernesto "Ché" Guevara died in such a war in 1967.

Castro's Marxist government brought mixed results. Citizens got free medical services. Nearly everyone learned to read and write. Cuba relied on Soviet aid and sugar exports to Eastern Europe. When those Communist regimes fell, the Cuban economy suffered. In 2008 Raúl Castro became president of Cuba. Cuban relations with the U.S. have not improved.

Central America (page 733)

Comparing and Contrasting

Compare and contrast the groups the United States supported in wars in El Salvador and Nicaragua.

El Salvador:

_____

_____

Nicaragua:

_____

_____

Both:

_____

Fear of communism led the United States to intervene in Central American politics in the 1970s and 1980s, supporting dictators.

In El Salvador in the 1970s, civil war broke out between Marxist guerrillas and right-wing death squads. Archbishop Oscar Romero and other Catholic priests were killed. The United States provided weapons and training to oppose the guerrillas. At least 75,000 people died before a peace settlement was reached in 1992.

The Somoza family controlled Nicaragua, with United States support. In 1979 Marxist guerrillas called Sandinistas won control of the country. The U.S. aided the **contras,** a group opposed to the Sandinistas' policies, to try to overthrow the government.

Manuel Noriega, the military leader of Panama, was involved in the drug trade. U.S. president George Bush sent U.S. troops to Panama in 1989, and Noriega was sent to prison. Control of the Panama Canal passed from the United States to Panama in 1999.

In a civil war in Guatemala, military dictators used death squads against native Maya people. Some fled to Mexico as refugees. The civil war ended in 1996.

Section Wrap-up

Answer these questions to check your understanding of the entire section.

1. Why did the United States provide military training and weapons for repressive regimes in Central America?

_____

_____

_____

2. Why did Mexico adopt a policy of privatization after the mid-1980s?

_____

_____

_____

Expository Writing

Analyze the effect of the Cuban Revolution on subsequent events in Central America. Choose a way to organize the information into smaller and simpler categories, to make your analysis easy for the reader to follow.

_____

_____

_____

_____

_____

_____

_____

_____

_____

_____

_____

_____

_____

_____

The Nations of South America

Big Idea

South American countries have experienced economic, social, and political problems, but democracy has advanced since the late 1980s. As you read, use a table like the one below to list factors leading to the change from military rule to civilian rule.

Argentina	Brazil	Chile	Venezuela

Notes | Read to Learn

Chile and Argentina (page 736)

Problems and Solutions

To solve the problem of foreign control of major industries, Allende and Perón _____ the industries.

Salvador Allende, a Marxist, became president of Chile in 1970. He increased wages and nationalized large corporations. He gained support in the Chilean congress. The American owners of the copper companies were angry about nationalization. Military forces killed Allende in 1973, and General Augusto Pinochet became dictator. He ended the congress and outlawed political parties.

The Pinochet regime was brutal. Thousands of opponents and other civilians were arrested and never seen again—imprisoned, tortured, or killed. Free elections finally removed Pinochet in 1989. Chile has since become a stable democracy, and its economy has improved.

Argentina was ruled by an oligarchy of large landowners, supported by the army. In 1943 army officers overthrew the oligarchy. The new labor secretary, Juan Perón, encouraged workers to join unions. He increased job benefits. He was elected president in 1946. He and his popular wife, Eva Perón, introduced social reforms. He tried to industrialize Argentina and free it from foreign investors. He nationalized major industries.

Perón's rule was authoritarian. So was the military regime that took power in 1976. A failed invasion of the British-controlled Falkland Islands in 1982 discredited the military regime. The next president, Raúl Alfonsín, restored democracy in Argentina. Argentina experienced a financial crisis in 2001–2002.

 **Notes** | **Read to Learn**

Brazil (page 739)

Analyzing Information

How did Brazil's "economic miracle" benefit and harm Brazil?

Benefit:

_____

_____

Harm:

_____

_____

Like other countries of Latin America, Brazil had severe economic problems after World War II. Democratically elected governments could not solve the problems. The military seized control in 1964. The military government reduced government interference in the economy. It encouraged the free market. Beginning about 1968, the economy grew quickly. Brazil experienced an "economic miracle." Most people in Brazil did not benefit from this economic growth. Inflation soared. Prices doubled in a year. The generals running the government were overwhelmed. They backed off, and democracy returned in 1985.

The new democratic government faced huge challenges. It had an enormous foreign debt. The inflation rate in 1987 was 800 percent. The government stabilized the economy in the 1990s, but the gap between rich and poor remained high. Luiz Inácio Lula da Silva, elected in 2002, was the first left-wing president of Brazil in four decades. He tried to make Brazil more independent in global trade. Da Silva was reelected in 2006. Brazil's economy has continued to improve.

Peru, Colombia, and Venezuela (page 739)

Synthesizing Information

In both Peru and Colombia, economic dependence on

_____

made the national economies unstable.

Dependence on exports made Peru unstable. After a military takeover in 1968, General Juan Velasco Alvarado tried to help the peasants. The government transferred most landed estates to **cooperatives,** farm organizations owned by and operated for the peasants. It nationalized foreign-owned industries. It froze food prices to help urban workers. The Shining Path, a Communist guerrilla group, killed many people. Alberto Fujimori was elected president in 1990. He promised reforms but became a dictator. He was removed from power in 2000.

Conservative coffee plantation owners ran the democratic government of Colombia. Dependence on coffee exports made the economy unstable. Poor peasants turned to a new cash crop—coca leaves, used to make cocaine. Marxist guerrilla groups made deals with drug **cartels** (groups of drug businesses) to oppose the government. The United States funded an antidrug program and sent troops to support it.

Military dictators promoted the oil industry in Venezuela. Democracy was restored by 1958. Economic problems and policies provoked riots in 1979. A group of army lieutenants led by Hugo Chávez attempted a coup in 1992. It failed, but Chávez became a folk hero. He was elected president in 1998 and again in 2006. In 2007 Chávez began to nationalize some industries.

Section Wrap-up

Answer these questions to check your understanding of the entire section.

1. List three economic policies undertaken by the government of Juan Velasco Alvarado in Peru.

_____

_____

_____

2. Which two exports are most important to the economy of Colombia?

_____

_____

_____

Persuasive Writing

Imagine that the leader of a Latin American country has come to you for economic policy advice. What would you advise the leader to do to improve the national economy and the lives of people living there? Consider the economic challenges that are most widespread in Latin America. Use facts to support your suggestions. Present and support your suggestions in a way that will make the reader agree with your opinion.

_____

_____

_____

_____

_____

_____

_____

_____

_____

_____

_____

_____

_____

_____

_____

Independence in Africa

Big Idea

After achieving independence from their colonial rulers, many African nations faced political, economic, social, and health challenges. As you read, complete a chart like the one below identifying the problems in Africa during its first stages of independence.

Problems in Africa	
Economic	
Social	
Political	

Notes

Read to Learn

Independence and New Nations (page 750)

Synthesizing Information

Majority Hutus killed half a million Tutsis in Rwanda.

Arabs attacked African tribal groups in the Darfur region of Sudan. These civil wars are examples of _____ conflict.

The United Nations Charter stated that colonial peoples should choose their own governments. Ghana, Nigeria, Kenya, Morocco, Tunisia, Algeria, and others were granted independence.

Whites ran South Africa. Afrikaners, descended from the Dutch, set up racial segregation laws called **apartheid.** The black African National Congress (ANC) leader Nelson Mandela was arrested in 1962.

Jomo Kenyatta of Kenya and Mobutu Sese Seko of the Democratic Republic of the Congo favored capitalism. Julius Nyerere of Tanzania, Kwame Nkrumah of Ghana, Sékou Touré of Guinea, and Patrice Lumumba of the Republic of Congo preferred an African form of socialism, based on tradition. **Pan-Africanism,** the ideal of black African unity, led to the Organization of African Unity (OAU) in 1963 and the African Union (AU) in 2002.

Africa suffered from single-export economies, foreign debt, population growth, rapid urbanization, poverty, pollution, and droughts. **AIDS,** or acquired immunodeficiency syndrome, is epidemic. Ethnic conflict led to bloody civil wars. Hutus and Tutsis killed each other in Rwanda in 1994. Arab militias killed black Africans in Darfur, Sudan, causing the UN to intervene in peacekeeping efforts.

 **Notes** | # Read to Learn

New Hopes (page 754)

Evaluating Information

Mandela said in 1964, "I have cherished the ideal of a democratic and free society in which all persons live together in harmony."

In his inaugural address in 1994, he promised to build "a rainbow nation at peace with itself and the world."

These are evidence of his _____.

Because of the many problems, more than 70 elected leaders were overthrown between 1957 and 1982. Many African states were under military or one-party rule in the 1980s. Some restored democracy.

Idi Amin ruled Uganda by terror and brutal repression throughout the 1970s. He was deposed in 1979. Dictatorships also came to an end in Ethiopia, Liberia, and Somalia. In those countries, bloody civil wars followed the fall of the dictators' regimes.

In South Africa, black leader Nelson Mandela spent almost 26 years in prison for his activity with the African National Congress. He was offered a conditional release in 1985 but refused, saying that prisoners are not free to negotiate. Bishop Desmond Tutu, who won the Nobel Peace Prize in 1984, and others worked to free Mandela and end apartheid.

Finally, international pressure forced the South African government to end its apartheid laws. Mandela was released from prison in 1990. In 1993 President F. W. de Klerk agreed to hold the first democratic national elections in the history of South Africa. The election made Nelson Mandela president in 1994.

Society and Culture (page 756)

Identifying the Main Idea

African culture and art are marked by a tension between _____ and _____.

In general, Western culture has had the most impact in the cities. Many cities are a direct product of colonial rule. Examples include Dakar, Senegal; Lagos, Nigeria; Cape Town, South Africa; Brazzaville, Congo; and Nairobi, Kenya. Most African cities look like cities on other continents. They have high-rise buildings, wide boulevards, neon lights, movie theaters, and traffic jams.

Most Africans live outside the major cities. Their lives are more traditional. Millions live in thatched houses without plumbing or electricity. They farm, hunt, or raise livestock the way their ancestors did. In times of drought or flood, some move to the cities for work.

Upon independence, in almost every country, women were allowed to vote and hold political office. Some, including Luisa Diogo in Mozambique, became leaders of their countries. Rural areas often still observe traditional practices toward women, including arranged marriages.

African artists and writers struggle to balance traditional and Western influences. Some make traditional art for the tourist industry. Novelists Chinua Achebe of Nigeria (*Things Fall Apart*) and Noni Jabavu of South Africa (*The Ochre People*) write about the tension between traditional and Western values.

Section Wrap-up

Answer these questions to check your understanding of the entire section.

1. What dramatic changes took place in South Africa in the 1990s?

_____

_____

_____

2. How did the ideal of African socialism differ from the socialism of the Soviet Union?

_____

_____

_____

Descriptive Writing

Imagine and describe a large African city and the countryside of the same African country. Use strong verbs, vivid scenes, and as many as possible of the five senses to give the reader the sense of being present. Highlight the contrasts between the city and the countryside.

_____

_____

_____

_____

_____

_____

_____

_____

_____

_____

_____

_____

_____

_____

Conflict in the Middle East

Big Idea

Recurring violence and continuing efforts at international mediation have been the norm in the Middle East for decades. As you read, create a table and fill in the important events in the history of Arab-Israeli conflicts.

Year	Event

Notes

Read to Learn

Palestine and the Mideast Crisis *(page 760)*

Detecting Bias

Leaders of Arab nations did not agree about Pan-Arabism. Write + or – to show whether the bias toward Pan-Arabism below is positive or negative.

____ *Arabs need to support one another.*

____ *Money from oil-rich countries could raise living standards in Arab countries with fewer resources.*

____ *If we unite, too much of our wealth will be drained off by poorer Arab countries.*

Many Jews migrated to Palestine. The United Nations proposed in 1947 that Palestine should be divided into Jewish and Arab states. Israel became a nation in 1948. Arab states did not recognize Israel. Palestinian refugees from Israel poured into neighboring countries.

Colonel Gamal Abdel Nasser, leader of Egypt, seized the Suez Canal Company from Britain and France in 1956. Britain, France, and Israel attacked Egypt but had to withdraw. Nasser promoted **Pan-Arabism,** or Arab unity. Egypt and Syria joined in 1958 as the United Arab Republic. It ended in 1961 when new leaders in Syria withdrew.

In 1967 Nasser blocked Israeli shipping through the Gulf of Aqaba. Fearing attack, Israel launched air strikes against Egypt and other Arab neighbors. Israel seized control of the Sinai Peninsula, the West Bank of the Jordan River, East Jerusalem, and the Golan Heights. Israel tripled its territory during this Six-Day War.

Egypt and Syria attacked Israel on the Jewish holiday of Yom Kippur, 1973. Israel defeated them. During the Yom Kippur War, Arab countries in the Organization of the Petroleum Exporting Countries (OPEC) raised oil prices. That caused economic problems in the West.

Egyptian president Anwar el-Sadat and Israeli prime minister Menachem Begin met with U.S. president Jimmy Carter at Camp David in 1978. Israel agreed to withdraw from the Sinai Peninsula. Many Arab countries still refused to recognize Israel.

Read to Learn

The Ongoing Crisis (page 763)

Drawing Conclusions

In making the case to invade Iraq in 2003, President George W. Bush claimed that Iraq had (1) weapons of mass destruction and (2) close ties to al-Qaeda. Other United Nations members doubted both claims.

Why did the United States attack on Iraq in 2003 have little world support?

_____

_____

_____

The Palestine Liberation Organization (PLO) formed to represent Palestinians. Al-Fatah, a guerrilla movement led by PLO leader Yasir Arafat, made terrorist attacks against Israel. In the 1980s, Palestinian Arabs in Israeli-occupied areas began an *intifada,* or uprising. In the Oslo Accords of 1993, the PLO recognized Israel, and Israel agreed to partial Palestinian self-rule. Progress was slow. A second *intifada* broke out after 2000. Arafat died in 2004 and was replaced by Mahmoud Abbas. Israel withdrew from the Gaza Strip in 2005. In 2006 Hamas, a Palestinian group that rejects Israel's right to exist, controlled the new parliament. In 2007 Hamas took control of Gaza and Abbas dissolved the government. Peace talks resumed.

Hezbollah, a radical Islamic group from Lebanon, captured two Israeli soldiers in 1982. Israel responded by bombing Lebanon. Hezbollah fired rockets into Israel. A cease-fire followed in 2006.

Iran was an oil-rich country under Shah Mohammad Reza Pahlavi, a U.S. ally. In 1979 the shah's government was replaced by an Islamic republic, led by Ayatollah Ruhollah Khomeini. Militants held 52 Americans hostage for more than a year. After Khomeini died in 1997, control passed between Islamic extremists and moderate reformers.

Iran and Iraq (led by Saddam Hussein) were at war from 1980 to 1988. In 1990 Iraq invaded Kuwait, on the Persian Gulf. The United States led forces that freed Kuwait in the Persian Gulf War of 1991.

Afghanistan had pro-Soviet leaders. Islamic groups opposed them. The Soviets invaded Afghanistan in 1979. The United States and Pakistan helped anti-Communist Islamic forces (known as the mujahideen) drive them out. An Islamic group called the Taliban seized control. The Taliban let Osama bin Laden train Islamic militants of al-Qaeda. Al-Qaeda attacks on the United States in 2001 led the United States to invade Afghanistan. The Taliban collapsed. In 2003 the United States attacked Iraq and removed Saddam Hussein. In 2007 the U.S. increased troops in Iraq to help end violence and internal struggles but withdrew the additional troops in 2008.

Society and Culture (page 767)

Predicting

If Islamic revivalism gains power in

Conservative religious forces in the Middle East have tried to replace foreign values and culture with those of Islam. This is called Islamic revivalism. Extremists want to remove all Western influence. Islamic revivalism began in Iran under Ayatollah Khomeini. It spread to other countries. Militant Muslims assassinated President Sadat of

Turkey, how will Turkish policies most likely change?

_____

_____

_____

_____

Egypt in 1981. The Turkish military has concerns that Islamic revivalism threatens the secular, pro-Western Turkish regime.

Muslim scholars debated issues around the role of women. Until the 1970s, the trend in urban areas was toward a greater role for women. Then it shifted toward more traditional roles, especially in Iran.

The first Arabic-language author to win the Nobel Prize in literature (1988) was Naguib Mahfouz. His *Cairo Trilogy* tells of a merchant family in Egypt in the 1920s.

Section Wrap-up

Answer these questions to check your understanding of the entire section.

1. Why did the United States invade Afghanistan in 2001?

_____

_____

_____

2. What is the goal of Islamic revivalism?

_____

_____

_____

Informative Writing

Tell the history of relations between Israel, its Arab neighbors, and Palestinians in Israeli-controlled areas. Present the information as a story that flows smoothly. Include the story elements of time, place, people, and events. Write the story factually, without showing your opinions.

_____

_____

_____

_____

_____

_____

Communist China

Big Idea

The policies of the Chinese Communist government set up in 1949 failed to bring prosperity. Since the 1980s, its economy has moved toward free enterprise, but political freedom is still very limited. As you read, use a chart like the one below to list Communism's effects on China's international affairs.

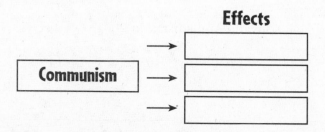

Effects

Communism →

→

→

 **Notes** | **Read to Learn**

Mao's China (page 776)

Comparing and Contrasting

How were the Great Leap Forward and the Cultural Revolution different and alike?

Great Leap Forward:

_____

_____

Cultural Revolution:

_____

_____

Both:

_____

_____

Civil war broke out in 1945 between China's two governments. Nationalists, led by Chiang Kai-shek, were based in southern and central China. Communists, led by Mao Zedong, were based in North China. Promises of free land led many peasants to support Mao. The Communists won in 1949. Chiang and the Nationalists fled to Taiwan.

The new government took land from wealthy landlords and gave it to poor peasants. They hoped collective farms would increase food production. It did not, but the population grew.

To speed up economic growth, Mao introduced the Great Leap Forward in 1958. Under this program, village-sized collective farms were combined into huge **communes** with more than 30,000 people each. The Great Leap Forward was a disaster. Peasants hated it. Food production decreased. Almost 15 million people died of starvation. In 1960 the government started returning to smaller collective farms.

Mao wanted to create a classless society by means of a **permanent revolution**. In 1966 he launched the Great Proletarian Cultural Revolution. His *Little Red Book* was regarded as the leading source of knowledge. Groups called Red Guards destroyed temples, books by foreigners, and foreign music. Intellectuals and artists were attacked.

 **Notes** | # Read to Learn

China After Mao *(page 778)*

Mao died in 1976. A group of practical reformers led by Deng Xiaoping took power. They ended the Cultural Revolution.

Deng Xiaoping called for modernization of industry, agriculture, technology, and national defense. The government invited foreign investors to China and sent students to study abroad. Peasants were allowed small-scale private enterprise. **Per capita** (per person) income doubled. Living standards rose.

Some people wanted democracy. Inflation and corruption increased discontent, especially in cities. In May 1989, student protesters called for an end to corruption and the resignation of China's aging Communist Party leaders. Many people in cities agreed. Massive protests took place in Tiananmen Square in Beijing. Tanks and troops killed between 500 and 2,000 protesters.

Human rights violations and China's desire to reunify with Taiwan have strained relations with the West. However, China hosted the 2008 Olympic Games in Beijing.

Chinese Society *(page 780)*

From the start, the Communist Party in China wanted to create a new kind of citizen. This new citizen would give as much as possible for the good of China.

During the 1950s, the role of women in China changed dramatically. Women were now allowed to take part in politics. They had equal rights with men. But Mao was afraid that loyalty to the family would interfere with loyalty to the state.

After Mao's death, family traditions returned. People had better living conditions and more personal freedom. In order to slow population growth the state began a **one-child policy** in 1979. Education benefits, child care, and housing were offered to couples with only one child. While the population growth rate has declined, this policy has also contributed to an aging population.

The Cold War in Asia *(page 781)*

China signed a pact of friendship with the Soviet Union in 1950. War soon broke out in Korea. Before 1945 Korea was under Japanese control. After World War II, the United States and the Soviet Union divided Korea into two zones. The plan was to hold elections after the war and reunify Korea. Instead, a Communist government emerged in North Korea and an anticommunist government in South Korea.

North Korea invaded South Korea in 1950. U.S. troops were sent to push the invaders back. United Nations troops crossed

What can one infer about the relative strength of the two sides in the Korean War? Explain.

_____

_____

_____

into North Korea. The Chinese sent troops to help North Korea push the UN forces back. After three years of fighting, the two sides agreed to a cease-fire. Korean leaders took part in the first North-South Summit in 2000. Tensions increased again with fears that North Korea was trying to make nuclear weapons.

Communist China had relied on the Soviet Union for technology and economic aid. By the late 1950s, however, China and the Soviet Union were no longer so friendly. Feeling threatened by the Soviets, the Chinese reached out to the United States. In 1972 Richard Nixon became the first U.S. president to visit Communist China. China and the United States resumed diplomatic relations in 1979. China joined the World Trade Organization in 2001.

Section Wrap-up

Answer these questions to check your understanding of the entire section.

1. What policies did Deng Xiaoping put in place of the Cultural Revolution?

_____

_____

2. How did the relationship between Communist China and the Soviet Union change over time?

_____

_____

Expository Writing

Form a theory, or model, about the relationship between economics and political actions or ideas in Communist China. Discuss how your model can be applied to different periods of Chinese history since 1949.

_____

_____

_____

_____

_____

_____

_____

_____

_____

South and Southeast Asia

Big Idea

British India and colonies throughout Southeast Asia gained independence following World War II, but independence was often followed by continued conflict. As you read, use a web diagram like the one below to identify challenges India faced after gaining independence.

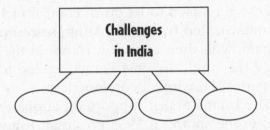

 **Notes**   **Read to Learn**

India Divided (page 782)

Determining Cause and Effect

Which issue was the cause of border clashes between India and Pakistan?

_____

_____

What was the effect of the civil war between East and West Pakistan?

_____

_____

With the end of British rule, India split into two nations. India was Hindu and Pakistan was Muslim. Upon independence in 1947, millions of Hindus and Muslims fled across the new borders. More than a million people were killed. A Hindu militant assassinated Mohandas Gandhi in 1948. In 1948 Sri Lanka gained independence but internal conflict has remained.

The former Indian National Congress became the Congress Party, led by Prime Minister Jawaharlal Nehru. He had moderate socialist ideals. He followed the **principle of nonalignment,** refusing to take sides in the Cold War or join any alliances.

Nehru's daughter, Indira Gandhi, was prime minister most years from 1966 to 1984. Poverty was widespread. Sikh rebels in Punjab province wanted independence. Gandhi refused and used military force. Two Sikh members of her bodyguard killed her in 1984. Her son, Rajiv Gandhi, was prime minister from 1984 to 1989; he was assassinated in 1991.

Muslim-Hindu conflict continued. India and Pakistan clashed over Kashmir. A cease-fire came in 2003.

East and West Pakistan were very different. The government was based in the west. In 1971 East Pakistan declared its independence. After a brief civil war, it became the new nation of Bangladesh. General Pervez Musharraf named himself president of Pakistan in 2001. He was reelected in 2007.

 **Notes** | **Read to Learn**

Southeast Asia (page 785)

Identifying the Main Idea

After World War II, most former

_____

in Southeast Asia became

_____

nations.

Most colonies in southeast Asia became independent nations after World War II. The Philippines gained independence from the United States in 1946. Indonesia, led by Sukarno, became independent of the Netherlands in 1949. Britain recognized the independence of Burma (now Myanmar) in 1948 and Malaya in 1957. The struggle for democracy continues in Myanmar, which is under military rule. Aung San Suu Kyi, leader of the democracy movement in Myanmar, received the Nobel Peace Prize in 1991.

France refused to let go of control of Indochina. Communists, led by Ho Chi Minh, seized power over much of Vietnam, with their capital at Hanoi in the north. France controlled the south. In 1954 France agreed to divide Vietnam into two parts. The conflict continued.

The United States supported nationalist leader Ngo Dinh Diem in the south. In 1965 President Johnson sent U.S. troops to prevent a complete Communist takeover. The war reached a **stalemate** with no significant gains for either side. The United States withdrew in 1973. Vietnam was reunified under Communist rule in 1975. Laos and Cambodia became Communist too. Pol Pot, leader of the Khmer Rouge in Cambodia, killed more than a million Cambodians.

Democracy in Southeast Asia (page 787)

Problems and Solutions

How did the people of the Philippines and Indonesia solve the problem of rule by authoritarian dictators?

_____

_____

_____

_____

Economic problems and internal disputes weakened democracy in parts of Southeast Asia. Some came under military or one-party rule. In the Philippines in 1986, a public uprising forced dictator Ferdinand Marcos to flee the country. Corazon Aquino, widow of a murdered opposition leader, became president. Corruption, a weak economy, and terrorism continued to challenge the Philippines.

In Indonesia, rioting in 1998 forced the authoritarian General Suharto to step down. Ethnic and religious conflicts trouble the nation. A tsunami in 2004 and an earthquake in 2005 caused severe damage.

Across the region, the rights and roles of women have changed. Virtually all nations of Southeast Asia grant women full legal and political rights, although old customs and attitudes survive in rural areas.

In India, the constitution of 1950 forbade **discrimination,** or prejudicial treatment based on gender. It called for equal pay for equal work. Child marriage was outlawed. Women in India were encouraged to attend school and enter the labor market.

Section Wrap-up

Answer these questions to check your understanding of the entire section.

1. List four countries of Southeast Asia that became independent, with their dates of independence and their former colonial rulers.

   _____

   _____

   _____

2. What did the 1950 constitution of India say about women's rights and roles?

   _____

   _____

   _____

Informative Writing

Tell highlights of the history of India and Pakistan from the time of independence to the present. Include elements in the relation between India and Pakistan. Recount events objectively as a smoothly flowing story, in approximately the order they happened. Discuss what happened, when it happened, why it happened, how it happened, and who was involved.

_____

_____

_____

_____

_____

_____

_____

_____

_____

_____

_____

_____

_____

_____

Japan and the Pacific

Big Idea

Since 1945 Japan and the four "Asian tigers" have become economic pow-
erhouses, while Australia and New Zealand remain linked culturally to
Europe. As your read, use a table like the one below to list the key areas
of industrial development in South Korea, Taiwan, and Singapore.

South Korea	Taiwan	Singapore

Notes

Read to Learn

The Transformation of Japan (page 788)

Distinguishing Fact from Opinion

*Circle the newspaper
headlines that report
facts (not opinions):*

JAPAN HAS WORLD'S
MOST DESIRABLE
WORKFORCE

JAPAN EXPORTS RECORD
NUMBER OF CARS

JAPANESE PRACTICES
UNWISE AND UNFAIR

MOST JAPANESE
FACTORIES LESS THAN
60 YEARS OLD

From 1945 to 1952, Japan was an **occupied** country. Allied
military forces led by U.S. general Douglas MacArthur held and
controlled it. He remodeled Japanese society on a Western
model. A new constitution established a parliamentary system,
guaranteed basic rights, and reduced the power of the emperor.

Since regaining its independence, Japan has become an economic giant. Japan is a stable democracy with two main political
parties—the Liberal Democrats and the Socialists. The central
government plays an active role in the economy. It establishes
price and wage policies and subsidizes key industries. This is
called **state capitalism.**

Allied plans to take apart the *zaibatsu* system were scaled
back during the Cold War. Land reform created a strong class of
free farmers. Cultural values of hard work, long hours, cooperation, and savings contributed to Japan's economic success.
Because the war destroyed Japanese industries, factories are
new and modern. Japan has become one of the largest exporting nations in the world. Though it suffered from a recession in
the 1990s, it remains a world economic power.

Some values are changing. Schools stress individualism and
play down patriotism or aggression. Women have legal rights
but still earn less than men.

The "Asian Tigers," Australia, and New Zealand (page 791)

Making Generalizations

In general, based on the examples of the Asian tigers, is political democracy necessary in order for an economy to thrive?

Yes   No
(circle one)

Explain your answer.

_____

_____

_____

_____

_____

South Korea, Taiwan, Singapore, and Hong Kong are sometimes called the "Asian tigers." Like Japan, they built successful industrial societies.

Dictators ruled both parts of Korea after the Korean War: Kim Il Sung in the north and Syngman Rhee in the south. Voters in South Korea elected General Park Chung Hee president in 1961. He promoted land reform and new industries. Chemicals, textiles, and shipbuilding were key areas of industrial development. Democracy grew slowly and arrived in the 1990s.

The island of Taiwan is the seat of the Republic of China. Chiang Kai-shek and his Nationalist followers fled there after losing to the Communists. They claimed that their government represented all the people of China. Land reform doubled food production. Manufacturing and commerce grew. By 2000 over three-quarters of the people lived in urban areas. Chiang ruled by decree. After his death in 1975, Taiwan moved toward representative government.

Singapore was once a British colony and later briefly part of Malaysia. It is now an independent state. It has a successful free-market economy based on shipbuilding, oil refineries, and electronics. Its port is one of the busiest in the world. Singapore is also a regional banking center. Its regime is authoritarian but stable.

Like Singapore, Hong Kong became an industrial powerhouse. Great Britain ruled Hong Kong for more than 150 years. In 1997 Britain returned control of Hong Kong to mainland China. China promised to allow Hong Kong to continue a capitalist system for the next 50 years.

Australia and New Zealand lie south and east of Asia. Culturally and politically, they have identified more with Europe than with Asia. Both are members of the British Commonwealth.

In recent years, however, Australia and New Zealand have drawn closer to their Asian neighbors. Immigration from East and Southeast Asia has increased. Trade relations with Asia are growing rapidly. The majority of Australia's exports today go to East Asia.

Section Wrap-up

Answer these questions to check your understanding of the entire section.

1. Name at least three causes that contribute to Japan's economic success.

_____

_____

_____

2. What recent factors have drawn Australia and New Zealand closer to their Asian neighbors?

_____

_____

_____

Persuasive Writing

What kind of trade policies do you think the United States should have in relation to Japan, the Asian tigers, and Australia and New Zealand? Make a recommendation and support it with information. Present your information so as to try to persuade the reader to share your opinion.

_____

_____

_____

_____

_____

_____

_____

_____

_____

_____

_____

_____

_____

Challenges of a New Century

Big Idea

Today's societies face many social, economic, and political challenges, and they must balance the costs and benefits of the technological revolution. As you read, complete a table like the one below to determine the cause and effect of global concerns.

Concern	Cause	Effect
Deforestation		
Greenhouse effect		
Weapons		
Hunger		

 **Notes**

Read to Learn

Technological Revolution *(page 802)*

Drawing Conclusions

Why are nuclear, biological, and chemical weapons called weapons of mass destruction?

_____

_____

_____

_____

Like the first and second Industrial Revolutions, the revolution in technology since World War II is changing people's lives. Computers were developed during World War II to crack enemy codes. The microprocessor made personal computers possible. Jumbo jets, the Internet, satellites, and cell phones make the world a global village.

Technology has also led to nuclear, biological, and chemical weapons. **Bioterrorism** is the use of these weapons in terrorist attacks. Chemical weapons were used during World War I and the Iran-Iraq war in the 1980s. Anthrax-filled letters were used to kill Americans in 2001.

The Human Genome Project unlocked the secrets of DNA, leading to new medical diagnoses and treatments. Bioethics deals with moral choices in medical research, such as controversial human cloning and stem-cell research. Global AIDS deaths have declined, though the disease remains a major global concern.

New genetically engineered grains in the Green Revolution increased the food supply. Fertilizers and pesticides increase crop yields but raise environmental concerns. Organic farming does not use chemicals.

Environmental Crisis (page 805)

Identifying the Main Idea

In the greenhouse effect, _____ in the atmosphere causes _____.

In her 1962 book *Silent Spring,* scientist Rachel Carson warned of the dangers of chemical pesticides. Her warnings gave rise to the new field of **ecology,** the study of the relationship between living things and their environment.

Deforestation is the clearing of forests for farmland and wood. Overgrazing and poor farming practices in dry areas cause **desertification,** turning soil into desert.

Chemical wastes pose another danger. Chlorofluorocarbons found in many products destroy the ozone layer, which shields Earth from ultraviolet rays. Forests die from acid rain caused by sulfur pollution. In the **greenhouse effect,** carbon dioxide in the atmosphere causes global warming.

The Kyoto Protocol is a treaty among most countries to reduce emissions that cause global warming. Accidents can cause ecological disasters. Economic development that conserves natural resources for future generations is called **sustainable development.**

Poverty and Civil Strife (page 807)

Making Inferences

Where does the most population growth occur?

_____

In a **global economy,** goods are produced, distributed, and sold on a worldwide scale. The global economy increased in the 1970s. One feature is the gap between rich and poor nations. Developed nations have well-organized industrial and agricultural systems. They have strong educational systems and use advanced technologies.

Poorer, developing nations—mostly in Africa, Asia, and Latin America—have farming economies with little technology. Most population growth is in developing nations. Millions die of hunger. Civil wars and ethnic conflicts also claim many victims.

Political and Social Challenges (page 809)

Evaluating Information

More recently, interest in democracy in Africa and Asia has _____.

The United Nations General Assembly adopted the Universal Declaration of Human Rights in 1948. It listed rights to which everyone is entitled. They included life, liberty, personal security, and freedom of movement, opinion, and expression. Human rights violations still occur in many parts of the world.

After World War II, many African and Asian leaders wanted democracies. Within a decade, military dictatorships or one-party governments took over. More recently, interest in democracy has revived.

Many countries have laws that require equality for women and men. Nevertheless, in many developing countries, women cannot get education or decent jobs.

Comparing and Contrasting

How are the goals of Islamic militants and the Irish Republican Army different and alike?

_____

_____

_____

_____

Terrorists often kill civilians and take hostages to achieve their political goals. Some terrorists are militant nationalists who want separate states. The Irish Republican Army wants to unite Northern Ireland (part of the United Kingdom) with the Irish Republic. Sometimes terrorism is state-sponsored. Iraq, Syria, Cuba, and North Korea have sheltered and supported terrorist organizations. Islamic militants are extremists who use violence to oppose Western influence in Muslim countries.

On September 11, 2001, commercial jets seized by terrorists flew into buildings in the United States, killing thousands. President George W. Bush announced a war on terrorism. The United States and allies attacked Afghanistan and later Iraq.

In October 2001, the United States passed an antiterrorist bill called the Patriot Act. It allowed secret searches and made it easier to monitor phone calls, e-mail, voice mail, and library records. The United States established a Department of Homeland Security. Airport security tightened around the world.

Section Wrap-up

Answer these questions to check your understanding of the entire section.

1. Define *bioethics* and give two examples of specific issues in bioethics.

_____

_____

2. What are the advantages and disadvantages of a global economy?

_____

_____

Persuasive Writing

What do you consider the most serious challenge facing the world in the twenty-first century, and what do you think should be done to address it? Try to make your reader agree with your opinion about the seriousness of the problem and what should be done. Support your case with facts and persuasive arguments.

_____

_____

_____

_____

New Global Communities

Big Idea

The global economy and new global threats have prompted international organizations and individuals to work on global problems. As you read, create a pyramid like the one below to depict how the United Nations is organized.

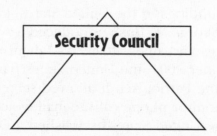

Security Council

 **Notes** | **Read to Learn**

The United Nations (page 812)

Making Generalizations

In general, do the challenges of the twenty-first century require nations to work together more closely or less closely to solve their problems?

Circle one:

MORE   LESS

Explain your answer.

_____

_____

_____

_____

Founded in 1945, the United Nations (UN) brings nations together to solve important problems. Its chief goals are peace and human dignity.

Representatives of all member nations form the General Assembly of the UN. It discusses issues and recommends action. The Security Council passes resolutions that require the UN to act. Of the 15 members of the Security Council, 5 are permanent—the United States, Russia, Britain, France, and China. Ten others are chosen by the General Assembly for limited terms. Each permanent member can veto a decision, which frequently leads to a stalemate.

The head administrator of the UN is the secretary-general. The UN has a number of specialized agencies that address economic and social problems. The UN has also provided **peacekeeping forces**—military forces from neutral member states—to settle conflicts and supervise truces.

The UN established the International Atomic Energy Agency (IAEA) in 1957. It works to prevent **nuclear proliferation**—the spread of nuclear weapons technology. The greatest risk comes from nations that have not signed (or have violated) the Nuclear Nonproliferation Treaty, such as India, Pakistan, and North Korea.

Population and Migration *(page 814)*

Determining Cause and Effect

The average age in Western Europe is rising because the _____ has gone down and _____ has gone up.

The population of the world reached 5 billion in 1988 and more than 6.7 billion in 2007. By 2050 it will probably increase to 9.2 billion or more. Growth is fastest in developing countries. India will surpass China as the most populous country in the world.

In wealthy regions such as Western Europe, the population is becoming smaller and older. As life expectancy rises and birthrates fall, populations worldwide will be older on average. People of working age will have to support more care for the elderly.

In less developed countries, population growth will increase migration and urbanization.

Many cities lack the infrastructure to support a larger population. About 200 million international migrants moved from one country to another in 2005. Millions were refugees from persecution, civil war, or famine. Even more people moved to find jobs. Latin Americans have moved to the United States. Guest workers from poorer countries work in Western Europe. Often they face backlash and become scapegoats for economic problems. Migration trends have changed in the 2000s. More women are migrating and more people are moving from one developing nation to another.

Globalization *(page 815)*

Synthesizing Information

Multinational corporations, the World Trade Organization, free-trade areas, and international nongovernmental organizations all illustrate the increase in _____.

Technology has brought **globalization,** the realization that different parts of the world depend on each other. In the global economy, the World Bank makes grants and loans for developing countries. The International Monetary Fund watches exchange rates and oversees the global financial system. **Multinational corporations**—companies with divisions in more than two countries—tie countries together.

Trade talks among countries led to the General Agreement on Tariffs and Trade (GATT). In 1995 nations that had signed GATT set up the World Trade Organization (WTO). Groups of nations form trading blocs. The largest is the European Union. The North American Free Trade Agreement (NAFTA) and the Asia Pacific Economic Cooperation (APEC) agreement set up other free-trade areas.

Ordinary citizens work together to address global issues—the environment, gender liberation, child labor, technology, and peace. Some organizations, such as the Red Cross, have members in many nations. Some individuals act at the **grassroots level,** in their own communities. **Nongovernmental organizations** include business and professional groups, foundations, and religious, peace, and **disarmament groups.** People have power to make a difference.

Section Wrap-up *Answer these questions to check your understanding of the entire section.*

1. Why is urbanization resulting from population growth a problem for many developing countries?

_____

_____

_____

2. Which feature of the United Nations Security Council frequently leads to stalemate?

_____

_____

_____

Expository Writing

Analyze the global economy. What has caused it? What challenges does it pose? How have nations and individuals responded? Organize your writing by classifying information, breaking down a larger topic into smaller categories. Define your categories or ideas to help your reader understand.

_____

_____

_____

_____

_____

_____

_____

_____

_____

_____

_____

_____

_____

_____

_____

_____